MILITARY TRIBUNALS AND PRESIDENTIAL POWER

BY THE SAME AUTHOR

American Constitutional Law (6th ed., 2005)

Presidential War Power (2d ed., 2004)

The Democratic Constitution (with Neal Devins, 2004)

The Politics of Executive Privilege (2004)

Nazi Saboteurs on Trial: A Military Tribunal & American Law (2003)

Religious Liberty in America: Political Safeguards (2002)

Political Dynamics of Constitutional Law (with Neal Devins, 3d ed., 2001)

Congressional Abdication on War and Spending (2000)

The Politics of Shared Power: Congress and the Executive (4th ed., 1998)

Constitutional Conflicts Between Congress and the President (4th ed., 1997)

Encyclopedia of the American Presidency (with Leonard W. Levy, 1994)

Constitutional Dialogues: Interpretation as Political Process (1988)

The Constitution Between Friends: Congress, the President, and the Law (1978)

Presidential Spending Power (1975)

President and Congress: Power and Policy (1972)

MILITARY TRIBUNALS AND PRESIDENTIAL POWER

American Revolution to the War on Terrorism

Louis Fisher

University Press of Kansas

Published by the University Press of Kansas (Lawrence, Kansas 66049), which
was organized by the Kansas Board of Regents and is operated and funded by
Emporia State University, Fort Hays State University, Kansas State University,
Pittsburg State University, the University of Kansas, and Wichita State University

Library of Congress Cataloging-in-Publication Data

Fisher, Louis.
Military tribunals and presidential power : American Revolution to the war on
terrorism
Louis Fisher.
    p. cm.
Includes bibliographical references and indexes.
ISBN 0-7006-1375-7 (cloth : alk. paper) — ISBN 0-7006-1376-5 (pbk. : alk. paper)
1. Military courts—United States—History. I. Title
KF7661.F57 2005
343.73′0143—dc22

2004025521

British Library Cataloguing-in-Publication Data is available.

Printed in the United States of America

10 9 8 7 6 5 4 3 2

The paper used in this publication meets the minimum requirements of the
American National Standard for Permanence of Paper for Printed Library Materials
Z39.48–1984.

To Jacob Landynski,
cherished teacher and friend

CONTENTS

PREFACE

After the terrorist actions of 9/11, President George W. Bush authorized the creation of military tribunals to try individuals who assisted in the attacks on New York City and Washington, D.C. The administration sought no assistance from Congress, the Armed Services and Judiciary Committees, or even the Judge Advocate General offices in the military services. Bush's military order closely tracked the model established by President Franklin D. Roosevelt, who appointed a military tribunal in 1942 to try eight German saboteurs. In *Ex parte Quirin* (1942), the Supreme Court unanimously upheld Roosevelt's tribunal (also called "military commissions").

These examples from the FDR and Bush administrations illustrate a trend over the past 60 years that has progressively moved military law away from statutory directives, enacted by the elected representatives in Congress, to independent and unilateral actions by executive officials. At the same time that executive actions skirt legislative control, they marginalize or eliminate review by the courts. At stake in the operation of tribunals are such fundamental values as democratic control, constitutional grants of power, the doctrine of separated powers, the system of checks and balances, an independent judiciary, and procedural protections for U.S. citizens and foreign nationals. Military tribunals in U.S. history have generally been hostile to civil liberties, procedural due process, and elementary standards of justice.

When President Bush authorized military tribunals, some supporters looked to *Quirin* as an "apt precedent." A close look at the Nazi saboteur case shakes the assumption that it is a reliable or attractive frame of reference. The decision was deeply flawed at the time it was released. In early 1945, when the Roosevelt administration again had to consider a tribunal to deal with two other spies from Germany, it decided that the 1942 model was unacceptable and abandoned it. In general, efforts in time of war to replace civilian courts with military tribunals have produced serious deficiencies in law, practice, and institutional checks. The Bush order on military tribunals augmented presidential power at the cost of legislative controls, judicial supervision, and democratic government. Tribunals are most

justified when civil courts are unavailable or not functioning and least justified when they are.

The eight Germans tried in 1942 were charged with four crimes: one
against the "law of war," two against the Articles of War, and one involving conspiracy. The prosecutors thus combined a mix of offenses that were
nonstatutory (law of war) and statutory (Articles of War). The distinction
here is fundamental. In federal law, the creation of criminal offenses is
reserved to the legislative branch, not to the President. The Constitution
vests in Congress the power to "constitute Tribunals inferior to the
supreme Court," to "make rules for the Government and Regulation of the
land and naval Forces," and to "define and punish Piracies and Felonies
committed on the high Seas, and Offences against the Law of Nations." By
enacting Articles of War, Congress decided not only the procedures but
also the punishments to be applied to the field of military law. Charging
individuals with violations of the "law of war" shifts the balance of power
from Congress to the executive.

Military tribunals also affect power relationships between the President
and the judiciary. Legal briefs filed by the Bush administration warned federal courts not to second-guess presidential judgments on the war against
terrorism. Federal judges initially deferred to the administration, but some
of the courts began to challenge the President's right to act unilaterally,
such as holding "enemy combatants" incommunicado, giving them no
opportunity to challenge their detentions in court, or to seek the assistance
of counsel. This concentration of military power in the hands of the executive branch, without effective legislative and judicial checks, forms the
central theme that defines the purpose of this book. Unchecked executive
power always poses a threat to individual rights and liberties.

Although the bulk of my analysis focuses on the history of military tribunals in the United States, my principal concern is the breadth of presidential power in time of war, at the cost of legislative and judicial control.
For that reason I extend the coverage to other actions by Presidents that
present military justifications to augment political power, such as invoking
martial law and using courts-martial to try U.S. citizens. Included within my
framework is the decision by President Bush to apply the concept of
"enemy combatant"—initially raised in the Nazi saboteur case—to two U.S.
citizens, Yaser Esam Hamdi and Jose Padilla. Here we have a presidential
decision to first take aim at noncitizens (the November 13 order authorizing tribunals) and then later extending executive power over U.S. citizens.
I also examine the trial of Zacarias Moussaoui in civil court because he
remained at all times the administration's candidate to be tried by tribunal.

This book looks comprehensively only at tribunals created by the United States, operating either in this country or abroad. No attempt is made to analyze in detail the kind of international tribunal used in concert with allies, such as the Leipzig trials after World War I or the Nuremberg trials after World War II. I touch briefly on the international trials in Tokyo, but those proceedings raise quite different issues and are not analyzed here with any thoroughness.

I use the word *tribunal* instead of *military commission,* which is preferred by administration officials and many attorneys. I regard the two terms as interchangeable, although in some cases persuasive reasons can be offered in favor of *commission.* However, *tribunal* seems to me to clearly carry the meaning of a court, capable of issuing binding decisions. In contrast, a *commission* is often a study body, authorized to submit recommendations but lacking authority to do more.

Once again, I express my appreciation to the University Press of Kansas for offering its support and encouragement to my writings. The first step in this project was my book *Nazi Saboteurs on Trial: A Military Tribunal and American Law,* which the Press published in 2003. At that time I indicated my intention to complete a second work on military tribunals "from George Washington to the present to judge their effectiveness and constitutionality." This book carries out that promise. As always, I worked closely with Mike Briggs of the Press and enjoyed the engaging process of defining and crystallizing the objectives of a book.

For outside reviewers, I was blessed with the guidance and advice of two seasoned experts in military law: Eugene R. Fidell and Scott Silliman. Fidell is president of the National Institute of Military Justice and actively litigates cases involving military law. Silliman, who teaches at the Duke University School of Law, served 25 years as a uniformed judge advocate in the Air Force. I express my appreciation once again to the Congressional Research Service and the Library of Congress for providing a rich, stimulating environment. As with my first book on military tribunals, I thank Jennifer Elsea of the American Law Division for trading documents, ideas, and puzzlements. I appreciate also the careful copyediting by Karen Hellekson. The views expressed in this book are personal, not institutional, and do not represent the positions of either CRS or the library.

I dedicate this book to Jacob Landynski, who taught me constitutional law at the New School for Social Research in the mid-1960s. I can still hear his lectures: crisp, incisive, focused. After my graduation, Jacob remained available for support, encouragement, and friendship. In May 2003, he was instrumental in having me invited to the New School to present an evening talk on the Iraq war and its implications for constitutional government. Earlier, he took me to his afternoon class on constitutional law. After introducing me, he walked to the front row, sat down, and turned the class over to me. Several months later, I learned, to my great shock, that Jacob had passed away. We are told that no one dies if they are remembered. Jacob remains with me a model of gentleness, kindness, generosity, intellectual integrity, and scholarly dedication. I am honored to have been in his presence.

1

THE LAW OF WAR

With the war of independence fast approaching, the Continental Congress in 1775 enacted Articles of War to specify procedures and punishments for the field of military law. At first the Articles were borrowed largely from British precedents, but Congress over the years continued to reenact and modify them. Through these statutes the legislative branch, operating under the principles of a republican form of government, established its control over military law and set limits on the actions taken by Presidents, military commanders, and executive officials. Congressional control of military law would be tested at times when the executive branch created military tribunals that lacked specific statutory authority or were only tenuously connected to legislative policy.

Articles of War

For nearly a thousand years, governments have announced codes and principles to maintain order and discipline among soldiers and sailors and to protect civilians and their property. An ordinance from Richard I in 1190 ordered that whoever murdered a man on ship "shall be bound to the dead man and thrown into the sea." If the murder occurred on land, the assailant would be bound to the dead man and buried in the earth. Other penalties covered lesser crimes, including injuries from a knife, blows with the hand, robbery, and uttering "disgraceful language or abuse."[1] In 1385, Richard II issued a more detailed guide of 26 instructions for members of the army.[2]

King Gustavus Adolphus of Sweden, in 1621, released a comprehensive list of 167 Articles of War, explaining the proper conduct for soldiers and the punishment for violations. Some of the fundamental values, phrased in one way or another, would find expression in other countries over the years. For example, "whosoever giveth advice unto the enemy any man-

1. William Winthrop, Military Law and Precedents 903 (1920).
2. Id. at 904–6.

ner or way, shall die for it."[3] Certain buildings and activities in a zone of combat were entitled to protection. "No man shall presume to pillage any Church or Hospitall," and no man "shall set fire upon any Hospitall, Churche, Schoole, or Mill, or spoyle them any way, except he be commanded."[4] No harm was to be inflicted on innocent civilians. "Our Commanders shall defend the countrey-people and Ploughman that follow their husbandry, and shall suffer none to hinder them in it."[5] The Articles were to be read every month before every regiment "to the end that no man shall pretend ignorance."[6] Some of these Articles adopted in 1621 were carried forth by the early British codes and later found expression in the Articles of War adopted by the United States.[7]

British Articles of War

Initially, American policy on military law depended to a large extent on British precedents dating back to the 1600s.[8] In the time of James II, in 1686, English military law established the procedures for a council of war, or court-martial. The court consisted of seven officers, usually at the rank of general, colonel, or captain. If not enough officers at that level were available, inferior officers could be called in. The presiding officer interrogated the prisoner about the facts behind the accusation, and, having heard his defense, ordered the prisoner to withdraw. At that point, each member of the court, "according to his Conscience, and the Ordinances or Articles of War," offered his judgment. Sentence depended on a plurality of votes.[9]

In Great Britain, Articles of War were issued by the army and ordained by the King pursuant to his royal prerogative.[10] The Articles spelled out the penalties for various acts by soldiers and sailors and established procedures for courts-martial. Punishments were meted out for disobedience,

---

3. Id. at 911 (Article 76).

4. Id. at 913 (Articles 96 and 97).

5. Id. at 914 (Article 113).

6. Id. at 918 (Article 167).

7. "Revision of the Articles of War," hearing before the House Committee on Military Affairs, 62d Cong., 2d Sess. 71 (1912) (testimony by Judge Advocate General E. H. Crowder). An appendix to this hearing shows the relationship of the Articles of Gustavus Adolphus to British and American Articles of War. Id. at 114–21.

8. See W. Y. Baldry, "Early Articles of War," 4 J. Soc. Army Hist. Res. 166 (1926); 6 id. 188 (1927).

9. Winthrop, Military Law and Precedents, at 919.

10. Id. at 18.

mutinous activity, and other conduct that threatened military discipline and effectiveness. Royal prerogative attempted to expand the jurisdiction of these military courts to cover civilians, forcing Parliament to reassert its power to prevent encroachments upon the civilian population.[11]

The British Articles of War were reviewed in 1715 to determine what alterations and additions might be necessary.[12] Included in this ongoing process of review and revision were the Secretary at War and the Judge Advocate General.[13] Throughout this period it was necessary to decide under what conditions a court-martial could be used against civilians. For example, a court-martial could try servants of soldiers and also sutlers (civilians who sold provisions at an army post).[14] Some offenses by sutlers were transferred to civil courts.[15]

Under British custom, Articles of War were read at least once a month to educate soldiers and sailors on military requirements and penalties. As amended by Parliament in 1749, the statute explained that the laws related to sea service "have been found by experience not to be so full, so clear, so expedient, or consistent with each other, as they ought to be."[16] As set forth in the opening paragraph, the purpose of the statute was to direct executive conduct by establishing articles and orders "for regulating and better government of his Majesty's navies, ships of war, and forces by sea." The Articles left no room for the executive branch to take contrary or conflicting actions in time of "emergency." The Articles applied "as well in time of peace as in time of war."[17]

The 1749 statute defined punishments for such actions as holding illegal correspondence with an enemy, failing to notify a superior officer about a message from the enemy, spying, giving money and other assistance to an enemy, disobeying orders, cowardice or neglect of duty, desertion, mutiny, murder, and robbery. Protections were extended to prisoners. If a ship were taken as prize, "none of the officers, mariners, or other persons on board her, shall be stripped of their cloaths, or in any sort pillaged, beaten, or evil-intreated, upon pain that the person or persons so offend-

---

11. David A. Schlueter, Military Criminal Justice: Practice and Procedure 20 (5th ed. 1999).

12. Frederick Bernays Wiener, Civilians Under Military Justice: The British Practice Since 1689, Especially in North America 9–10 (1967).

13. Id. at 10–11.

14. Id. at 12.

15. Id. at 13.

16. 19 Statutes at Large 325 (1765).

17. Id. at 326.

ing, shall be liable to such punishment as a court-martial shall think fit to inflict."[18] Parliament amended the Articles of War at other times, as in 1757.

Military Justice in the Colonies

When George Washington served as an officer in the American colonies under British rule, it was his duty to have recruits understand the Articles of War. In an order dated December 25, 1755, he directed that the men "have the Articles of War read to them."[19] The following year, he noted the dissolution of a general court-martial and his approval of the sentence handed down by a court-martial, "which was unanimous in opinion." He appointed a court-martial to try a sergeant "for retreating with a party without Orders" and of men "confined for throwing away their Arms in the retreat of the party."[20]

During the French and Indian War, fought from 1754 to 1763, Washington found that colonial legislation governing military actions was often so general or incomplete that he had to "guess at every thing."[21] He pointed out that the law on mutiny and desertion did not authorize a court-martial "against any officer or soldier who is charged with cowardice, holding correspondence with the enemy, quitting or sleeping upon a post, nay, many other crimes, which are provided against in the articles of war."[22] Here Washington underscored the weaknesses of colonial legislation compared to the comprehensive nature of the British Articles of War.

He often urged "the necessity of enforcing the articles of war in all its parts, where it is not incompatible with the nature of this service."[23] In 1756 he described the purpose of the British Articles of War as preserving "the rights and liberties of the people against the arbitrary proceedings of the military officers."[24] When colonial legislation over martial law expired, he offered his view "that we can prepare no Law more fit than that provided by Act of Parliament, as a military code for the government or our Troops."[25]

18. Id. at 328 (Art. 9).

19. 1 The Writings of George Washington 257 (John C. Fitzpatrick ed. 1931) (hereafter "Washington").

20. Id. at 354.

21. Id. at 356 (emphasis in original).

22. Id. at 356–57.

23. Id. at 467.

24. Id.

25. 2 Washington 30.

In issuing general instructions to company captains in 1757, Washington directed them to hold courts-martial for trying and punishing noncommissioned officers and soldiers, and that "in all other respects you are to govern yourselves exactly agreeable to the articles of War, and the rules and customs of the Army."[26] Discipline, he reminded them, "is the soul of an army. It makes small numbers formidable; procures success to the weak, and esteem to all."[27]

The War of Independence

In the steps leading to a political break with England, the American colonies became aware of the lack of procedural safeguards for individuals tried for a crime. The declaration and resolves of the First Continental Congress, agreed to on October 14, 1774, objected that colonists "may be transported to England, and tried there upon accusations for treasons and misprisions, or concealments of treasons committed in the colonies."[28] The declaration referred to "the great and inestimable privilege of being tried by their peers of the vicinage, according to the course of that law."[29] Various British practices had "deprive[d] the American subject of trial by jury."[30]

Courts-martial marked an exception to trial by a jury of peers, but at least a court-martial required the government to set forth charges against an individual, assemble a body of officers to render a judgment, and follow written procedures for review. Moreover, a court-martial applied to soldiers, not civilians. Those standards would change fundamentally after the terrorist attacks of 9/11, when the Bush administration claimed that the military could hold U.S. citizens as "enemy combatants" and detain them indefinitely without charging them of specific crimes, offering legal counsel, or trying them in court.

With conflicts escalating between England and America, several of the colonies began to enact Articles of War and procedures for courts-martial. On April 5, 1775, the Provisional Congress of Massachusetts Bay adopted 53 Articles, drawing heavily from British precedents.[31] Similar articles were

26. Id. at 114.
27. Id.
28. Documents of American History 82 (Henry Steele Commager ed. 1973) (hereafter "Commager").
29. Id. at 83.
30. Id. at 84.
31. Winthrop, Military Law and Precedents, at 947–52.

passed by the Provincial Assemblies of Connecticut and Rhode Island, the Congresses of Rhode Island and New Hampshire, the Pennsylvania Assembly, and the Convention of South Carolina.[32]

A year before declaring independence, the Continental Congress met on June 14, 1775, to create a committee "to bring in a dra't of Rules and regulations for the government of the army."[33] The committee consisted of George Washington, Philip Schuyler, Silas Deane, Thomas Cushing, and Joseph Hewes. A day later, Congress unanimously elected Washington as general to command all the continental forces.[34] Moving quickly, a congressional committee on June 17 drafted instructions that combined a mix of discretion for Washington with adherence to "the rules and discipline of war" and to such directions as Congress may adopt. The instructions were grounded in the principle of legislative control:

> You are hereby vested with full power and authority to act as you shall think for the good and welfare of the [military] service.
> . . . And you are to regulate your conduct in every respect by the rules and discipline of war, (as herewith given you,) and punctually to observe and follow such orders and directions, from time to time, as you shall receive from this, or a future Congress of these United Colonies, or committee of Congress.[35]

Two days later, additional legislative instructions gave great latitude to Washington, with the understanding that Congress could always intervene at a later stage to reverse, modify, or narrow his decisions:

> And whereas all particulars cannot be foreseen, nor positive instructions for such emergencies so before hand given but that many things must be left to your prudent and discreet management, as occurrences may arise upon the place, or from time to time fall out, you are therefore upon all such accidents or any occasions that may happen, to use your best circumspection and (advising with your council of war) to order and dispose of the said Army under your command as may be most advantageous for the obtaining the end for which these forces have been raised, making it your special care in

---

32. Schlueter, Military Criminal Justice, at 24.
33. 2 Journals of the Continental Congress 90 (1905) (hereafter "Journals").
34. Id. at 91.
35. Id. at 96.

discharge of the great trust committed unto you, that the liberties of America receive no detriment.[36]

On June 30, 1775, Congress adopted rules and regulations for the military, spelling out national policy in a series of 69 Articles. The principles of warfare were drawn largely from the British Articles of War, but they were (unlike the early British tradition) "wholly statutory, having been, from the beginning, enacted by Congress as the legislative power."[37] Congress established standards to deal with mutiny, sedition, insubordination, desertion, and assistance to enemies, all to be judged and punished by court-martial.[38] Congress set forth the conditions for a death sentence and for punishment short of capital offenses, including "whipping not exceeding *thirty-nine* lashes, fine not exceeding two months pay of the offender, imprisonment not exceeding one month."[39] Congress promulgated these standards *in advance* by legislation, rather than leave them to the discretion and judgment of military commanders or executive officials.

The following month, George Washington noted in general orders: "to morrow the Rules and Articles formed by the Hon: the Continental Congress for the Government of the Troops of the Twelve United Colonies."[40] A year later, he directed that the Articles of War "are to be read, at least once a week, to every Company in the Army, that neither Men nor Officers may plead Ignorance against any of the Rules, and Regulations therein contained."[41]

British and American commanders understood that the laws of war allowed for successful military action but did not justify barbarity or cruelty. The guidelines were not merely moral but practical. If England overstepped the boundaries of appropriate military conduct, it would inflame the local populace and create a growing band of insurgents. General Washington remained alert to excesses committed by his troops. In general orders issued on January 1, 1777, he prohibited soldiers from "plundering any person whatsoever, whether Tories or others." He expected that "humanity and tenderness to women and children will distinguish brave Americans, contending for liberty, from infamous mercenary ravagers,

---

36. Id. at 101.
37. Winthrop, Military Law and Precedents, at 21.
38. 2 Journals 111–23.
39. Id. at 119 (emphasis in original).
40. 3 Washington 411.
41. 4 Washington 527.

whether British or Hessians."[42] In various letters he "remonstrated sharply" on the treatment of American prisoners of war.[43] He referred to a lieutenant from Virginia who, after a slight wound on his thigh, "was overtaken and murthered in a most cruel manner."[44] Commenting elsewhere on the conduct of the Hessians, he said "our people who have been prisoners generally agree that they received much kinder treatment from them, than from the British Officers and Soldiers."[45] Tempted at times to retaliate in kind against the British, he concluded that "Humanity and Policy forbid the measure. Experience proves, that their wanton Cruelty injures rather than benefits their cause."

When America issued its Declaration of Independence on July 4, 1776, it identified "a long train of abuses and usurpations" and charged King George III with "affect[ing] to render the Military independent of and superior to the Civil Power."[46] Through this indictment, the colonies set forth the principle that military commanders were at all times subordinate to legislative bodies, including specifications set forth in the Articles of War and any arrangement for military tribunals. The Declaration also charged that the King had "depriv[ed] us in many cases, of the benefits of Trial by Jury" and had "transport[ed] us beyond Seas to be tried for pretended offenses."[47]

Other colonies and states adopted similar principles. The Virginia Bill of Rights, on June 12, 1776, stated that "in all cases the military should be under strict subordination to, and governed by, the civil power, and described trial by jury as "preferable to any other, and ought to be held sacred." Moreover, it offered these specific views on court proceedings:

> That in all capital or criminal prosecutions a man hath a right to demand the cause and nature of his accusation, to be confronted with the accusers and witnesses, to call for evidence in his favour, and to a speedy trial by an impartial jury of his vicinage, without whose unanimous consent he cannot be found guilty; nor can he be compelled to give evidence against himself; that no man be deprived of his liberty, except by the law of the land or the judgment of his peers.[48]

42. 6 Washington 466.
43. 7 Washington 15–16.
44. Id. at 103.
45. Id. at 108.
46. Commager at 101.
47. Id.
48. Id. at 104.

The Massachusetts Bill of Rights of 1780 identified the basic procedural rights available to the accused: "No subject shall be held to answer for any crimes or offence, until the same is fully and plainly . . . described to him; or be compelled to accuse, or furnish evidence against himself." Every subject "shall have a right to produce all proofs that may be favorable to him; to meet the witnesses against him face to face, and to be fully heard in his defense by himself, or his counsel, at his election." Finally, no subject "shall be arrested, . . . or deprived of his life, liberty, or estate, but by the judgment of his peers, or the law of the land."[49] Trial by jury was required except for the military: "And the legislature shall not make any law that shall subject any person to a capital or infamous punishment, excepting for the government of the army and navy, without trial by jury."[50] Courts-martial applied only to those in the military and were governed solely by legislative authority: "No person can in any case be subject to law-martial, or to any penalties or pains, by virtue of that law, except those employed in the army or navy, and except the military in actual service, but by authority of the legislature."[51]

During the war, both sides depended on military courts to deal with spies. The Continental Congress adopted a resolution on August 21, 1776, stating that all persons not owing allegiance to America, "found lurking as spies in or about the fortifications or encampments of the armies of the United States," shall suffer death or punishment by sentence of a court-martial.[52] A month later, the British apprehended Capt. Nathan Hale of the Continental Army, who was behind British lines on Long Island. Hale had been dressed in civilian clothes and carried documents concerning British fortifications. Found guilty by a military court, he was hanged.[53]

John Adams and Thomas Jefferson were part of a committee charged with revising the Articles of War in 1776. They decided it was better to present the entire list at one time rather than report individual Articles. As Adams explained, the reporting and enactment of these Articles laid "the foundation of a discipline which, in time, brought our troops to a capaci-

---

49. Id. at 108 (Art. XII).
50. Id. at 109.
51. Id. at 109 (Art. XXVIII).
52. 5 Journals 693.
53. "Brief for the Respondent," United States ex rel. Ernest Peter Burger [Ex parte Quirin], 39 Landmark Briefs and Arguments of the Supreme Court of the United States: Constitutional Law 472 (Philip B. Kurland and Gerhard Casper eds. 1975) (hereafter "Landmark Briefs").

ty of contending with British veterans, and a rivalry with the best troops of France."[54]

The national legislature in America maintained control over the Articles of War. The Articles of Confederation, agreed to by Congress on November 15, 1777, and ratified by the states on March 1, 1781, placed control over military law in the Congress, empowering it to make "rules for the government and regulation of the said land and naval forces, and directing their operations."[55] The Continental Congress adopted amendments to the Articles, including the requirement that no sentence of a general court-martial could be executed until a report was first made to Congress, the Commander in Chief, or the continental general commanding in the state.[56] The general could suspend a death sentence "until the pleasure of Congress can be known."[57] Congress specifically approved a death sentence for James Molesworth, who had been convicted of being a spy.[58] As Commander in Chief, George Washington adhered to the Articles of War enacted by the Continental Congress and reviewed sentences issued by courts-martial.[59]

At times, Washington disapproved a sentence by a court-martial because he concluded that it lacked a legal basis. On April 15, 1778, he discussed a general court-martial of Samuel Carter, an inhabitant of New Jersey, for taking arms to the enemy. Washington decided that the sentence "was illegally constituted" and it was necessary to disapprove it "for that reason." He wanted Carter delivered to the civil authority of New Jersey because he "knew they had Laws fully competent to the punishment of offenders of such a nature." Washington said he was "not fully satisfied of the legality of trying an inhabitant of any State by Military Law, when the Civil authority of that State has made provision for the punishment of persons taking Arms with the Enemy."[60]

Changes in the military code required legislative action. Washington advised Congress on December 8, 1779, that any alteration "can only be defined and fixed by Congress."[61] To that end, he submitted recommendations to Congress. Early in 1781 he pointed out that the "highest corpo-

---

54. 3 The Works of John Adams 69 (1851).
55. 4 Washington 114.
56. 7 Journals 264–65.
57. Id. at 266.
58. Id. at 210.
59. 13 Washington 136–40.
60. 11 Washington 262.
61. 17 Washington 239.

ral punishment we are allowed to give is an hundred lashes; between that and death there are no degrees."[62] Various examples demonstrated that the former punishment was inadequate. Courts-martial "to preserve some proportion between the crime and the punishment are obliged to pronounce the sentence of death," but too frequent recourse to capital sentences "render[ed] their execution in most cases inexpedient."[63] Washington thought it would be useful if courts-martial could sentence delinquents to labor at public works or perhaps transfer the individuals "from the land to the sea service, where they have less opportunity to indulge their inconstancy."[64]

Trial of Major André

In 1780, in the midst of the war of independence, American soldiers apprehended a British spy, Major John André. General Washington reported the matter to Maj. Gen. Nathanael Greene, alerting him to transactions "of a most interesting nature such as will astonish You."[65] André, a British intelligence officer, had met with the American general Benedict Arnold on the morning of September 22, 1780, after maintaining a secret correspondence with him. At the time, Arnold served as commandant at West Point and was prepared to betray his country and surrender the fort for £20,000. When American soldiers captured André the next day, he had in his boots papers (in Arnold's handwriting) concerning West Point. Washington learned that the soldiers who arrested André were offered "a large sum of money for his release, and as many goods as they would demand, but without effect. Their conduct gives them a just claim to the thanks of their country."[66]

Washington urged "every precaution of attention" to prevent André's escape.[67] While not wishing him "to be treated with insult," Washington explained that "he does not appear to stand upon the footing of a common prisoner of War and therefore he is not intitled [sic] to the usual indulgences they receive."[68] By substituting civilian clothes for his military uniform, André's appearance "in a disguised habit" placed him in the category

62. 21 Washington 178.
63. Id. at 178–79.
64. Id. at 179.
65. 20 Washington 85.
66. Id. at 92.
67. Id. at 86.
68. Id. at 87.

of a spy.[69] André argued that he should be treated as a prisoner of war, not a spy, because he came to Arnold under a flag of truce and obeyed orders that Arnold had a right to give. However, flags do not sanction treason or spying, and André's argument that he came behind enemy lines legally was contradicted by his decision to change from his officer's uniform to civilian clothes and to adopt an assumed name.[70]

Washington designated a board of officers to try André. The board, consisting of 14 officers, met at an old Dutch church at Tappan, New York, with the Judge Advocate present to assist with the examination.[71] The board, setting forth the facts, recommended that André be sentenced to death:

> That he came on Shore from the Vulture Sloop of war in the night of the Twenty first of September Instant on an interview with General Arnold in a private and secret manner. Secondly that he changed his dress within our lines, and under a feigned name and in a disguised habit passed our Works at Stoney and Verplanks points the Evening of the Twenty second of September Instant, and was taken the morning of the Twenty third of September Instant, at Tarry Town, in a disguised habit, being then on his way to New York, and when taken he had in his possession Several papers which contained intelligence for the Enemy. The Board having maturely considered these Facts do also report to His Excellency General Washington, that Major André Adjutant General to the British Army ought to be considered as a Spy from the Enemy, and that agreable [sic] to the Law and usage of Nations it is their opinion he ought to suffer death.[72]

André petitioned Washington to be shot, which was the preferred treatment for officers and those of higher class. He resigned himself to his fate, but "would be happy, if possible, to be indulged a professional death."[73] Repelled by "the idea of a felon's death,"[74] André directed these sentiments to Washington: "Sympathy towards a soldier will surely induce your Excel-

---

69. Id. at 101.

70. James Thomas Flexner, The Traitor and the Spy: Benedict Arnold and John André 384 (1991 ed.).

71. Winthrop Sargent, The Life of Major John André 347 (1871).

72. 20 Washington 103–4.

73. Sargent, The Life of Major John André, at 368.

74. Id. at 371.

lency and a military tribunal to adapt the mode of my death to the feelings of a man of honor. Let me hope, Sir, that if ought in my character impresses you with esteem toward me, if ought in my misfortunes marks me the victim of policy and not of resentment, I shall experience the operation of those feelings in your heart, by being informed that I am not to die on a gibbet."[75]

Washington decided that "the practice and usage of war, circumstanced as he was, were against the indulgence."[76] The customary method of dealing with spies was by hanging. On October 2, 1780, André climbed aboard a wagon that was destined to be driven beneath the gallows' pole, took the rope from the hangman and adjusted it around his neck, and tied a handkerchief around his eyes. Asked if he had any final words, he said: "All I request of you, gentlemen, is that you will bear witness to the world that I die like a brave man."[77] As the wagon rolled away, André took leave of this world.

A month later, Congress voted to recognize "the virtuous and patriotic conduct" of the three soldiers who arrested André, granting them the annual amount of 200 dollars in specie, and ordering the minting of a silver medal with the inscription "Fidelity" on one side and the motto "Vincit amor patriæ" on the other.[78] Benedict Arnold escaped to England, where he died in 1801.

Congressional Oversight

After America's victory over the British, strong pressures built to disband the Continental Army. Before that could happen, measures had to be taken to settle accounts, make payments, and decide the type of military force that could protect the frontier settlements against Indian attacks and secure areas still vulnerable to British influence. Congress debated whether to rely on a national army or a militia furnished by the states. A powerful prejudice stood in the way of a standing army, but serious deficiencies plagued a part-time militia of volunteers.[79]

---

75. Id. at 390.

76. 20 Washington 131.

77. Sargent, The Life of Major John André, at 395. For further accounts, see Joshua Hett Smith, Narrative of the Death of Major André (1969 ed.; originally published in 1808); Malcolm Decker, Ten Days of Infamy: An Illustrated Memoir of the Arnold-André Conspiracy (1969).

78. 18 Journals 1009–10.

79. Richard H. Kohn, Eagle and Sword 40–53 (1975).

On June 2, 1784, Congress discharged what remained of the Continental Army. It kept in place 25 privates to guard the stores at Fort Pitt and 55 to guard the stores at West Point and other magazines. It also kept the officers needed to supervise these men, but no officer above the rank of captain.[80] On the following day, Congress called on four states (Connecticut, New York, New Jersey, and Pennsylvania) for 700 troops, to be "properly officered."[81] These troops were to be subject to all the rules and regulations that had applied to the Continental Army.[82]

The Continental Congress, learning of unauthorized initiatives taken by military commanders, found it necessary to reenter the arena to clarify national policy. The military was supposed to notify Congress of any death sentence and await legislative approval. In March 1786, however, Congress discovered that Major John P. Wyllys on the western frontier had executed several soldiers found guilty of desertion.[83] He decided that capital punishment was "absolutely necessary" to deal with the problem of desertions.[84] In the midst of one court-martial proceeding, three men had deserted. They were captured and brought back to the garrison, and Wyllys "ordered them immediately to be put to death, which was done." After those executions, no further desertions occurred, a result he attributed to the severity of the punishment.[85]

Congress learned of the impractical requirement in the existing Articles of War, which required a general court-martial of 13 officers in all cases of capital crimes, followed by the approval of Congress, the Commander in Chief, or the general commanding a separate department. The small number of troops in remote outposts made it difficult "and almost impossible" to form a general court-martial of that size.[86] Secretary at War Henry Knox told Congress that "a full investigation of all the circumstances attending this transaction should be made immediately in order that Congress may ground thereon their ultimate determination respecting the same." He also recommended that Wyllys be suspended until the further order of Congress. He directed that two men sentenced by court-martial under Wyllys be released, "their trial having been illegal." Knox recognized that if Congress disagreed with his judgment, it could reverse him.[87]

---

80. 27 Journals 524.
81. Id. at 530, 536–40.
82. Id. at 539–40.
83. 30 Journals 115.
84. Id. at 119.
85. Id. at 120.
86. Id.
87. Id. at 121.

The War Power Transformed

These disputes over the Articles of War should not obscure more fundamental changes in the war power. In breaking with England, America not only parted company physically and politically but dispensed as well with British precedents toward the war power. John Locke counseled that all of the external power of government should be placed with the executive.[88] Similarly, William Blackstone defined the king's prerogative to include all of foreign and military affairs: the power to make war or peace, to raise and regulate fleets and armies, to make treaties, to appoint ambassadors, and to issue letters of marque and reprisal (authorizing private citizens to undertake military actions).[89]

When the framers declared their independence from England, they vested all executive powers in the Continental Congress. The ninth article of the Articles of Confederation provided: "The United States, in Congress assembled, shall have the sole and exclusive right and power of determining on peace and war." The single exception to that principle lay in the sixth article, which allowed states to engage in war if invaded by enemies or when threatened with invasion by Indian tribes.

The war power of the Continental Congress extended to both "perfect" and "imperfect" wars: to wars that were formally declared by Congress, and those that were merely authorized. As a federal court of appeals noted in 1782, a perfect war "destroys the national peace and tranquillity, and lays the foundation of every possible act of hostility," whereas an imperfect war "does not entirely destroy the public tranquillity, but interrupts it only in some particulars, as in the case of reprisals."[90] The power over perfect and imperfect wars would be transferred to Congress by the Constitution of 1787.

Not a single one of the Blackstone's prerogatives over war and foreign affairs would be vested solely in the President. The power to go to war was not left to a solitary decision by the President, but to collective decision making through parliamentary deliberations. The powers to declare war, to raise armies and navies, to decide foreign commerce, and to issue letters of marque and reprisal were placed in Article I, defining the powers of Congress. The power over treaties and appointing ambassadors was shared between the President and the Senate. The framers recognized that

---

88. John Locke, Second Treatise on Civil Government §§ 146–48 (1690).
89. 2 William Blackstone, Commentaries on the Laws of England 238–62 (1803).
90. Miller v. The Ship Resolution, 2 Dall. (2 U.S.) 19, 20 (1782).

in times of emergency, especially when Congress was not in session, the President would have the power "to repel sudden attacks."[91] This grant of defensive power did not extend to offensive operations. Elbridge Gerry said he "never expected to hear in a republic a motion to empower the Executive alone to declare war."[92] George Mason spoke "agst giving the power of war to the Executive, because not [safely] to be trusted with it."[93]

The framers placed the war power in Congress because of their belief in a republic, popular control, and representative democracy. Their study of history convinced them that executives, in their search for fame and personal glory, had an appetite for war and entered into hostilities that were ruinous for the nation. John Jay warned in *Federalist* No. 4 that "absolute monarchs will often make war when their nations are to get nothing by it, but for purposes and objects merely personal, such as a thirst for military glory, revenge for personal affronts, ambition, or private compacts to aggrandize or support their particular families or partisans. These and a variety of other motives, which affect only the mind of the sovereign, often lead him to engage in wars not sanctified by justice or the voice and interests of his people."

The delegates at the Philadelphia Convention agreed to make the President Commander in Chief, but that title must be understood in the context of military responsibilities assigned to Congress. The constitutional language provides: "The President shall be Commander in Chief of the Army and Navy of the United States, and of the Militia of the several States, when called into the actual Service of the United States." Congress, not the President, does the calling. Article I gave Congress the power to provide "for calling forth the Militia to execute the Laws of the Union, suppress Insurrections and repel invasions."

In *Federalist* No. 74, Alexander Hamilton explained part of the purpose for making the President Commander in Chief. The direction of war "most peculiarly demands those qualities which distinguish the exercise of power by a single head." The power of directing war and emphasizing the common strength "forms a usual and essential part in the definition of the executive authority." In *Federalist* No. 69, Hamilton offered a modest definition of commander-in-chief powers, claiming that the office "would amount to nothing more than the supreme command and direction of the military and

91. 2 The Records of the Federal Convention of 1787, at 318–19 (Max Farrand ed. 1937).
92. Id. at 318.
93. Id. at 319.

naval forces, as first general and admiral of the Confederacy." He used this language to allay fears in the states about the scope of presidential power. However, as Washington's aide during the revolutionary war, Hamilton understood that "command and direction" are more than clerical tasks. They can be powerful determinants of the scope and duration of a war.

Designating the President as Commander in Chief represented an important technique for preserving civilian supremacy over the military. The person leading the armed forces would be the civilian President, not a military officer. One of the complaints included in the Declaration of Independence was that George III had "affected to render the Military independent of and superior to the Civil Power." Attorney General Edward Bates explained in 1861 that the President is Commander in Chief not because he is "skilled in the art of war and qualified to marshal a host in the field of battle." He is Commander in Chief for a different reason. Whatever soldier leads U.S. armies to victory against an enemy, "he is subject to the orders of the *civil magistrate,* and he and his army are always 'subordinate to the civil power.'"[94]

America inherited military tribunals from British precedents and its own experiences during the Revolutionary War, but it also adopted the fundamental principle that military tribunals and the war power flowed from legislative judgments reached by the people's representatives. That principle was respected for the next 70 years until the outbreak of civil war, which placed many of the decisions to create military tribunals in the hands of President Lincoln and his military commanders. Congress had little to say, and only after the war did it begin to reassert its constitutional authority and responsibility. In the years before the Civil War, Congress took note of initiatives by Gen. Andrew Jackson and Gen. Winfield Scott, who authorized the creation of military tribunals.

94. 10 Op. Att'y Gen. 74, 79 (1861) (emphasis in original).

2

AMERICAN PRECEDENTS

After ratification of the Constitution, one of the first duties of the new Congress was to pass legislation in 1789 to establish rules for the military. Subsequent legislation added further details on congressional policy. Throughout this formative period, it was the understanding of executive officials and military commanders that statutory policy would define standards of conduct within the army and naval forces. New conflicts would arise with the use of military tribunals by Andrew Jackson and during the Mexican War, but even here, it was recognized that whatever initiatives military commanders might take, when driven by necessity, Congress could always revisit the issue and override executive precedents with new legislation.

Constitutional Powers

No one questioned the authority of Congress to define the rules of war. Under Section 8 of Article I of the Constitution, Congress is empowered to "define and punish Piracies and Felonies committed on the high Seas, and Offences against the Law of Nations," and it is the responsibility of Congress to "make rules for the Government and Regulation of the land and naval Forces." Vesting rule-making authority in Congress marked a dramatic break with English precedents. British kings were accustomed to issue, on their own authority, Articles of War and military rules.[1]

At the Philadelphia Convention, the Rules and Regulation Clause was adopted with little debate.[2] The delegates understood that the language was being picked up bodily "from the existing Articles of Confederation."[3] Joseph Story, who served on the Supreme Court from 1811 to 1845, explained that the power of Congress to make rules for the military is "a

---

1. William Winthrop, Military Law and Precedents 18–19 (1920).
2. 2 The Records of the Federal Convention of 1787, at 323 (Max Farrand ed. 1937) (hereafter "Farrand").
3. Id. at 330.

natural incident to the preceding powers to make war, to raise armies, and to provide and maintain a navy."[4] He noted that in Great Britain, the King, "in his capacity of generalissimo of the whole kingdom, has the sole power of regulating fleets and armies."[5] Story continued: "The whole power is far more safe in the hands of congress, than in the executive; since otherwise the most summary and severe punishments might be inflicted at the mere will of the executive."[6]

Just as the Rules and Regulation Clause empowers Congress to legislate on militia law within the United States, so does the constitutional provision dealing with "Offenses against the Law of Nations" authorize Congress to pass legislation dealing with law in an international context. At the time of America's break with England, the phrase *law of nations* referred to a body of international law that regulated the conduct of individual nations. Writers of the sixteenth and seventeenth centuries spoke of two legal categories: the law of nature (*jus naturae,* or certain universal principles) and the law of nations (*jus gentium,* including treaties and other conventions). Some nations recognized that "international law" can cover a body of obligations that are independent of and superior to domestic legislation.[7]

When America declared its independence from Britain, it recognized the force of the law of nations. Although the Articles of Confederation made no express mention of the power of the Continental Congress regarding offenses against the law of nations, Congress had been active in giving it scope. It enacted national policy for captures, seizures, prizes, and reprisals of all ships and goods taken during hostilities and created a Court of Appeals in Cases of Captures.[8] The judicial rules for decisions "shall be the resolutions and ordinances of the United States in Congress assembled, public treaties when declared to be so by an act of Congress, and the law of nations, according to the general usages of Europe."[9] Captains and commanders of private armed vessels were instructed to "tak[e] care not to infringe or violate the laws of nations, or laws of neutrality."[10]

At the Philadelphia Convention, James Madison discussed the relation-

4. Joseph Story, Commentaries on the Constitution of the United States 418 (Ronald D. Rotunda and John E. Nowak eds. 1987).

5. Id.

6. Id.

7. 1 John Bassett Moore, A Digest of International Law 1–2 (1906).

8. 19 Journals of the Continental Congress 314–16 (1781) (hereafter "Journals"), 360–61; 20 Journals 761–67; 21 Journals 1136–37, 1152–58.

9. 21 Journals 1158 (1781).

10. 19 Journals 361.

ship between the war power and the law of nations and explained why the Constitution vests both in Congress. In drafting a constitution, it was important to "prevent those violations of the law of nations & of Treaties which if not prevented must involve us in the calamities of foreign wars."[11] In *Federalist* No. 3, John Jay warned that "either designed or accidental violations of treaties and the laws of nations afford just causes of war."[12] Under British precedents and the prerogative powers enunciated by Blackstone, the King exercised exclusive control over defining the law of nations; that duty under the Constitution would be discharged by Congress, not the President.

Congress passed legislation in 1790 to prescribe punishments for certain crimes against the United States. One provision established fines and imprisonment for any person who attempted to prosecute or bring legal action against an ambassador or other public minister from another country. Persons who took such actions were deemed "violators of the law of nations" who "infract the law of nations."[13] As James Kent noted in his *Commentaries,* an action against an ambassador or public minister "tends to provoke the resentment of the sovereign who the ambassador represents, and to bring upon the state the calamities of war."[14]

Statutory Framework

A treatise by Alexander Macomb in 1809 described U.S. martial law as flowing from congressional action in the same manner as domestic law: "Martial law, as it exists in this country, forms part of the Laws of the Land; and it is enacted by the same authority which is the origin of all other statutory regulations." As a consequence, it has "the same positive obligation on those whom it is intended to bind, as the Common and Statute Law has on all the citizens of the United States."[15] The source of martial law in America, Macomb noted, derives from rules and Articles of War enacted by Congress.

Legislation in 1789 stated that military troops "shall be governed by the rules and articles of war which have been established by the United States in Congress assembled, or by such rules and articles of war, as may here-

---

11. 1 Farrand 316.
12. The Federalist 99 (Benjamin Fletcher Wright ed. 1961) (emphasis in original).
13. 1 Stat. 117–18, sections 25–28 (1790).
14. 1 James Kent, Commentaries on American Law 170 (1826).
15. Alexander Macomb, A Treatise on Martial Law and Courts-Martial 7 (1809).

after by law be established."[16] This language incorporated the Articles of War previously adopted by the Continental Congress and gave notice that Congress, under its constitutional authority, would legislate as necessary in the future.

Congress retained the provisions of the Continental Congress rules until changing conditions forced new legislation. On January 13, 1804, the House appointed a committee "to revise the rules and articles for the government of the Army of the United States."[17] After the committee reported a bill on March 8, floor debate began on March 15.[18] The debate was quite brief, giving one member an opportunity to successfully challenge language that sought to punish military officers or soldiers who used "traitorous or disrespectful words" against the President, the Vice President, Congress, the Chief Justice, or state legislatures.[19] No further action was taken until November 30, when the House again appointed a committee to revise the rules and articles of the army.[20]

A new bill, reported on December 12,[21] passed the House on December 17 after the adoption of several amendments.[22] The bill was referred to a Senate committee, reported with amendments, and came to the floor.[23] Senator John Quincy Adams vented his exasperation:

> It is a very long bill, and a very strong disposition appeared to carry it through all its stages without reading it at all. . . . Its defects of various kinds were numerous, and among the most conspicuous was a continual series of the most barbarous English that ever crept through the bars of legislation. In many instances the articles prescribing oaths, and even penalties of death, were so loosely and indistinctly expressed as to be scarcely intelligible, or liable to double and treble equivocation. Besides this, there were many variations from the old Articles, which I did not approve.[24]

Adams insisted that the bill be read in stages, paragraph by paragraph. The chairman of the reporting committee bridled at this suggestion. Late in

16. 1 Stat. 96, sec. 4 (1789).
17. Annals of Cong., 8th Cong. 882 (1804).
18. Id. at 1123.
19. Id. at 1190–91.
20. Annals of Cong., 8th Cong., 2d Sess. 726 (1804).
21. Id. at 808.
22. Id. at 835–36, 858–59.
23. Id. at 27, 33, 42.
24. 1 Memoirs of John Quincy Adams 338 (1874).

the afternoon, a motion was made to recommit the bill to a select committee, but not to the one that reported it. The chairman of the reporting
committee announced that he had offered all the amendments he thought
necessary, and if it was to be recommitted, it should be to a different committee.[25] On January 25, 1805, the amended bill went to a committee of
three, chaired by Adams.[26] He reported the bill for floor action, but further
consideration would await the next session of Congress.[27]

On December 6, 1805, Rep. Joseph B. Varnum reminded the House that
the rules and regulations for the army "had never been revised since the
era of the present Government; and that consequently the rules and regulations established during the Revolutionary war still continued in force,
though our circumstances had materially changed."[28] The House appointed a committee of seven to prepare a bill, which was reported on December 18.[29] This time the bill, after House and Senate amendments, passed
Congress and became law.[30]

The bill, enacted on April 10, 1806, consisted of 101 Articles of War. Many
of the provisions defined the punishments and procedures to be followed
by courts-martial. Prisoners, for example, were not required to testify: "When
a prisoner arraigned before a general court martial shall, from obstinacy and
deliberate design, stand mute or answer foreign to the purpose, the court
may proceed to trial and judgment as if the prisoner had regularly pleaded
not guilty."[31] No person "shall be sentenced to suffer death, but by the concurrence of two thirds of the members of a general court martial."[32]

The 1806 statute, reflecting the André precedent, provided that in time
of war "all persons not citizens of, or owing allegiance to the United States
of America, who shall be found lurking as spies, in or about the fortifications or encampments of the armies of the United States, or any of them,
shall suffer death, according to the law and usages of nations, by sentence
of a general court martial."[33] The sentence of death for spies was well
known by all nations, including the Nazi saboteurs who made their way to
American shores wearing parts of a German uniform. In case they were

25. Id. at 339.
26. Annals of Cong., 8th Cong., 2d Sess. 42.
27. Id. at 64, 66.
28. Annals of Cong., 9th Cong., 1st Sess. 264 (1805).
29. Id. at 294.
30. House action at 326–27, 332–33, 337–38, 339, 729, 760, 838, 849, 878; Senate
action at 48, 143, 163, 167, 181–82, 200–201, 207, 210.
31. 2 Stat. 368 (1806) (Art. 70).
32. Id. at 369 (Art. 87).
33. Id. at 371 (Art. 101(2)).

captured, they could claim the right to be treated not as spies but as prisoners of war.

Experience during the War of 1812 underscored the urgent need for Congress to clarify the procedures for courts-martial. President James Madison, in a message of December 7, 1813, recommended that Congress prepare "a revision of the militia laws."[34] The House of Representatives responded by directing that the President's message "as relates to a revision of the Militia laws, be referred to a select committee."[35] The committee reported legislation on February 15, 1814,[36] and it reached the floor on March 29 for debate. Rep. John W. Taylor (D-N.Y.) explained that "different opinions had been entertained as to the jurisdiction of courts martial, which ought to be conclusively settled—and such was the object of this bill."[37] Although some members objected that the provisions on courts-martial were "not according with the principles of the Constitution, and possibly as hazarding the existence of civil liberty,"[38] the bill passed 88 to 53.[39] The Senate agreed to the bill, with some amendments, and the two houses produced a compromise measure that went to President Madison for his signature.[40]

Congress reentered the field of military law in 1830 to correct a conflict of interest problem with courts-martial. Maj. Gen. Alexander Macomb brought charges against Col. Roger Jones, Adjutant General of the Army, for issuing special orders and publishing material in the *Army Register* without first receiving Macomb's review and approval.[41] Not only did Macomb bring the charges, he appeared before the court-martial as the principal prosecution witness and later approved the proceedings that decided on a reprimand for Jones.[42] Similar controversies would later emerge with military tribunals.

Congress found Macomb's action so open to abuse that it amended the Articles of War to prevent future repetitions. Article 65, as adopted in 1806,

---

34. 2 A Compilation of the Messages and Papers of the Presidents 523 (James D. Richardson ed. 1925) (hereafter "Richardson").

35. Annals of Cong., 13th Cong., 1st Sess.–2d Sess. 785 (1813).

36. Id. at 1431.

37. Annals of Cong., 13th Cong., 2d Sess. 1930 (1814).

38. Id. at 1930.

39. Id. at 1931.

40. Id. at 2022, 2026. For Senate action, see Annals of Cong., 13th Cong., 1st Sess.–2d Sess. 545, 546, 548, 632, 638, 639, 640, 691–92, 737, 762–63, 764, 766 (1813–14). Public law: 3 Stat. 134 (1814).

41. H. Doc. No. 104, 21st Cong., 1st Sess. 3–4, 10–11, 14 (1830).

42. Id. at 10–12, 45. The material in the House document also appears at 4 American State Papers: Military Affairs 450–78 (1860).

had authorized any general officer commanding an army to appoint general courts-martial. Only in cases of loss of life or the dismissal of a commissioned officer would the proceedings be transmitted to the Secretary of War, to be laid before the President for confirmation or approval. All other sentences could be confirmed and executed by the officer who ordered the court to assemble.[43] House debate in 1830 pointed out the opportunity for mischief when "the general or colonel ordering the court is himself the accuser and prosecutor, when it would be obviously inconsistent with the common principles of justice, that the members of a court who are to sit in judgment upon the accused should be detailed by an individual interested in the event of the trial, and who, under the influence of that feeling, might select officers hostile to the party accused, or peculiarly attached to himself."[44]

Congress enacted legislation to provide that whenever an officer is the accuser or prosecutor of any officer under his command, "the general court-martial for the trial of such officer shall be appointed by the President of the United States."[45] This statute corrected the conflict of interest problem within the military but not within the executive branch. For example, in the Nazi saboteur case of 1942, President Franklin D. Roosevelt issued a military order and proclamation to create a military tribunal, appointed the generals who served on the tribunal, and appointed the prosecutors (the Attorney General and the Judge Advocate General) and the colonels who served as defense counsel. All of those officials were subordinate to the President. After the tribunal completed its deliberations and reached a verdict, the court transcript then went to Roosevelt as the final reviewing authority.[46]

Treatises on martial law examined the possible friction or competition between civil and military courts. To Macomb, the military law contained in the Articles of War "does not in any respect either supercede or interfere with the civil and municipal laws of the country."[47] He identified a provision in Article of War 33 that whenever any commissioned officer or soldier was accused of a capital crime, and of having committed an offense against the persons or property of a U.S. citizen, the military had a duty to transfer the person to a civil magistrate for trial. Military law was "so much subordinate to the civil" that military authorities were "expressly required"

43. 2 Stat. 367 (1806).
44. Cong. Debates, 21st Cong., 1st Sess. 575 (1830).
45. 4 Stat. 417 (1830).
46. See Chapter 5 for further details.
47. Macomb, A Treatise on Martial Law, at 27.

to use their "utmost endeavors" to deliver the accused person to the civil magistrate.[48]

Andrew Jackson in New Orleans

During the War of 1812, Andrew Jackson resorted to martial law when he commanded American forces at New Orleans. On December 15, 1814, anticipating a British invasion of the city, he issued a statement alerting residents to "his unalterable determination rigidly to execute the martial law in all cases which may come within his province."[49] The general order for martial law was released the next day, requiring anyone entering the city to report to the Adjutant General's office. Failure to do so would result in arrest and detention. No person could leave the city "without a permission in writing signed by the General or one of his staff." Street lamps would be extinguished at 9 PM, after which individuals found in the streets "shall be apprehended as spies and held for examination."[50]

After Jackson's victory over the British, the citizens of New Orleans expected him to rescind the order for martial law. It was not to be. Martial law continued, even with peace negotiations underway at Ghent. An article in the local newspaper by Louis Louallier insisted that persons accused of a crime should be heard before a civil judge, not military tribunals, and called Jackson's policy "no longer compatible with our dignity and our oath of making the Constitution respected."[51] Jackson had him arrested on March 5, 1815, for inciting mutiny and disaffection in the army. Louallier's lawyer went to U.S. District Judge Dominick Augustin Hall to request a writ of habeas corpus, which the judge granted after concluding that martial law could no longer be justified. Jackson directed his military officers that "should any person attempt by serving a writ of Habeas corpus" for Louallier, that person was to be arrested and confined.[52] Reaching the remark-

---

48. Id. at 28–29.

49. 3 Papers of Andrew Jackson 205 (Harold D. Moser ed. 1991).

50. Id. at 206–7. See also Robert V. Remini, The Battle of New Orleans: Andrew Jackson and America's First Military Victory, at 57–59 (2001 paper ed.).

51. Robert V. Remini, Andrew Jackson and the Course of American Empire, 1767–1821, at 310 (1977). I've seen a variety of spellings: Louallier, Louiallier, and Louailler. The first appears to be more reliable because of contemporary usage. See Henry P. Dart, ed., "Andrew Jackson and Judge D. A. Hall," 5 La. Hist. Q. 509, 538–45 (1922).

52. 2 Correspondence of Andrew Jackson 183 (letter to Lt. Col. Mathew Arbuckle, March 5, 1815).

able conclusion that Hall had engaged "in aiding abetting and inciting mutiny within my camp," Jackson ordered his arrest and confinement.[53] Judge Hall found himself locked up in the same barracks as the writer.[54]

A court-martial acquitted Louallier, in part because he challenged the jurisdiction of the court to try someone who was not a member of the militia or the army. As to the charge of spying, the court considered it far-fetched that a spy would publish his views in a newspaper that circulated in Jackson's camp. Jackson disagreed with the acquittal and kept Louallier in jail. As for Judge Hall, Jackson recognized that the military court was unlikely to convict a federal judge. He thus ordered Hall out of the city, not to return until the official announcement of peace or until the British left the southern coast.[55] On March 12, Jackson's troops marched Hall four miles outside of New Orleans and left him there. On the following day, after official confirmation of the peace treaty arrived, Jackson revoked martial law and released Louallier.[56]

Judge Hall made his way back to the city, prepared to even the score with Jackson. On March 22, he ordered Jackson to appear in court to show why he should not be held in contempt for refusing to obey the court's writ of habeas corpus and for having imprisoned Hall.[57] Jackson appeared with an aide, submitted a written statement why he was not in contempt, and withdrew. His aide objected that the court lacked jurisdiction to consider sanctions against Jackson. In a prepared statement for the court, Jackson argued that if he had exercised power "wantonly or improperly" (which he denied), he would be liable not to a court for contempt but "to his government for an abuse of power & to those individuals whom he has injured, in damages proportioned to that injury."[58]

Jackson returned to the court on March 31 to answer interrogatories. He told Judge Hall that he would not respond to the questions because when he attempted "to shew cause why an attachment for a contempt of this Court ought not to run against me," Hall "tho't proper to refuse me this constitutional right—you would not hear my defence, although you were advised that it contained sufficient cause to show that no attachment ought

53. Id.

54. Remini, Andrew Jackson and the Course of American Empire, 1767–1821, at 310.

55. 2 Correspondence of Andrew Jackson 189 (letter to Capt. Peter Ogden, March 11, 1815, and order to Judge Hall, March 11, 1815).

56. 3 Papers of Andrew Jackson 310; Remini, Andrew Jackson and the Course of American Empire, 1767–1821, at 312.

57. Dart, "Andrew Jackson and Judge D. A. Hall," at 545.

58. 3 Papers of Andrew Jackson 332.

to run." Under the circumstances, Jackson agreed to appear before the court to receive the sentence "& have nothing further to add." He cautioned that his remarks were not intended to show "any disrespect to the Court," but denied an opportunity to explain "the reasons and motives which influenced my conduct, so it is expected that censure will form no part of that punishment which your honor may imagine it your duty to pronounce."[59] After further proceedings, Hall fined Jackson $1,000, which Jackson paid.[60]

Jackson offered a definition of emergency power that bears an eerie resemblance to a formulation later used by Lincoln. Rights enjoyed under peaceful conditions, Jackson said, may have to be surrendered in times of crisis, so "that we may secure the permanent enjoyment of the former. Is it wise, in such a moment, to sacrifice the spirit of the laws to the letter, and by adhering too strictly to the letter, lose the substance forever, in order that we may, for an instant, preserve the shadow?"[61] Lincoln asked Congress on July 4, 1861: "are all the laws, but one, to go unexecuted, and the government itself go to pieces, lest that one be violated?"[62]

On March 10, 1842, Senator Lewis F. Linn (D-Mo.) introduced a bill to remit the fine imposed on Jackson. He proposed that the fine of $1,000 with costs imposed by Judge Hall "be refunded to him, with legal interest."[63] In his Second Annual Message, delivered on December 6, 1842, President John Tyler urged Congress to pass the bill. "Without designing any reflection on the judicial tribunal which imposed the fine," Tyler said that "the remission at this day may be regarded as not unjust or inexpedient." The size of the fine was not significant from "a pecuniary point of view," but "it can hardly be doubted that it would be gratifying to the war-worn veteran, now in retirement and in the winter of his days, to be relieved from the circumstances in which that judgment placed him." Given Jackson's record in defending New Orleans, Tyler believed that the remission of the fine "would be in accordance with the general feeling and wishes of the American people."[64]

---

59. Id. at 342–43.

60. Id. at 343; John Spencer Bassett, The Life of Andrew Jackson 228–29 (1931). For other accounts of the contempt proceedings, see John Reid and John Henry Eaton, The Life of Andrew Jackson 384–90 (1817), and Jonathan Lurie, "Andrew Jackson, Martial Law, Civilian Control of the Military, and American Politics: An Intriguing Amalgam," 126 Mil. L. Rev. 133 (1989).

61. 3 Papers of Andrew Jackson 313.

62. 4 The Collected Works of Abraham Lincoln 30 (Roy P. Basler ed. 1953) (emphasis in original).

63. Cong. Globe, 27th Cong., 2d Sess. 304 (1842).

64. 5 Richardson 2062.

Some versions of the bill were drafted to avoid any possible reproach directed against Judge Hall, such as by stating that "nothing herein contained shall be intended to be so construed as to imply any censure upon the judge who imposed said fine, or in any way to question the propriety of his decision in said case."[65] However, qualifications of that nature were stripped from the bill that became law in 1844.[66] Debate on the bill was extensive and spirited because lawmakers differed sharply on whether more credit was due to Jackson for defending the city or to Hall for defending the Constitution.[67]

Arbuthnot and Ambrister

A few years later, when commanding troops in Florida in 1818 during the Seminole War, Gen. Jackson again turned to a military tribunal. This time the trial involved two British subjects, Alexander Arbuthnot and Robert Christy Ambrister, charged with inciting and aiding the Creek Indians to war against the United States. Arbuthnot was also charged with acting as a spy and inciting the Indians to murder two men. He pleaded not guilty to all charges, while Ambrister pleaded not guilty to aiding and abetting the Creeks but guilty with justification to the charge that he led and commanded the Lower Creeks in carrying on a war against the United States.[68]

The "special court" consisted of eleven officers, headed by Maj. Gen. Edmund P. Gaines. Arbuthnot asked for legal representation and was granted counsel; the record does not indicate whether Ambrister requested counsel or was granted one. In the trial of Arbuthnot, the court heard from three witnesses for the prosecution and accepted a number of documents to be entered into the record. After Arbuthnot or his attorney cross-examined two of the witnesses, the court found him guilty of all charges except "acting as a spy." By a two-thirds majority, the court sentenced him "to be suspended by the neck until he is dead."[69]

---

65. Cong. Globe, 28th Cong., 1st Sess. 87 (1843).

66. 5 Stat. 651 (1844).

67. E.g., statement by Rep. Alexander H. Stephens, Cong. Globe, 28th Cong., 1st Sess. 87 (1843). For the debate, see id. at 18, 87–96, 111–15, 117–20, 206, 230, 245, 250–51, 263, 267–69, 274, 278. Also, see the separate floor statements in the Appendix to the Congressional Globe, 28th Cong., 1st Sess. 26–28, 32–37, 43–48, 58–63, 88–89, 112–13, 145, 194–96, 206–11, 226–30 (1844). See also Abraham D. Sofaer, "Emergency Power and the Hero of New Orleans," 2 Cardozo L. Rev. 233 (1981).

68. 1 American State Papers: Military Affairs 721, 731 (1832).

69. Id. at 730.

Ambrister's trial proceeded in similar fashion, with the court finding him guilty on most charges but not guilty on one of the specifications. He was sentenced "to suffer death by being shot, two-thirds of the court concurring therein." One of the members of the court requested reconsideration of his vote on the sentence, forcing a revote. The court then decided to sentence Ambrister to "receive fifty stripes on his bare back" and be confined with ball and chain to hard labor for 12 months.[70] Jackson overrode the court and directed that Ambrister be shot, an order that was carried out.

In his State of the Union Message on November 16, 1818, President James Monroe made reference to the trial of Arbuthnot and Ambrister and forwarded a number of documents to Congress related to the case.[71] The following year, the House Committee on Military Affairs issued a report highly critical of the trials. The committee could find "no law of the United States authorizing a trial before a military court for offences such as are alleged" against the two men, except that of "acting as a spy," for which Arbuthnot was found not guilty.[72] It acknowledged that the law of nations recognized that "where the war is with a savage nation, which observes no rules, and never gives quarter, we may punish them in the persons of any of their people whom we may take, (these belonging to the number of the guilty,) and endeavor, by this rigorous proceeding, to force them to respect the laws of humanity; but wherever severity is not absolutely necessary, clemency becomes a duty." Having examined the documentation, the committee was unable to find "a shadow of necessity for the death of the persons arraigned before the court."[73]

In looking through the general order of April 29, 1818, issued by Jackson for the executions, the committee discovered "this remarkable reason" to justify the deaths: "It is an established principle of the law of nations, that any individual of a nation, making war against the citizens of another nation, they being at peace, forfeits his allegiance, and becomes an outlaw and a pirate." The committee associated piracy with actions on the high seas, over which Jackson's military court would have no jurisdiction. The committee found similar difficulty in applying the charge of "outlaw" to Arbuthnot and Ambrister, for that term "applies only to the relations of individuals with their own Government."[74]

---

70. Id. at 734.
71. 2 Richardson 612. These documents are reprinted in Annals of Cong., 15th Cong., 2d Sess., starting at page 2136.
72. 1 American State Papers: Military Affairs 735.
73. Id.
74. Id.

The committee drew particular attention to the execution of Ambrister, "who, after having been subjected to a trial before a court which had no cognizance or jurisdiction over the offences charged against him, was shot by order of the commanding general [Jackson], contrary of the forms and usages of the army, and without regard to the finding of that court, which had been instituted as a guide for himself." The committee also criticized the military court that tried the two men: "A court-martial is a tribunal erected with limited jurisdiction, having for its guidance the same rules of evidence which govern courts of law; and yet Arbuthnot is refused by the court-martial, before whom he was on trial for his life, the benefit of Ambrister, who had not been put upon his trial at that time, and whose evidence would have been received by any court of law, as legal, if not credible." The committee further rebuked the court for allowing a leading question to one of the witnesses for the prosecution, William Hambly. By allowing this question and response, the court relied on an expression of opinion and belief rather than a statement of facts, "upon which alone could the court act." Hearsay evidence "in a case of life and death," the committee said, "was never before received against the accused in any court of this country."[75]

Having completed this evaluation, the committee disapproved the proceedings in the trial and execution of Arbuthnot and Ambrister. A minority report from the committee largely defended Jackson's actions, discovering "much which merits applause, and little that deserves censure." It faulted Jackson only for not accepting the judgment of the military court, which first sentenced Ambrister to be shot but later changed that to corporal punishment and confinement at hard labor. Jackson disapproved the change and ordered his execution. To the minority, it would have been "more correct for General Jackson, after submitting his case to a court-martial, not only to examine the facts as to his guilt, but to determine the punishment to be inflicted," thus acquiescing in the court's final decision.[76]

In 1819, the House debated a resolution to disapprove the "proceedings in the trial and execution" of Arbuthnot and Ambrister.[77] The debate continued for several weeks, stretching from January 18 to February 8. The resolution to censure Jackson was rejected in the Committee of the Whole by

75. Id.

76. Id. at 739. The committee report also appears at Annals of Cong., 15th Cong., 2d Sess. 515–27 (1819). The trial material, in the form printed in the American State Papers, was first published as The Trials of A. Arbuthnot and R. C. Ambrister, Charged with Exciting the Seminole Indians to War Against the United States of America (1819).

77. Annals of Cong., 15th Cong., 2d Sess. 583 (1819).

a vote of 54 to 90. The full House concurred with that judgment, voting 108 to 62 to support the trial and execution of Arbuthnot, and 107 to 63 to support the trial and execution of Ambrister.[78]

Having escaped the House censure, Jackson had to weather a critical Senate report issued on February 24, 1819, by a select committee created to examine the conduct of the Seminole War. In reviewing the executions of Arbuthnot and Ambrister, the committee said it "cannot but consider it as an unnecessary act of severity, on the part of the commanding general, and a departure from that mild and humane system towards prisoners, which, in all our conflicts with savage or civilized nations, has heretofore been considered, not only honorable to the national character, but conformable to the dictates of sound policy." As prisoners of war and subjects of a country "with whom the United States are at peace," the two men were entitled to be treated at least on a par with Indians. "No process of reasoning," said the committee, "can degrade them below the savages with whom they were connected." The committee further noted: "Humanity shudders at the idea of a cold-blooded execution of prisoners, disarmed, and in the power of the conquerer." The committee rejected the theory that Arbuthnot and Ambrister were "outlaws and pirates," and pointed out that Jackson, having created a military court to try them, set aside the sentence of whipping and confinement "and substituted for that sentence his own arbitrary will."[79] The Senate adjourned sine die on March 3 without taking action on the committee report.

Commenting on this trial later in his respected *Military Law and Precedents,* William Winthrop remarked that if any officer ordered an execution in the manner of Jackson, he "would now be indictable for murder."[80] William E. Birkhimer, in his 1904 treatise, defended Jackson's conduct. To Birkhimer, Jackson had asked the special court only for its *opinion,* both as to guilt and punishment, and the delivery of that opinion could not divest Jackson of the authority he possessed from the beginning: to proceed summarily against Arbuthnot and Ambrister and order their execution.[81] Birkhimer's analysis would allow generals to either execute civilians without trial or to dispense with the fact-finding and judgment that result from trial proceedings.

---

78. Id. at 1132, 1136.

79. S. Doc. No. 100, 15th Cong., 2d Sess. 11–12 (1819). This committee report is reprinted at Annals of Cong., 15th Cong., 2d Sess. 256–68 (1819). The language quoted in my paragraph appears on page 267.

80. Winthrop, Military Law and Precedents 465 (italics in original).

81. William E. Birkhimer, Military Government and Martial Law 354 (1904).

The Mexican War

Military tribunals were used during the war against Mexico, when American forces found themselves in a foreign country without a reliable judicial system to try offenders. Gen. Winfield Scott, placed in command of U.S. troops in Mexico, was concerned about the lack of discipline and misconduct among American soldiers, especially the volunteers. Before he left Washington, D.C., he drafted an order calling for martial law in Mexico for both American soldiers and Mexican citizens. He showed the draft order to Secretary of War William Marcy and Attorney General Nathan Clifford. Neither official expressed disapproval or opposition.[82] Marcy turned to Congress to recommend legislation that would authorize a military tribunal, but lawmakers declined to act.[83]

Scott knew from military history that lawless and undisciplined action by American soldiers in Mexico would invite and incite guerrilla uprisings. He was familiar with the mistakes of French soldiers, under Napoleon's command, when they reached Spain. Reacting to their record of plunder and rape, Spanish residents revolted and sparked a cycle of violence and atrocities. Napoleon escalated the conflict by threatening to cut off the ears of Spanish clergy suspected of helping the guerrillas. Scott intended to enforce discipline across the board to avert guerrilla war. He designed the martial law order to guarantee Mexican property rights and to recognize the sanctity of religious structures.[84]

During congressional debate in late 1846, lawmakers discussed the situation in Mexico and the scope of martial law. Rep. James Seddon (D-Va.) insisted that war had to respect moral obligations: "in more barbarous ages, when the maxim originated, it may have been true that *inter arma leges silent*." Yet Seddon rejected the idea that conquerors could seize whatever they liked and reduce the population to slavery: "such savage courses are long since obsolete." In the midst of war, "law does now speak, to humanize and restrain, as in the gentler times of peace, it is felt to elevate and civilize." Of all the nations, he said, "we should be, and are, I believe, the last to depart from or evade the obligations of this high code."[85]

On February 19, 1847, Gen. Scott issued General Orders No. 20, proclaiming a state of martial law at Tampico. Certain specified acts commit-

82. Timothy D. Johnson, Winfield Scott: The Quest for Military Glory 165 (1998).
83. 2 Justin H. Smith, The War with Mexico 220 (1919).
84. Johnson, Winfield Scott, at 166–68.
85. Cong. Globe, 29th Cong., 2d Sess. 23 (1846).

ted by civilians or military persons would be tried before military tribunals. He was particularly concerned about the behavior of "the wild volunteers" who, as soon as they crossed the Rio Grande, "committed, with impunity, all sorts of atrocities on the persons and property of Mexicans."[86] Scott could discover "no legal punishment for any of those offences, for by the strange omission of Congress, American troops take with them beyond the limits of their own country, no law but the Constitution of the United States, and the rules and articles of war." Those legal standards "do not provide any court for the trial or punishment of murder, rape, theft, &c., &c.—no matter by whom, or on whom committed."[87]

Scott never questioned the ultimate authority of Congress to control military tribunals. To "suppress these disgraceful acts abroad," he issued the martial law order "until Congress could be stimulated to legislate on the subject."[88] Under his order, "all offenders, Americans and Mexicans, were alike punished—with death for murder or rape, and for other crimes proportionally."[89] His order also provided for a special American tribunal "for any case to which an American might be a party."[90] Scott said that his order "worked like a charm; that it conciliated Mexicans; intimidated the vicious of the several races, and being executed with impartial rigor, gave the highest moral deportment and discipline ever known in an invading army."[91]

Scott sought clarifying authority from Congress but was unsuccessful. Four days before proclaiming martial law, Marcy wrote to Scott that it was not reasonable to expect enactment of an additional Article of War "giving authority to military tribunals to try and punish certain offences not expressly embraced in the existing articles." Marcy had discussed the matter with the chairman of a Senate committee and was advised that the chairman, after considering the matter, saw no need for legislation. The right to punish for such offenses "necessarily resulted from the condition of things when an army is prosecuting hostilities in an enemy's country."[92]

Martial law and military tribunals sent the same message to Mexican citizens and U.S. soldiers. Misconduct by either side could result in swift and severe punishment. One American soldier, after getting drunk, was found

86. 2 Memoirs of Lieut.-General Scott 392 (1864).
87. Id. at 393.
88. Id.
89. Id. at 395.
90. Id.
91. Id. at 396.
92. H. Exec. Doc. No. 56, 30th Cong., 1st Sess. 63–64 (1848).

guilty by a tribunal of beating a Mexican woman. He received 12 lashes and confinement at hard labor, in ball and chain, for the remainder of the war.[93] Another American, convicted of raping and robbing a Mexican woman, was hanged.[94] Those actions helped assure the local population that they would be treated fairly and given protection. It was Scott's intent to act firmly and evenhandedly to minimize resistance and guerrilla activity.

The martial law order represented a blend of executive initiative and statutory authority. The first paragraph stated that in the war between the United States and Mexico there were "many grave offences, not provided for in the Act of Congress 'establishing rules and articles for the government of the armies of the United States,'" enacted in 1806.[95] A supplemental code, he said, "is absolutely needed."[96] He called this "*unwritten code*" martial law, "an addition to the *written* military code, prescribed by Congress in the rules and articles of war."[97] All offenders "shall be promptly seized, confined, and reported for trial, before military commissions, . . . appointed, governed, and limited, as nearly as practicable, as prescribed by the 65th, 66th, 67th, and 97th, of the said rules and articles of war."[98] Scott's order distinguished between the competing jurisdictions of military tribunals and courts-martial. No tribunal "shall try any case clearly cognizable by any court martial."[99]

Scott also looked to state policy to limit the reach of his order. No sentence of a tribunal "shall be put in execution against any individual belonging to this army, which may not be, according to the nature and degree of the offence, as established by evidence, in conformity with known punishments, in like cases, in some one of the States of the United States of America."[100] Furthermore, any punishment for the sale, waste, or loss of ammunition, horses, arms, clothing, "or accouterments" by soldiers would be governed by Articles of War 37 and 38.[101]

On September 17, 1847, Scott republished General Orders No. 20 after making certain changes. He listed a number of offenses, including assassination, murder, poisoning, rape, and theft, that could be punished by civil

93. Johnson, Winfield Scott, at 179.
94. H. Exec. Doc. No. 56, at 125–26.
95. 2 Memoirs of Lieut.-General Scott 540–41.
96. Id. at 542.
97. Id. (emphasis in original).
98. Id. at 544.
99. Id.
100. Id.
101. Id.

courts but not by military courts. The written military code "does not provide for the punishment of any *one* of those crimes, even when committed by individuals of the Army upon the persons or property of other individuals of the same."[102] Every military tribunal created to deal with these crimes "will be appointed, governed, and limited, as nearly as practicable," by specified Articles of War. The proceedings of the tribunals would "be duly recorded in writing, reviewed, revised, disapproved or approved, and the sentences executed—all, as near as may be, as in the cases of the proceedings and sentences of courts-martial; provided, that no military commission shall try any case clearly cognizable by any court-martial."[103] Tribunals in Mexico resulted in the trials of 117 individuals. Most were Americans: either soldiers (74) or Americans who were not soldiers (12). The overall conviction rate for Mexican nationals was slightly lower than for Americans.[104]

Judicial Supervision

The Supreme Court reviewed and overturned some of the actions taken by military authorities during the Mexican War. In describing the power of Commander in Chief, the Court said that the President "is authorized to direct the movements of the naval and military forces placed *by law* at his command, and to employ them in the manner he may deem most effectual to harass and conquer and subdue the enemy."[105] The Court thus looked to legislation to define the limits of presidential power in time of war. The President "may invade the hostile country, and subject it to the sovereignty and authority of the United States. But his conquests do not enlarge the boundaries of the Union, nor extend the operation of our institutions and laws beyond the limits before assigned to them by the legislative power."[106]

The Court reviewed language in a congressional statute of July 30, 1846, to determine whether duties were properly imposed upon a schooner at Tampico, Mexico. It decided that Tampico was not a part of the United States but rather a foreign port, and that Congress had not established a

102. Birkhimer, Military Government and Martial Law, at 581 (emphasis in original).
103. Id. at 582.
104. David Glazier, "Kangaroo Court or Competent Tribunal? Judging the 21st Century Military Commission," 89 Va. L. Rev. 2005, 2031–32 (2003).
105. Fleming v. Page, 9 How. (50 U.S.) 603, 615 (1850) (emphasis added).
106. Id.

customhouse at Tampico, nor had it authorized the appointment of a collector.[107] The President had no independent authority to enlarge the boundaries of the United States: "This can be done only by the treaty-making power or the legislative authority, and is not a part of the power conferred upon the President by the declaration of war. His duty and his power are purely military."[108]

In another Mexican War case, the Court granted damages to a U.S. civilian trader for the seizure of his property by a U.S. military officer, who was operating under orders of a superior officer on grounds of necessity. The Court first decided that the merchant was not trading with the enemy, and that decisions by military officers in time of war could be reviewed by courts. It was the duty of a court "to determine under what circumstances private property may be taken from the owner by a military officer in a time of war. And the question here is, whether the law permits it to be taken to insure the success of any enterprise against a public enemy which the commanding officer may deem it advisable to undertake. And we think it very clear that the law does not permit it."[109]

A third case from the Mexican War focused directly on presidential authority to create courts outside the United States. The dispute arose from the seizure of an American vessel suspected of trading with the enemy. The vessel was condemned as a lawful prize by a military officer who had been authorized by the President to exercise admiralty jurisdiction in cases of capture, operating out of a court in Monterey, California. The Supreme Court held that, under the Constitution, the judicial power of the national government is vested in the Supreme Court and in such inferior courts as Congress shall establish. Every court of the United States, therefore, "must derive its jurisdiction and judicial authority from the Constitution or the laws of the United States. And neither the President nor any military officer can establish a court in a conquered country, and authorize it to decide upon the rights of the United States, or of individuals in prize cases, nor to administer the laws of nations."[110]

The courts established in Mexico during the war by the U.S. military "were nothing more than the agents of the military power, to assist it in preserving order in the conquered territory, and to protect the inhabitants in their persons and property while it was occupied by the American

107. Id. at 616.
108. Id. at 615.
109. Mitchell v. Harmony, 13 How. (54 U.S.) 115, 135 (1851).
110. Jecker v. Montgomery, 13 How. (54 U.S.) 498, 515 (1852).

arms." These military courts "were not courts of the United States, and had no right to adjudicate upon a question of prize or no prize."[111] Any sentence of condemnation by the admiralty court in Monterey "is a nullity, and can have no effect upon the rights of any party."[112]

Scope of Executive Authority

Throughout the first seven decades, scholars and executive officials recognized that the ultimate constitutional authority to create and regulate military tribunals lay with Congress, not the President. Macomb, in his 1809 treatise on martial law, warned that the President or commanding officer "can no more interfere with the procedure of Courts-Martial, in the execution of their duty, than they can with any of the fixed courts of justice."[113] Through the power of pardon, the President may "entirely remit the punishment" decided by a court-martial, "but he can no more decree any particular alteration of their sentence, than he can alter the judgment of a civil court, or the verdict of a jury."[114] Constitutionally, the President could lessen or cancel a sentence but could not increase the penalty or rewrite the judgment.

In 1818, Attorney General William Wirt issued a legal memorandum on the authority needed to order a new trial before a military court. Article of War 87 expressly stated that "no officer, non-commissioned officer, soldier, or follower of the army, shall be tried a second time for the same offence."[115] During the proceedings of a court-martial, the Judge Advocate refused to arraign Capt. Nathaniel N. Hall because he had already been tried by a court-martial on the same charge. The sentence of the first court had been disapproved by the President.[116] The question presented to Wirt was whether a President "has the right, under these circumstances, to order a new trial."[117]

It is a "clear principle," Wirt reasoned, that the President "has no powers except those derived from the constitution and laws of the United States; if the power in question, therefore, cannot be fairly deduced from these

111. Id.
112. Id.
113. Macomb, A Treatise on Martial Law 8–9.
114. Id. at 9.
115. 2 Stat. 369 (1806).
116. 1 Op. Att'y Gen. 233 (1818).
117. Id. at 234.

sources, it does not exist at all."[118] The Constitution made the President Commander in Chief, but

> in a government limited like ours, it would not be safe to draw from this provision inferential powers, by a forced analogy to other governments differently constituted. Let us draw from it, therefore, no other inference than that, under the constitution, the President is the national and proper depository of the final appellate power, in all judicial matters touching the police of the army; but let us not claim this power for him, unless it has been communicated to him by some specific grant from Congress, the fountain of all law under the constitution.[119]

Wirt observed that Congress had granted the President an appellate role over military trials. A statute enacted in 1802 provided that officers, noncommissioned officers, and other members of the military "shall be governed by the rules and articles of war, which have been established" by Congress, "or by such rules and articles as may be hereafter, by law, established." Nevertheless, any sentence of a general court-martial "extending to the loss of life, the dismission of a commissioned officer, or which shall respect the general officer, shall, with the whole proceedings of such cases, respectively, be laid before the President of the United States, who is hereby authorized to direct the same to be carried into execution, or otherwise, as he shall judge proper."[120]

To judge the reach of this power, Wirt looked for guidance to the enactments of the Continental Congress, to British precedents, and to the values that infused the War of Independence.[121] America, projecting a system of rules "on more liberal and bolder principles in favor of the citizen," and acting in the spirit of "enlarged views of human liberty," could not have "narrowed the rights and privileges of the American citizen, and surrendered him to a military despotism more severe than that which they were throwing off."[122] He concluded that it was inappropriate to deny the President the right to grant a new trial when it would benefit the party accused.[123]

118. Id.
119. Id.
120. 2 Stat. 134, sec. 10 (1802). Wirt inaccurately refers to this as "the 14th section of the act."
121. 1 Op. Att'y Gen. 235–36.
122. Id. at 237.
123. Id. at 240.

In this case, the prisoner expressly asked for a new trial. Wirt offered his opinion that the President "is vested by the laws with the power of ordering a new trial for the benefit of the prisoner."[124] The President possessed that discretion "by the laws," not by some inherent power. On the other hand, the President could not order a new trial if the accused were acquitted. A new trial is appropriate not when "ordered *against him*—it is only *for him*."[125]

The President, as Commander in Chief, exercises authority over the military services. In an 1820 opinion, Wirt explained that the Departments of War and of the Navy "are the channels through which his orders proceed to them, respectively, and the Secretaries of those departments are the organs by which he makes his will known to them."[126] Through this hierarchical control, the President may direct obedience to his orders, unless Congress has already given contrary orders to executive officials by statute. Thus, the President may suspend, modify, or rescind any order issued by military officers, "except where a direct authority has been given by Congress to an officer to perform any particular function—for example, for a commanding officer to order courts-martial in certain cases."[127] The paramount political institution here was Congress, not the President.

In 1857, Attorney General Caleb Cushing offered his views on whether the Governor of the Washington Territory possessed legal power to proclaim martial law. Finding little reliable guidance on the meaning of martial law, he concluded that the Governor lacked authority to suspend the laws and to substitute the military for civil government.[128] Turning to the authority to suspend the writ of habeas corpus, he determined that it belonged exclusively with Congress.[129] Cushing recognized that state constitutions had different language dealing with suspension of the writ, but reached the same judgment that the only power authorized to make the suspension was the legislature.[130]

American experiences during the nation's first seven decades underscored the primary control by Congress through the legislative process. Exceptions occurred, as with the initiatives taken by Andrew Jackson in New Orleans

---

124. Id. at 242.
125. Id. at 241 (emphasis in original).
126. 1 Op. Att'y Gen. 380–81 (1820).
127. Id. at 381.
128. 8 Op. Att'y Gen. 365, 374 (1857).
129. Id. at 372.
130. Id. at 373.

and in the trial of Arbuthnot and Ambrister, but those actions left a shadow of illegitimacy over executive power. Winfield Scott's use of martial law
in Mexico met with greater acceptance because he was forced to operate
in a foreign country and used military tribunals effectively to forestall guerrilla warfare. He also expressly recognized the authority of Congress, at
any time, to review and modify his initiatives. Constitutional values and the
power of Congress over war would be subjected to much greater strain
during the Civil War.

3

THE CIVIL WAR

Military tribunals flourished during the Civil War after President Lincoln suspended the writ of habeas corpus and authorized martial law in several regions. Congress passed legislation to authorize, retroactively, his emergency orders and proclamations. Later, in 1863, it passed a habeas corpus bill that required the executive branch to submit to federal courts the names of military prisoners. In the midst of war, however, federal judges were largely marginalized. Occasional judicial efforts to curb executive power were either circumvented or ignored. Only after the war did the Supreme Court in the *Milligan* case decide that military tribunals could not function when civil courts were open and operating. In addition to the crises precipitated by the Civil War, Lincoln had to supervise and ameliorate military tribunals created in Minnesota to prosecute members of the Dakota tribe.

Lincoln's Emergency Actions

In April 1861, with Congress in recess, Lincoln issued proclamations to call out the state militia, increase the size of the army and navy, suspend the writ of habeas corpus in selected territories, and place a blockade on the rebellious states.[1] When Congress assembled in special session on July 4, he explained that the outbreak of civil war left him no choice but "to call out the war power of the Government and so to resist force employed for the destruction by force for its preservation."[2] His measures, "whether strictly legal or not, were ventured upon under what appeared to be a popular demand and a public necessity, trusting then, as now, that Congress would readily ratify them." Lincoln believed that "nothing has been done beyond the constitutional competency of Congress."[3]

---

1. 7 A Compilation of the Messages and Papers of the Presidents 3214–30 (James D. Richardson ed. 1925) (hereafter "Richardson").
2. Id. at 3224.
3. Id. at 3225.

Those words acknowledged that Lincoln had exercised not only the powers available to the President but also the powers vested in Congress. Especially was that so by suspending the writ of habeas corpus. The power to suspend appears in Article I: "The Privilege of the Writ of Habeas Corpus shall not be suspended, unless when in Cases of Rebellion or Invasion the public Safety may require it." Although the power of suspension is in Article I, Lincoln said that the Constitution "itself is silent as to which or who is to exercise this power; and as the provision was plainly made for a dangerous emergency, it can not be believed the framers of the instrument intended that in every case the danger should run its course until Congress could be called together, the very assembling of which might be prevented, as was intended in this case, by the rebellion."[4]

Having questioned the legality of his actions, Lincoln identified the process needed to bring his proclamations and orders into harmony with the Constitution: a statute passed by Congress. Even in times of emergency, the superior lawmaking body is Congress, not the President. Congress debated his request at length, with members eventually supporting Lincoln with the explicit understanding that his acts, standing alone, were illegal.[5] Legislation on August 6 provided that "all the acts, proclamations, and orders" of President Lincoln after March 4, 1861, respecting the army and navy and calling out the state militia "are hereby approved and in all respects legalized and made valid, to the same intent and with the same effect as if they had been issued and done under the previous express authority and direction of the Congress of the United States."[6]

Suspending Habeas Corpus

The day after Congress assembled in special session, Attorney General Edward Bates submitted to Lincoln his analysis of the President's authority to suspend the privilege of the writ of habeas corpus. From British times, prisoners relied on the writ to appeal to a judge that they were being unjustly held. Once a judge issued a writ, the custodian of a prisoner must bring the person before the court and defend the detention. Bates concluded that in times of "a great and dangerous insurrection," the President has discretion to arrest and hold in custody persons "known to have criminal intercourse with the insurgents, or persons against whom there is

4. Id. at 3226.
5. E.g., remarks by Senator Breckinridge at Cong. Globe, 37th Cong., 1st Sess. 137–42 (1861) and Senator Howe, id. at 393.
6. 12 Stat. 326 (1861).

probable cause for suspicion of such criminal complicity."[7] In case of such an arrest, Bates said, Presidents are justified in refusing to obey a writ of habeas corpus issued by a court.

Much of Bates's argument rested on the President's oath of office to "preserve, protect and defend the Constitution of the United States."[8] The President could not defend the Constitution "without putting down rebellion, insurrection, and all unlawful combinations to resist the General Government."[9] On the manner in which the insurrection is suppressed, "the President must, of necessity, be the sole judge."[10] Bates conceded that concentrating such power in the presidency is dangerous, especially "in the hands of an ambitious and wicked President," but "all power is dangerous ... [and] liable to abuse." Power can be abused by the other branches as well, because "a legislature may be factious and unprincipled, and a court may be venal and corrupt."[11] Presidents, lawmakers, or judges who abuse power are "liable to impeachment and condemnation."[12]

Short of impeachment and condemnation, Bates concluded that the decision to suppress an insurrection "is political and not judicial."[13] Under those conditions, Presidents could ignore a writ of habeas corpus issued by a federal judge. Just as the President has no judicial powers, so does the judiciary have "no political powers, and claims none, and therefore (as well as for other reasons already assigned) no court or judge can take cognizance of the political acts of the President, or undertake to revise and reverse his political decisions."[14] Bates qualified his opinion by saying that if the constitutional language meant "a repeal of all power to issue the writ, then I freely admit that none but Congress can do it." In case of "a great and dangerous rebellion, like the present," the President's power to suspend the privilege at times was "temporary and exceptional."[15]

Bates went far beyond the position advanced by Lincoln, who never argued that his decision to take emergency actions after Fort Sumter was unquestionably constitutional and could not be challenged by any other branch, much less shared. As his message to Congress made plain, Lincoln

7. 10 Op. Att'y Gen. 74, 81 (1861).
8. Id.
9. Id. at 82–83.
10. Id. at 84.
11. Id.
12. Id. at 85.
13. Id. at 86.
14. Id.
15. Id. at 90. See Sydney G. Fisher, "The Suspension of Habeas Corpus During the War of the Rebellion," 3 Pol. Sci. Q. 454 (1888).

had good reason to doubt the legality and constitutionality of his decision and therefore sought sanction from the only branch capable of granting it: Congress.

Later, both Lincoln and Bates acknowledged congressional power to pass legislation that defines when and how a President may suspend the writ of habeas corpus during a rebellion. On March 3, 1863, Congress enacted a bill authorizing the President, during the rebellion, to suspend the privilege of the writ of habeas corpus "whenever, in his judgment, the public safety may require it." If suspended, no military or other officer could be compelled to answer any writ of habeas corpus and return to a court the person detained under authority of the President. Under the terms of the statute, a judicial order would lack force.

In *Ex parte Milligan* (1866), the Supreme Court would rely on this statute to curb executive power. Congress had placed an important restriction on the President. The statute directed the Secretary of State and the Secretary of War, "as soon as may be practicable," to furnish federal judges with a list of the names of all persons, "citizens of states in which the administration of the laws has continued unimpaired in the said Federal courts," who are held as prisoners by order of the President or executive officers.[16] Submitting this list was not discretionary; it was mandatory. Failure to furnish the list could result in the discharge of a prisoner.[17]

The legislative history of the statute explains why lawmakers found it necessary to act. The bill started out in the House to indemnify the President for suspending the writ of habeas corpus, implying that the President and executive officers might have committed illegal acts. It was admitted during legislative debate that "there is not entire unanimity of opinion as to which branch of the Government possesses the constitutional power to declare such suspension."[18] As the bill moved through the Senate, it picked up additional language to establish procedures for lawsuits brought against executive or military officers in cases of arrest.[19] Senators challenged the theory that the President possessed independent authority to suspend the writ of habeas corpus.[20] After Senate passage, the House refused to concur in the amendments and insisted on going to conference.[21] It was in

16. 12 Stat. 755 (1863).
17. Id. at 756, sec. 3.
18. Cong. Globe, 37th Cong., 3d Sess. 21 (1862) (remarks of Rep. Vallandigham). See also pages 14, 20, 22.
19. Id. at 529.
20. Id. at 529–52.
21. Id. at 916, 1056–89, 1097, 1102–7.

conference that language was added to require the Secretaries of State and War to submit to federal courts the names of military prisoners.[22]

Martial Law in Missouri

In St. Louis, Brig. Gen. William S. Harney responded to a writ of habeas corpus by notifying a federal district judge on May 15, 1861, that the individual directed to be brought before the court was not imprisoned in his territory or under his control or command. While declaring his wish to sustain the Constitution and the laws of the United States and Missouri, he found himself "in such a position that in deciding upon a particular case I must take to what I am compelled to regard as the higher law, even by so doing my conduct shall have the appearance of coming in conflict with the forms of law."[23] This language indicated that the military would not brook judicial interference.

On August 30, Maj. Gen. John C. Frémont issued a proclamation stating that circumstances in Missouri were sufficiently urgent to compel him to "assume the administrative powers of the State" and declare martial law. Persons within a prescribed territory with arms in their hands would be tried by court-martial "and if found guilty will be shot." His proclamation was directed particularly to those who attempted to destroy railroad tracks, bridges, or telegraph lines.[24] The state of emergency, he said, was "not intended to suspend the ordinary tribunals of the country where law will be administered by civil officers in the usual manner and with their customary authority while the same can be peaceably administered."[25]

Lincoln reacted with alarm to Frémont's proclamation, fearful that the decision to shoot Confederates would lead, tit for tat, to the shooting of Union soldiers. He told Frémont on September 2 that no one was to be shot without the President's consent.[26] Lincoln also took sharp exception to language in the proclamation that threatened to confiscate property and liberate slaves held by traitorous owners. Such a policy, he warned, "will

---

22. Id. at 1354. See also James G. Randall, "The Indemnity Act of 1863: A Study in the Wartime Immunity of Government Officers," 20 Mich. L. Rev. 589 (1922).

23. 2:1 The War of the Rebellion: A Compilation of the Official Records of the Union and Confederate Armies 115 (1894) (hereafter "War of the Rebellion"). 2:1 stands for Series 2, vol. 1.

24. Id. at 221.

25. Id. at 222.

26. 4 The Collected Works of Abraham Lincoln 506 (Roy P. Basler ed. 1953) (hereafter "Lincoln").

alarm our Southern Union friends, and turn them against us."[27] The nation's capital already had Virginia to the South among the Confederate states. There was great risk that another neighboring state, Maryland, would join the southern cause. The capital could be surrounded by hostile forces. When Frémont asked Lincoln on September 8 to expressly direct him to modify the language, Lincoln responded with an unambiguous order to make the change.[28]

Later, in a private letter of September 22, Lincoln explained that Frémont's language regarding confiscation of property and the liberation of slaves was "*purely political,* and not within the range of *military* law, or necessity."[29] Temporary possession of private property or slaves might be justified, but not a permanent change in ownership. Such changes must be settled by laws "made by law-makers, and not by military proclamations."[30] Lincoln continued: "I do not say Congress might not with propriety pass a law, on the point, just such as General Frémont proclaimed. I do not say I might not, as a member of Congress, vote for it. What I object to, is, that I as President, shall expressly or impliedly seize and exercise the permanent legislative functions of the government."[31]

Those remarks were somewhat disingenuous of Lincoln. His primary reason for objecting to Frémont's proclamation was that it might lead to the loss of Kentucky, which "is nearly the same as to lose the whole game. Kentucky gone, we can not hold Missouri, nor, as I think, Maryland."[32] Several years later, with the Union more secure, Lincoln did not wait for congressional action to free the slaves. He moved unilaterally under his powers as Commander in Chief to issue the Emancipation Proclamation.[33]

Military tribunals assembled in September 1861 to consider charges ranging from treason to a variety of actions (such as bridge burning) that fell within the broad category of "the laws of war."[34] Other charges brought before these tribunals included the destruction of railroad ties, tracks, and railroad cars, giving aid and comfort to bridge burners, and destroying telegraph lines.[35] Convictions of treason were overturned by the Office of

27. Id.
28. Id. at 507 (n. 3), 517–18.
29. Id. at 531 (emphasis in original).
30. Id.
31. Id. at 532.
32. Id.
33. Louis Fisher, Presidential War Power 49 (2d ed. 2004).
34. 2:1 War of the Rebellion 282–89.
35. Id. at 402–5, 407.

Adjutant General because "not triable by a military commission."[36] Some defendants were allowed to have the assistance of counsel.[37]

In order to clarify Frémont's proclamation, military officials in St. Louis sought written authority from President Lincoln to declare and enforce martial law. Lincoln responded on November 21, 1861: "If General McClellan and General Halleck deem it necessary to declare and maintain martial law at Saint Louis the same is hereby authorized."[38] Halleck, failing to receive this message from Lincoln, asked for written authority on November 30. Lincoln answered on December 2: "As an insurrection exists in the United States and is in arms in the State of Missouri you are hereby authorized and empowered to suspend the writ of habeas corpus within the limits of the military division under your command and to exercise martial law as you find it necessary in your discretion to secure the public safety and the authority of the United States."[39]

Toward the end of the year, military officials in Missouri discussed the role of civil courts. On December 26, U.S. Army headquarters in St. Louis declared martial law in the city and "in and about all railroads" in the state. The order explained that it was not intended "to interfere with the jurisdiction of any civil court which is loyal to the Government of the United States and which will aid the military authorities in enforcing order and punishing crimes."[40] Yet military leaders placed little trust in the civil courts. On January 1, 1862, Gen. Halleck said that civil courts "can give us no assistance as they are very generally unreliable. There is no alternative but to enforce martial law."[41] On that same day, a general order from Army headquarters in St. Louis stated that "crimes and military offenses are frequently committed which are not triable or punishable by courts-martial and which are not within the jurisdiction of any existing civil court."[42] That finding opened the door to "a duly constituted military tribunal."[43] Offenses within the jurisdiction of civil courts "whenever such loyal courts exist will not be tried by a military commission."[44]

36. Id. at 405.
37. Id. at 285, 293, 407.
38. Id. at 230.
39. Id. at 233.
40. Id. at 155.
41. Id. at 247.
42. Id.
43. Id. at 248.
44. Id.

Procedural Checks

Correspondence and general orders during this period explained how military tribunals differed from courts-martial and civil courts. A tribunal "can be ordered only by the General-in-Chief of the Army or by a general commanding a department." Proceedings by officials under that rank, such as colonels, would be "null and void."[45] Tribunals "should as a general rule be resorted to only for cases which cannot be tried by a court-martial or by a proper civil tribunal." Moreover, the proceedings of a tribunal "should be regulated by the rules governing courts-martial so far as they may be applicable and the evidence should in all cases be fully recorded."[46] Treason, an offense defined by the Constitution, "is not triable by a military commission."[47]

Tribunals were instruments to enforce not so much the Articles of War, enacted by Congress and delegated to courts-martial, but rather the customary international standards known as the "laws of war." It was a well-established principle, said Gen. Halleck, that "insurgents and marauding, predatory and guerrilla bands are not entitled" to an exemption from military tribunals. These men are "by the laws of war regarded as no more nor less than murderers, robbers and thieves." Wearing military uniforms "cannot change the character of their offenses nor exempt them from punishment." If a prisoner of war "has committed acts in violation of the laws of war such as murder, robbery, arson, &c., the fact of his being a prisoner of war does not exempt him from trial and punishment by a military commission." In this type of case the charge "should be 'violation of the laws of war,' and not violation of the 'Rules and Articles of War,' which are statutory provisions modifying the laws of war only in the particular cases to which these provisions apply."[48]

Other analyses during this period discuss the need to keep military tribunals within the American system of law. Gen. Halleck received these thoughts from Charles C. Whittelsey, an attorney: "With our Constitution all military law is the creature of the Constitution and of the laws of Congress."[49] A general order on January 1, 1862, emphasized the need for strict procedures on military tribunals. They needed to be "ordered by the same

---

45. Id. at 242.
46. Id.
47. Id.
48. Id. at 242–43.
49. Id. at 246.

authority" as for courts-martial and "be constituted in a similar manner and their proceedings be conducted according to the same general rules as courts-martial in order to prevent abuses which might otherwise arise."[50]

An Army circular on February 14, 1862, announced that persons in arms against the United States were to be arrested and held for trial before a military tribunal. The specific acts of concern were "violation of the laws of war such as destruction of railroads and bridges or private property, firing into trains, assassinations, &c."[51] For those who assisted the Confederate cause, their property—including horses, mules, wagons, beef cattle, and forage—could be seized and turned over to military authorities.[52] Later that year, on September 24, President Lincoln issued a proclamation to subject whoever discouraged volunteer enlistments or militia drafts to trial and punishments "by courts-martial or military commissions." He also suspended the writ of habeas corpus for persons arrested or imprisoned "by any military authority or by sentence of any court-martial or military commission."[53]

Lincoln, with the assistance of the office of adjutant general, reviewed and often overturned the work of tribunals. A tribunal in St. Louis charged a civilian with giving aid and comfort to the enemy and sentenced him to be shot. After the trial proceedings were presented to the White House, it was there held that "Nothing is proved against the prisoner after he had taken the oath of allegiance, except the utterance of very disloyal sentiments. No *acts* are shown which would warrant the sentence of death. The sentence is remitted."[54] Another tribunal in Missouri found an individual guilty of murder and "a bad and dangerous man" (for being a member of a guerrilla band). He was ordered to be shot. Lincoln disapproved the sentence because the record was "fatally defective."[55] Also turned aside, for the same reason, was a tribunal's order that an individual be shot for murder and for threatening to kill two other people.[56]

A tribunal in Virginia in 1863 sentenced an individual to death. He was released after the Adjutant General's Office determined that the sentence "is inoperative, on account of informality in the proceedings of the Com-

50. Id. at 248.
51. Id. at 263.
52. Id. at 264.
53. 7 Richardson 3299–300.
54. General Orders No. 230, included in U.S. War Department, General Orders 1863, vol. 5 (Nos. 201–300), Library of Congress, at 2–3, 6 (emphasis in original).
55. Id. at 3–5, 6.
56. Id. at 5–6.

mission." The record did not show that the order convening the tribunal had been read to the prisoner or in his hearing; that he was given the opportunity to object to any member of the commission; that the charge against him had been put in writing; "or that he had, in advance of the examination of the witnesses, any knowledge of the offence for which he was to be tried; nor is it shown that the prisoner was allowed to plead to the charge against him as recited in the order convening the Commission." The office concluded that in a proceeding involving life, "such irregularities are wholly inexcusable, and make the execution of the death sentence legally impossible."[57]

A tribunal in Missouri sentenced eight men to death for various offenses. Lincoln approved the sentence of one and directed that it be carried out. For the other seven, however, it was found that the sentence of death was "inoperative" because the officer ordering the tribunal failed to approve it. All seven were released.[58] In other cases, tribunals sentenced rebel soldiers, in uniform, to death for treason. Those proceedings were disapproved by Lincoln because "the record shows clearly that the accused are prisoners of war."[59]

Laws Recognizing Tribunals

The tribunals created during the Civil War originated from the executive branch, not from Congress. Nevertheless, several statutes enacted from 1862 to 1864 recognized the existence and operation of tribunals. Legislation on July 17, 1862, authorized the President to appoint, by and with the advice and consent of the Senate, a judge advocate general, "to whose office shall be returned, for revision, the records and proceedings of all courts-martial and military commissions, and where a record shall be kept of all proceedings had thereupon."[60]

Legislation in 1863 specified procedures for enrolling and calling out the military forces. One section of the statute provided that in time of war, insurrection, or rebellion, "murder, assault and battery with an intent to kill, manslaughter, mayhem, wounding by shooting or stabbing with an intent

57. General Orders No. 257, included in U.S. War Department, General Orders 1863, vol. 5 (Nos. 201–300), Library of Congress.

58. General Orders No. 267, included in U.S. War Department, General Orders 1863, vol. 5 (Nos. 201–300), Library of Congress.

59. General Orders No. 145, included in U.S. War Department, General Orders 1863, vol. 4 (Nos. 1–200), Library of Congress, at 1–3, 4.

60. 12 Stat. 598, sec. 5 (1862).

to commit murder, robbery, arson, burglary, rape, assault and battery with an intent to commit rape, and larceny, shall be punishable by the sentence of a general court-martial or military commission," when committed by persons who were members of the military service and subject to the Articles of War.[61] This section did not give tribunals jurisdiction over citizens who were not in the military. The statute also provided that all persons, in time of war or rebellion against the United States, found lurking or acting as spies in or about any U.S. fortifications, posts, quarters, or encampments "shall be triable by a general court-martial or military commission, and shall, upon conviction, suffer death."[62]

An 1864 statute amended procedures for carrying out executions and imprisonment. Legislation two years earlier stated that no sentence of death or imprisonment "shall be carried into execution until the same shall have been approved by the President."[63] That law was amended the next year to make presidential approval unnecessary for carrying out the sentence of a court-martial against anyone convicted as a spy or deserter or of mutiny or murder. Sentences could be executed with the approval of the commanding general in the field.[64] The 1864 law broadened the proceedings to include not only courts-martial but also "the sentences of military commissions." The sentences would now apply not only to spies, deserters, mutineers, and murderers but also to "guerilla [sic] marauders for robbery, arson, burglary, rape, assault with intent to commit rape, and for violation of the laws and customs of war."[65]

Also in 1864, legislation dealing with the Quartermaster's Department included a section on inspectors, who were expected to perform their duties in "a faithful and impartial manner." For any corruption, willful neglect, or fraud in their official conduct, they were liable to punishment by fine and imprisonment, "by sentence of court-martial or military commission."[66]

The Dakota Trials

In 1862, the Dakota (or Sioux) community in Minnesota erupted after years of grievances by initiating war against American settlers. The hostilities had

61. Id. at 736, sec. 30 (1863).
62. Id. at 737, sec. 38.
63. 12 Stat. 598, sec. 5 (1862).
64. Id. at 735, sec. 21 (1863).
65. 13 Stat. 356, ch. 215, sec. 1 (1864).
66. Id. at 397, sec. 6 (1864).

many causes, ranging from the loss of Indian lands by treaty to crop failures and starvation during the winter of 1861–62.[67] Also contributing to the tension were late payments of funds from Congress.[68] Five weeks of fighting resulted in the deaths of 77 American soldiers, 29 citizen-soldiers, approximately 358 settlers, and an estimated 29 Dakota soldiers.[69]

Col. Henry H. Sibley created a five-member military tribunal to investigate the incidents and pass judgment, even though all members of the tribunal had fought in the war against the Dakota.[70] The trials began on September 28 and concluded on November 3, reviewing charges against 392 Dakota "with as many as 42 tried in a single day."[71] Some of the proceedings lasted a mere five minutes.[72] The tribunal convicted 323 and recommended the hanging of 303. Sibley labored under the misconception that he had authority to order executions.[73]

President Lincoln, learning of the trials on October 14, directed that no executions be made without his approval. Federal law, in fact, made that a requirement. For all courts-martial and military tribunals, "no sentence of death, or imprisonment in the penitentiary, shall be carried into execution until the same shall have been approved by the President."[74] On November 10, Lincoln received a dispatch providing the names of the Indians condemned to death. He directed Maj. Gen. John Pope, Sibley's commanding officer, to submit the "full and complete record" of the convictions.[75]

When Secretary of the Navy Gideon Welles received the news on October 14 about the military tribunals, he said he was "disgusted with the whole thing; the tone and opinions of the dispatch are discreditable." He did not doubt that the Indian actions were "horrible" but wondered what the whites might have done to provoke them. Behind the dispatch Welles saw a pretext for taking more Indian land: "The Sioux and Ojibbeways are bad, but the Winnebagoes have good land which white men want and mean to have."[76]

---

67. Kenneth Carley, The Sioux Uprising of 1862, at 2–5 (1976).

68. Id. at 5–6; Carol Chomsky, "The United States–Dakota War Trials: A Study in Military Injustice," 43 Stan. L. Rev. 13, 16–17 (1990).

69. Chomsky, "The United States–Dakota War Trials," at 21–22.

70. Id. at 22–24.

71. Id. at 27.

72. Carley, The Sioux Uprising of 1862, at 69.

73. 1:13 War of the Rebellion 708, 717, 722.

74. 12 Stat. 598, sec. 5 (1862).

75. 5 Lincoln 493.

76. 1 Diary of Gideon Welles 171 (1911).

Gen. Pope telegraphed Lincoln on November 11, warning that "if the guilty are not all executed I think it nearly impossible to prevent the indiscriminate massacre of all the Indians—old men, women, and children." In addition to the list of the condemned, Pope noted that there were 1,500 women, children, and elderly Indians still held prisoner, and "I fear that so soon as it is known that the criminals are not at once to be executed that there will be an indiscriminate massacre of the whole."[77]

Lincoln turned to Judge Advocate General Joseph Holt for advice: "I wish your legal opinion whether if I should conclude to execute only a part of them, I must myself designate which, or could I leave the designation to some officer on the ground?"[78] Holt answered that the President had to make the decision and could not transfer that judgment to others: "I am quite sure that the power cannot be delegated, and that the designation of the individuals, which its exercise involves, must necessarily be made by yourself."[79] Holt was unaware of any previous attempt to delegate "this delicate and responsible trust."[80]

To decide how to proceed with the executions, Lincoln adopted this general policy: "Anxious to not act with so much clemency as to encourage another outbreak, on the one hand, nor with so much severity as to be real cruelty, on the other, I caused a careful examination of the records of trials to be made, in view of first ordering the execution of such as had been proved guilty of violating females."[81] Only two examples of that category surfaced. He then directed that the examination look for those "who were proven to have participated in *massacres,* as distinguished from participation in *battles.*"[82] That class, including the two convicted of female violation, yielded 40 names. For one of the violators, the tribunal recommended a jail sentence of ten years.[83] This leniency resulted when the individual turned state's evidence against other defendants. He served three years in prison before being released.[84]

Lincoln received several letters from soldiers and civilians, urging that the 303 executions be carried out in accordance with the tribunal's judgment. One letter warned that if Lincoln failed to permit the executions to

---

77. 1:13 War of the Rebellion 788.
78. 5 Lincoln 537–38.
79. Id. (n. 1).
80. Id.
81. S. Ex. Doc. No. 7, 37th Cong., 3d Sess. 1 (1862).
82. Id. at 1–2 (emphasis in original).
83. Id. at 2. This document also appears at 5 Lincoln 550–51.
84. Carley, The Sioux Uprising of 1862, at 68.

take place "under the forms of law, the outraged people of Minnesota will dispose of these wretches without law. These two peoples cannot live together. We do not wish to see mob law inaugurated in Minnesota, as it certainly will be, if you force the people to it."[85] Another letter to Lincoln claimed that the "Indian's nature can no more be trusted than the wolf's. Tame him, cultivate him, strive to Christianize him as you will, and the sight of blood will in an instant call out the savage, wolfish, devilish instincts of the race."[86] Notwithstanding these strident appeals, of the 303 slated for execution, Lincoln ordered the death sentence only for 39 and commuted or pardoned the rest.[87] Because subsequent evidence cast doubt on the guilt of one of the accused, 38 were executed.[88]

Congress later passed legislation to provide $928,411 for the relief of persons damaged by the "depredations and injuries by certain banks of Sioux Indians."[89] It also appropriated funds to Sioux Indians who, "at the risk of their lives, aid[ed] in saving many white men, women, and children from being massacred," and who were, because of their assistance, forced to abandon their homes and property.[90]

The military tribunal for the Dakota trials has been the subject of several critiques, partly because of the accelerated nature of the proceedings and the prejudice of tribunal members. In addition, the tribunal could have granted, as a privilege and not as a right, counsel to the defendants, to assure that they understood the charges and could respond adequately. This was particularly necessary for defendants who had little command of English. In later military trials against Indians, counsel was provided.[91]

There is also a question whether Col. Sibley possessed authority to convene the tribunal. Article of War 65 made it clear that in cases of capital crimes, the officer who convened a court-martial could not also be the accuser. Gen. Pope and Judge Advocate General Holt concluded that Sibley was an accuser, "and Sibley did not disagree."[92] Sibley's defense was that Article 65 applied only to the court-martial of an inferior soldier, not to a military tribunal of outsiders. Yet the Army had determined, by January 1,

85. S. Ex. Doc. No. 7, at 4.

86. Id. at 5.

87. Id. at. 2, 6–7.

88. Chomsky, "The United States–Dakota War Trials," at 34. See also David A. Nichols, Lincoln and the Indians: Civil War Policy and Politics 94–118 (2000).

89. 13 Stat. 92–93 (1864).

90. Id. at 427 (1865).

91. Chomsky, "The United States–Dakota War Trials," at 52–53.

92. Id. at 56.

1862, that military tribunals should be conducted with the same procedures as courts-martial.[93] Whether for soldiers or for outsiders, the purpose of Article 65 was to prevent actual or perceived bias.

Monitoring by the Courts

Decisions by military tribunals were reviewed by a few federal courts, the most prominent cases involving John Merryman, Clement Vallandigham, and Lambdin Milligan. During the war, it became clear that courts would have little role in placing constraints either on martial law or military tribunals. Only after the war did courts begin to assert their independent powers and impose some limits on executive actions.

John Merryman

John Merryman was not merely a vocal opponent of the Union forces. He was also suspected of being the captain of a secession group and giving assistance to plans to destroy railroads and bridges. Arrested by military authorities on May 25, 1861, he was imprisoned at Fort McHenry in Baltimore, Maryland. His counsel sought a writ of habeas corpus from Chief Justice Roger Taney, sitting as circuit judge. On the following day, Taney issued the writ to the commandant of the fort, directing him to bring Merryman to the circuit courtroom in Baltimore on May 27. The commandant declined to produce Merryman. Taney then prepared an attachment to hold the officer in contempt, but the court's marshal was unable to enter the gate of the prison to serve the writ.[94]

Taney realized that he could not prevail in an open confrontation with Lincoln. He settled for writing an opinion that expressed his views on presidential power and constitutional procedures, concluding that a military officer had no right to arrest and detain a person "not subject to the rules and articles of war, for an offence against the laws of the United States, except in aid of the judicial authority, and subject to its control." For that reason, Merryman was "entitled to be set at liberty and discharged immediately from imprisonment."[95] Lacking the political power to implement his decision, Taney could only state his conclusion that the Constitution gave

93. Id. at 56, n. 269.
94. Ex parte Merryman, 17 Fed. Cas. 144, 147 (No. 9,487) (C.C. Md. 1861).
95. Id.

Congress, not the President, the power to suspend the privilege of the writ.[96] Taney ended with these observations:

> I have exercised all the power which the constitution and laws confer upon me, but that power has been resisted by a force too strong for me to overcome. . . . I shall, therefore, order all the proceedings in this case, with my opinion, to be filed and recorded in the circuit court of the United States for the district court of Maryland, and direct the clerk to transmit a copy, under seal, to the president of the United States. It will then remain for that high officer, in fulfillment of his constitutional obligation to "take care that the laws be faithfully executed," to determine what measures he will take to cause the civil process of the United States to be respected and enforced.[97]

Taney's experience convinced a district judge in New York that once a military officer declined to obey a writ of habeas corpus, it was the better part of wisdom for a court to take no further action and to deny a motion to execute the writ.[98] As for Merryman, he was not brought before a military tribunal. Instead, he was indicted in a civil court for treason or conspiracy to commit treason and released on bail, at $40,000. Merryman was never brought to trial.[99]

Clement Vallandigham

On April 13, 1863, Gen. Ambrose Burnside issued General Orders No. 38, warning that the death penalty would be imposed on those who not only gave physical aid to the Confederacy but even expressed "sympathies" for the enemy.[100] Less than a month later, on May 5, military authorities arrested Clement L. Vallandigham and charged that in a public speech four days earlier, he had expressed sympathy for the South and uttered "disloyal sentiments and opinions, with the object and purpose of weakening the power of the Government in its efforts for the suppression of an unlawful

96. Id. at 148.

97. Id. at 153. See Sherrill Halbert, "The Suspension of the Writ of Habeas Corpus by President Lincoln," 2 Am. J. Legal Hist. 95 (1958).

98. Ex parte McQuillon, 16 Fed. Cas. 347 (No. 8,924) (S.D. N.Y. 1861).

99. Carl B. Swisher, The Taney Period, 1836–64, at 853–54 (1974); Dean Sprague, Freedom Under Lincoln 43–44 (1965).

100. Michael Kent Curtis, "Lincoln, Vallandigham, and Anti-War Speech in the Civil War," 7 Wm. Mary Bill Rts. J. 105, 119 (1998).

rebellion."[101] His speech described the Civil War as "wicked, cruel, and unnecessary," waged not for the preservation of the Union but "for the purpose of crushing our liberty and to erect a despotism," to free blacks, and enslave whites.[102]

Vallandigham, a former member of Congress from Ohio, was tried before a military tribunal. An experienced trial lawyer, he called witnesses, cross-examined witnesses for the prosecution, had the assistance of counsel, and offered a witness on his own behalf.[103] In his testimony, he denied that the tribunal had jurisdiction over him because he was not in the land or naval forces or in the militia. He insisted that he be tried before a civil court with customary constitutional rights and protections. Moreover, he said that the charge brought by the tribunal was not known to the Constitution or to federal law, and that his criticism of government policy was delivered at an open and public meeting, lawfully and peaceably assembled, upon full notice.[104]

The tribunal found him guilty except for his comments that Lincoln and his officers had rejected peaceful overtures to win back the southern states, and that the administration was attempting to establish a despotism "more oppressive than ever existed before." He was placed in close confinement in a federal fort, to be held there for the duration of the war. After Gen. Burnside approved the finding and sentence, President Lincoln commuted the sentence and ordered the Army to put Vallandigham beyond the Union's military lines.[105]

Lincoln was not happy with Burnside's initiative. He sent this telegraph to Burnside on May 29, 1863: "All the cabinet regretted the necessity of arresting, for instance, Vallandigham, some perhaps, doubting, that there was a real necessity for it—but, being done, all were for seeing you through with it."[106] In a June 12 letter to a group in Albany, New York, Lincoln shared his thoughts about Vallandigham's case. He said that if he had been seized and tried "for no other reason than words addressed to a public meeting, in criticism of the course of the administration," he would concede that the arrest was wrong. But Lincoln said that Vallandigham did more: "he was laboring, with some effect, to prevent the raising of troops, to encourage desertions from the army, and to leave the rebellion without

---

101. Ex parte Vallandigham, 1 Wall. (68 U.S.) 243, 244 (1864).
102. Id.
103. Id. at 245–46.
104. Id. at 246.
105. Id. at 247–48.
106. 6 Lincoln 237.

an adequate military force to suppress it." He was "warring upon the military," giving the military the jurisdiction it needed "to lay hands upon him," and he was "damaging the military power of the country."[107] Yet by Lincoln's reasoning, no criticism of an administration would ever be safe, or lawful, because the government could always charge that statements made in public were "damaging" to the military power.

During the course of his confinement, Vallandigham sought a writ of habeas corpus from the Supreme Court, which heard the case on January 22, 1864, and decided it on February 15. After reviewing the types of courts over which it had appellate powers, it concluded that the petition of certiorari to hear the case "we think not to be within the letter or spirit of the grants of appellate jurisdiction to the Supreme Court." Nor were the operations of a military tribunal covered by the "law or equity" provision of Article III of the Constitution, or within the meaning of Section 14 of the Judiciary Act of 1789.[108] Under this reasoning, the Court held that it had no jurisdiction to review the proceedings of a military tribunal.[109]

One month after Lincoln banished Vallandigham to the Confederacy, Burnside suppressed publication of the *Chicago Times* newspaper because it had published stories critical of the administration. Lincoln, unwilling to play backstop for further Burnside blunders, revoked his order and allowed the newspaper to resume publication.[110]

The Milligan Case

In 1864, military authorities arrested Lambdin P. Milligan, a U.S. citizen from Indiana, on charges of conspiracy. Found guilty before a military tribunal, he was sentenced to be hanged.[111] He presented a petition of habeas corpus to a federal judge, asking that he be discharged because the military lacked jurisdiction over him. He argued that he was entitled to trial by jury before a civilian court. By the time the case reached the Supreme Court, the Civil War was over. The Court ruled that the laws and usages of war can never be applied to citizens in states where the civilian courts are open and their process unobstructed.[112] The Court held that the statute of March 3, 1863, gave federal courts "complete jurisdiction to adjudicate

---

107. Id. at 266.
108. Ex parte Vallandigham, 1 Wall. (68 U.S.) at 251.
109. Id. at 253–54.
110. Curtis, "Lincoln, Vallandigham, and Anti-War Speech in the Civil War," at 132–34.
111. 2:8 War of the Rebellion 6–11, 543–49.
112. Ex parte Milligan, 71 U.S. (4 Wall.) 2 (1866).

upon this case."[113] Milligan's trial and conviction by a tribunal "was illegal," and under the terms of the statute he was entitled to be discharged from custody.[114]

Four justices dissented, but not on the Court's jurisdiction to hear and decide the case. On that point, they agreed with the majority.[115] The dissenting justices regarded the matter completely settled by the March 3, 1863, legislation.[116] They disagreed only on the broader claim of the Court that tribunals could not operate when civil courts were open and functioning, and that it was not in the power of Congress to authorize tribunals during such periods. To the minority, Congress "had power, though not exercised, to authorize the military commission which was held in Indiana."[117]

Although this decision is generally praised today as one of the great landmarks in defense of civil liberties, it was not so popular when issued. Critics charged that the Court had thrown its weight against those in the North who intended to carry out a program of Reconstruction in the South. Numerous newspapers compared the decision to the Dred Scott case.[118] The 5–4 split within the Court invited criticism that the ruling was "not a judicial opinion; it is a political act."[119]

In response to this decision, Congress passed legislation to limit the Court's jurisdiction to hear cases involving military law. Despite the fact that civil lawsuits were already pending regarding the conduct of U.S. officials during and immediately after the war, Congress gave indemnity to all officials who implemented presidential proclamations from March 4, 1861, to June 30, 1866, with respect to martial law and military trials. The statute provided: "And no civil court of the United States, or of any State, or of the District of Columbia, or of any district or territory of the United States, shall have or take jurisdiction of, or in any manner reverse any of the proceedings had or acts done as aforesaid."[120]

Milligan appeared to sound the death knell for military tribunals when civil courts were operating, but tribunals continued to function in the South under martial law during the Reconstruction period. From the end of April 1865, to January 1, 1869, there were 1,435 trials by military tribunals, and

113. Id. at 117.
114. Id. at 130, 131.
115. Id. at 132.
116. Id. at 133.
117. Id. at 137.
118. 2 Charles Warren, The Supreme Court in United States History 428–32 (1937).
119. Id. at 432.
120. 14 Stat. 432, 433 (1867).

others occurred in Texas and Mississippi in 1869 and 1870.[121] The *Milligan* decision would be revisited by the Court in 1942 when it decided the Nazi saboteur case.

Other Judicial Rulings

A number of district and circuit courts carefully examined the legality of habeas corpus suspensions during the Civil War. In 1862, a district court held that the President is not vested by the Constitution with power to suspend the privilege of the writ of habeas corpus at any time, without the authority of an act of Congress.[122] Quoting Blackstone, the court declared: "Of great importance to the public is the preservation of this personal liberty; for if once it were left in the power of any, of the highest magistrate, to imprison whomever he or his officers thought proper . . . there would soon be an end of all other rights and immunities."[123] Blackstone acknowledged that suspension might be a necessary measure when the state is in danger, but "the happiness of our constitution is, that it is not left to the executive power to determine when the danger of the state is so great as to render this measure expedient; for it is the parliament only, or legislative power, that, whenever it sees proper, can authorize the crown, by suspending the habeas corpus act for a short and limited time, to imprison suspected persons without giving any reason for so doing."[124]

The district court relied on *Ex parte Merryman* to show that the power of suspension "is a legislative and not an executive power, and must be exercised, or its exercise authorized, by congress."[125] Looking to other decisions, including those by the Supreme Court, the district court regarded it as an "unanswerable argument" that the President, without congressional authority, "has no constitutional power to suspend the privilege of the writ of habeas corpus in the United States."[126]

Also in 1862, a circuit court in Vermont held that the War Department had no authority to issue an order suspending the writ of habeas corpus. At the time, neither Congress nor the President had declared that the public safety required the establishment of martial law or the suspension of

---

121. Mark E. Neely Jr., The Fate of Liberty: Abraham Lincoln and Civil Liberties 176–77 (1991).

122. Ex parte Benedict, 3 Fed. Cas. 159 (No. 1,292) (D. N.Y. 1862).

123. Id. at 163.

124. Id.

125. Id. at 165.

126. Id. at 171.

habeas corpus in loyal states.[127] The court also held that Lincoln had acted properly in issuing his proclamation of September 24, 1862, proclaiming martial law and suspending the writ of habeas corpus.[128]

In 1863, after Congress had passed the statute of March 3, 1863, authorizing the President to suspend the writ of habeas corpus, two district courts upheld Lincoln's actions. In the first, the court held that his proclamation of September 15, 1863, suspending the writ, was "valid and efficient in law."[129] Lincoln grounded his proclamation on the March 3, 1863, statute.[130] Similarly, a district court in Massachusetts looked to the broad language of the statute as reason to alleviate judicial concern. The statutory grant of authority was total: "No case is excepted. Not one is withheld from the operation of this power. All come within its scope, and the cases now before me are clearly comprehended in this language."[131]

After the war was over, federal courts became less tolerant of military tribunals that operated without specific statutory authority or that tried to use statutory authority to impose ex post facto punishments. In 1866, a circuit court in New York remarked that a trial before a tribunal took place seven months after hostilities had terminated and the rebel army had surrendered, and that the trial "was not had under the rules and articles of war, as established by the United States in congress assembled."[132] Lacking statutory authority, the trial "must have been had under what is known as 'martial law,'" with martial law generally defined as "neither more nor less than the will of the general who commands the army. It overrides and suppresses all existing civil laws, civil officers and civil authorities, by the arbitrary exercise of military power." Martial law, said the court, "is regulated by no known or established system or code of laws, as it is over and above all of them. The commander is the legislator, judge, and executioner."[133] The same concentration of power in the executive branch is found in the Nazi saboteur case of 1942 and the military tribunals authorized by President George W. Bush.

In 1867, a circuit court in Missouri reviewed a congressional statute of March 2, 1867, which authorized military tribunals for certain rebel states.[134]

127. Ex parte Field, 9 Fed. Cas. 1, 3 (No. 4,761) (C.C. Vt. 1862).
128. Id. at 5–9.
129. In re Dunn, 8 Fed. Cas. 93 (No. 4,171) (S.D. N.Y. 1863).
130. 3 Stat. 734 (1863).
131. In re Fagan, 8 Fed. Cas. 947, 949 (No. 4,604) (D. Mass. 1863).
132. In re Egan, 8 Fed. Cas. 367 (No. 4,303) (C.C. N.Y. 1866).
133. Id.
134. 14 Stat. 428 (1867).

President Andrew Johnson vetoed the bill, in part because of the authority vested in military commanders, but he was overridden.[135] Someone arrested in New Orleans in 1865 was tried by a military tribunal under this statute. The circuit court held that the statute used to prosecute the individual was unconstitutional because it was ex post facto.[136] "No clearer case," said the court, of an ex post facto law "could be framed." The effect of the law was "to hold men in confinement for offenses not punishable at the time they were committed, and to detain such persons in a servitude imposed by a court which had no jurisdiction to try them."[137]

Spotlight on Andersonville

A nine-member military tribunal convened at Washington, D.C., on August 23, 1865, to hear charges of conspiracy and murder against eight Southerners who administered the Andersonville prison, a "name that has come to stand for human misery wrought by war."[138] Thousands of Union soldiers held in this Georgia prison died from overcrowding, sun exposure, inadequate food, polluted water, lack of medicine, and disease. After reviewing the trial record, Judge Advocate General Holt said that language could not be found "to denounce, even in faint terrors, the diabolical combination for the destruction and death, by cruel and fiendishly ingenious processes, of helpless prisoners of war who might fall into their hands, which this record shows was plotted and deliberately entered upon, and, as far as time permitted, accomplished by the rebel authorities and their brutal underlings at Andersonville prison." He could find in criminal history "no parallel to this monstrous conspiracy." A system for murdering men "more revolting in its details could not have been planned."[139]

Both sides, prosecution and defense, conceded that conditions at the prison were inhumane. The focus at the trial should have been on establishing the personal culpability of Capt. Henry Wirz, superintendent of the prison. As his counsel told the court: "We may admit that the horrors of Andersonville are indescribable by tongue or pen, yet still we may be able to show, as we confidently hope to do, that for those horrors Captain Wirz

---

135. 8 Richardson 3696–3709.

136. In re Murphy, 17 Fed. Cas. 1030 (No. 9,947) (C.C. Mo. 1867).

137. Id. at 1032.

138. Lewis L. Laska and James M. Smith, "'Hell and the Devil': Andersonville and the Trial of Captain Henry Wirz, C.S.A., 1865," 68 Mil. L. Rev. 77, 78 (1975).

139. H. Ex. Doc. No. 23, 40th Cong., 2d Sess. 809 (1867).

is not in any way responsible."[140] Yet the prosecution used a broad brush to make him embody all the evils of the Civil War, including the assassination of Lincoln. The presentation by Judge Advocate General Holt ranged far and wide:

> When we remember that the men here charged, and those inculpated, but not named in the indictment, are some of them men who were at the head of the late rebellion, from its beginning to its close, and as such chiefs, sanctioned the brutal conduct of their soldiers as early as the first battle of Bull Run; who perpetrated unheard-of cruelties at Libby and Belle Isle; who encouraged the most atrocious propositions of retaliation in their congress; who sanctioned a guerilla [sic] mode of warfare; who instilled a system of steamboat burning and firing of cities; who employed a surgeon in their service to steal into our capital city infected clothing; who approved the criminal treatment of the captured prisoners at Fort Pillow, Fort Washington, and elsewhere; who were guilty of the basest treachery in sending paroled prisoners into the field; who planted torpedoes in the paths of our soldiers; who paid their emissaries for loading shell in the shape of coal, and intermixing them in the fuel of our steamers; who ordered an indiscriminate firing upon our transports and vessels and railroad trains, regardless of whom they contained; who organized and carried to a successful termination a most diabolical conspiracy to assassinate the President of the United States—when we remember these things of these men, may we not without hesitancy bring to light the conspiracy here charged?[141]

Holt reminded the tribunal members of the efforts of John A. Bingham, who "delivered for the prosecution in the trial of the conspirators for the assassination of President Lincoln" the argument on conspiracies.[142] Lincoln's assassination had the effect of canceling the initial public support for mercy toward the South and replacing it with "a demand for vengeance," not only against those who conspired against Lincoln "but against all the former leaders of the Confederacy."[143] Secretary of War Stanton helped promote the idea of a conspiracy in the South, directed by Jefferson Davis

140. Id. at 415.
141. Id. at 749.
142. Id. at 749–50.
143. Laska and Smith, "Hell and the Devil," at 83.

and the Confederacy, that supplied the driving force for the assassination of Lincoln.[144] When evidence for that theory could not be assembled,[145] there remained a determination to make some southerners pay a price.

The weight of that prejudice fell on Wirz.[146] He was "hurried to his death by vindictive politicians, an unbridled press, and a nation thirsty for revenge."[147] John Howard Stibbs, one of the nine members of the tribunal, published an article in 1911 recounting his experience. He said that the evidence presented at the trial "satisfied the Court beyond a doubt that while this prison was being made ready, if not before, a conspiracy was entered into by certain persons, high in authority in the Confederate service, to destroy the lives of our men, or at least subject them to such hardships as would render them unfit for further military service."[148] The target of the trial was therefore not Wirz but the "conspiracy." Unable to substantiate the latter, the tribunal settled on Wirz.

The documentary record reveals efforts by Wirz to improve camp conditions. When he arrived at the prison in early 1864, drainage of the grounds had been neglected and there were inadequate shelters.[149] His dispatches to headquarters called attention to the poor quality of bread and the lack of buckets for issuing rations.[150] Subsequent dispatches asked for axes, wheelbarrows, lumber, lime, iron, and sheet iron for baking pans.[151] Evidence indicated that Wirz had tried to improve the conditions of prisoners "with the few resources diverted to him from the main war effort . . . and in the face of indifference on the part of his superiors."[152] He attempted to construct dams that would subdivide a stream running through the camp into areas for drinking, bathing, and sanitation, but lacked equipment to complete the job.[153]

The prosecution relied heavily on the testimony and inspection reports prepared by Col. A. C. Chandler, who visited the camp during the war and

144. Darrett B. Rutman, "The War Crimes and Trial of Henry Wirz," 6 Civil War Hist. 117, 121 (1960).

145. William Hanchett, The Lincoln Murder Conspiracies 78–82 (1983).

146. The two charges (the second containing 13 specifications) are reproduced at 2:8 War of the Rebellion 785–89.

147. Rutman, "The War Crimes and Trial of Henry Wirz," at 118.

148. John Howard Stibbs, "Andersonville and the Trial of Henry Wirz," 9 Iowa J. Hist. Pol. 33, 35 (1911).

149. 2:7 War of the Rebellion 167–68.

150. Id. at 207.

151. Id. at 521.

152. Laska and Smith, "Hell and the Devil," at 115.

153. Rutman, "The War Crimes and Trial of Henry Wirz," at 119.

identified a number of deficiencies.[154] The court record, however, includes a report that Chandler prepared shortly after Wirz had assumed responsibility.[155] Chandler said that Wirz, on the job for seven months, was "entitled to commendation for his untiring energy and devotion to the multifarious duties of his position, for which he is pre-eminently qualified." He joined Gen. J. H. Winder in recommending Wirz for promotion.[156] The person Chandler wanted removed from duty was not Wirz but Winder. What was urgently needed, Chandler said, was someone "who unites both energy and good judgment with some feeling of humanity and consideration for the welfare and comfort . . . of unfortunates placed under his control."[157] At the trial, Chandler described Winder as "very indifferent to the welfare of the prisoners, indisposed to do anything, or to do as much as I thought he ought to do, to alleviate their sufferings."[158]

Chandler told the tribunal that during one of his visits to Andersonville, he decided to make inquiries directly of the prisoners. Having been a prisoner himself, he knew the "unwillingness of prisoners to make complaints in the presence of those who have power over them, and for that reason, I took the men aside and questioned them so that Wirz could not hear me as to any complaints they had to make, and none of them made any complaints against him."[159]

At the trial, Wirz was found guilty on most of the charges.[160] President Andrew Johnson approved the proceedings and sentences and ordered that Wirz be hanged on November 10, 1865. The execution was carried out as ordered, with Wirz's body interred in Washington, D.C., by the side of one of the Lincoln conspirators, George A. Atzerodt.[161]

Conspirators of Lincoln's Assassination

The most controversial Civil War tribunal is the trial of eight people charged with conspiring to assassinate President Lincoln. On May 1, 1865, President

154. H. Ex. Doc. No. 23, at 224–50.
155. Id. at 224–26 (Chandler report of January 5, 1864).
156. Id. at 226 (Chandler report of August 5, 1864).
157. Id. at 227.
158. Id. at 240.
159. Id.
160. He was found guilty of the first charge (conspiracy) and of 10 out of 13 specifications of the second charge (murder); 2:8 War of the Rebellion 791.
161. H. Ex. Doc. No. 23, at 815.

Johnson ordered nine military officers to serve on the tribunal to try the suspects, even though civil courts were open and operating.[162] The tribunal convened on May 9 to try seven men and one woman: David E. Herold, G. A. Atzerodt, Lewis Payne, Mary E. Surratt, Michael O'Laughlin, Edward Spangler, Samuel Arnold, and Samuel A. Mudd.[163] They were charged with conspiring with the intent to kill Lincoln, Vice President Johnson, Secretary of State William H. Seward, and Gen. Ulysses S. Grant.[164] Four received prison sentences and four were sentenced to death by public hanging: Herold, Atzerodt, Payne, and Surratt.[165] Johnson approved the sentences on July 5 and ordered the executions to take place two days later.[166] On the morning of the scheduled executions, Surratt's attorneys applied for and received a writ of habeas corpus, but Attorney General James Speed advised the civil court that Johnson had suspended the writ.[167] Commentary on these trials has generally criticized the appearance of prejudgment and the spirit of vengeance.[168]

Johnson asked Speed for a legal opinion on whether the persons charged with the conspiracy could be tried before a military tribunal or must be tried before a civil court. Speed acknowledged that although martial law had been declared in the District of Columbia at the time of Lincoln's assassination, "the civil courts were open and held their regular sessions, and transacted business as in times of peace."[169] Yet Speed concluded that the conspirators "not only may but ought to be tried by a military tribunal."[170] It was within the power of Congress to prescribe how tribunals "are to be constituted, what shall be their jurisdiction, and mode of procedure." If Congress failed to create such tribunals, "then, under the Constitution, they must be constituted according to the laws and usages of civilized warfare."[171]

---

162. 8 Richardson 3532–33.

163. Id. at 3540.

164. Id. at 3540–41.

165. Id. at 3543–45.

166. 8 Richardson 3545–46; 8 The Papers of Andrew Johnson 357 (1989).

167. 16 The Papers of Andrew Johnson 486 (2000); Hanchett, The Lincoln Murder Conspiracies, at 70.

168. James L. Swanson and Daniel R. Weinberg, Lincoln's Assassins: Their Trial and Execution (2001); Hanchett, The Lincoln Murder Conspiracies (1986); Elizabeth Steger Trindal, Mary Surratt: An American Tragedy (1996); David Miller DeWitt, The Judicial Murder of Mary E. Surratt (1895); James H. Johnston, "Swift and Terrible: A Military Tribunal Rushed to Convict After Lincoln's Murder," Washington Post, December 9, 2001, at F1.

169. 11 Op. Att'y Gen. 297, 297 (1865).

170. Id. at 298.

171. Id.

Speed further reasoned that "when war comes, the laws of war come with it," and Presidents had substantial constitutional authority to act under the laws of war.[172] Some of the offenses against the laws of war are crimes, punishable in the civil courts, "and some not."[173] He recognized that murder (and attempted murder) are crimes punishable in the civil courts, but added that "in committing the murder an offence may also have been committed against the laws of war; for that offence he must answer to the laws of war, and the tribunals legalized by that law."[174]

Clearly Speed makes a jump here, without ever explaining why murder and attempted murder could not, or should not, be tried in civil court. Appealing more to emotion than to logic, he said that the fact that civil courts "are open does not affect the right of the military tribunal to hold as a prisoner and to try." Civil courts "have no more right to prevent the military, in time of war, from trying an offender against the laws of war than they have a right to interfere with and prevent a battle."[175] The analogy here is strained. Courts are created to try offenders, not to engage in military battles.

Opinions of Attorneys General usually have a specific date: month, day, and year. Speed's opinion is merely marked "July, 1865," which is two months after President Johnson created the tribunal and the same month that the tribunal rendered its verdicts and carried out the hangings. Given the timing of Speed's opinion, it looks like an after-the-fact analysis to justify not what could or should happen, legally, but what had happened or was about to happen.[176]

Edward Bates, who served as Attorney General under Lincoln from 1861 to 1863, held a low opinion of Speed. He said Speed came into office "with not much reputation as a lawyer, and perhaps, no strong confidence in his own opinions," vulnerable to falling under the influence of Cabinet officers such as Secretary of War Stanton and Secretary of State Seward, "to give such opinions as were wanted!"[177] Bates considered the military tribunal for the conspirators a great mistake:

Such a trial is not only unlawful, but it is a gross blunder in policy:
It denies the great, fundamental principle, that ours is a government

172. Id. at 312.
173. Id.
174. Id. at 312–13.
175. Id. at 315.
176. For a cutting analysis of the Speed opinion by former Attorney General Edward Bates, see The Diary of Edward Bates, 1859–1866, at 498–503 (Howard K. Beale ed. 1933).
177. Id. at 483.

of *Law,* and that the law is strong enough, to rule the people wisely
and well; and if the offenders be done to death by that tribunal, however truly guilty, they will pass for martyrs with half the world.

I do not doubt that that unwise determination was the work of Mr.
Stanton. He believes in mere force, so long as he wields it, but cow-
ers before it, when wielded by any other hand.[178]

Bates objected to military tribunals because the people who serve "are
selected by the military commander *from among his own subordinates,*
who are bound to obey him, and responsible to him; and therefore, they
will, commonly, find the case as required or desired by the commander
who selected them."[179] Courts-martial, he said, exist because of a statute
enacted by Congress "and the members thereof have *legal* duties and
rights," whereas military tribunals "exist only by the will of the commander, and that will is their only known rule of proceeding."[180] Judge R. A
Watts, who served as acting Assistant Adjutant General at the trial, described
the tribunal as "a law unto itself. It made its own rules of procedure. It was
the sole judge of the law, as well as of the facts. . . . It was empowered not
only to decide the question of guilt but it also had the power, and it was
its duty, to fix the penalties."[181]

Clemency for Surratt

The public hanging of Mary Surratt created a political embarrassment for
President Johnson. Several years after her execution, Judge Advocate General Holt claimed that he presented Johnson with a petition, signed by five
members of the military tribunal, recommending that in consideration of
her age and sex she be imprisoned for life rather than hanged. Johnson
denied that he had seen the document or had anyone discuss it "until some
days *after,* the Execution of Mrs. Surratt."[182] Public knowledge that a majority of the tribunal had recommended imprisonment for Surratt sparked a
"growing sentiment that she had been unjustly put to death."[183]

---

178. Id. (emphasis in original).

179. Id. at 502 (emphasis in original).

180. Id. (emphasis in original).

181. Judge R. A. Watts, "The Trial and Execution of the Lincoln Conspirators," 6 Mich.
Hist. Mag. 81, 99 (1922).

182. 16 The Papers of Andrew Johnson 440 (2000) (emphasis in original); Hanchett,
The Lincoln Murder Conspiracies, at 87–88.

183. Hanchett, The Lincoln Murder Conspiracies, at 88.

Johnson's term ended on March 4, 1869. Returning to Tennessee, he decided in 1872 to run for Congress. During the campaign, Holt published a lengthy article on August 26, 1873, insisting that he had presented the clemency petition to Johnson and it had been discussed with several members of the Cabinet, after which Johnson decided that execution was the proper course.[184] Holt tried unsuccessfully to get Speed to comment publicly on Johnson's handling of the petition.[185] Johnson published a lengthy rebuttal on November 11, 1873, disputing Holt's account of the clemency offer.[186] Johnson said that only after there had been public notice of the petition had he sent for the papers on August 5, 1867, more than two years after the executions.[187] If Holt in 1867 had disagreed with Johnson on the presentation of the petition, Johnson asked why Holt had not issued an immediate challenge and sought the corroboration of Stanton and Seward while they were alive. By 1873, both were dead.

Samuel A. Mudd

In recent decades, portions of the Lincoln conspiracy trial were replayed in federal court. Samuel A. Mudd, found guilty of harboring some of the conspirators, was sentenced to be imprisoned at hard labor for life.[188] In 1868, a district court in Florida held that his case was properly tried by a military tribunal.[189] On February 8, 1869, President Johnson granted Mudd a full and unconditional pardon.[190]

More than a century later, Mudd's grandson challenged the jurisdiction of the military tribunal that convicted the Lincoln conspirators. In 1992, the Army Board for Correction of Military Records noted that Mudd never

184. Vindication of Hon. Joseph Holt, Judge Advocate General of the United States Army (1873).

185. Allen Thorndike Rice, "New Facts About Mrs. Surratt," 147 No. Am. Rev. 83 (1888). See also documents put together by Speed's son, John Speed: "The Assassins of Lincoln," 147 No. Am. Rev. 314 (1888). For other commentary on the trial, see John W. Curran, "Lincoln Conspiracy Trial and Military Jurisdiction over Civilians," 9 Notre Dame Lawyer 26 (1933), and Thomas R. Turner, "What Type of Trial? A Civil Versus a Military Trial for the Lincoln Assassination Conspirators," 4 Papers of the Abraham Lincoln Association 29 (1982).

186. 16 The Papers of Andrew Johnson 475–89 (2000).

187. Id. at 483–84.

188. 8 Richardson 3545.

189. Ex parte Mudd, 17 Fed. Cas. 954 (No. 9,899) (D. Fla. 1868).

190. Andrew Johnson Papers, Library of Congress, Reel 50, Series 8C; 15 The Papers of Andrew Johnson 424 (1999).

served in the military, was a civilian at the time of Lincoln's assassination, and lived in the nonsecessionist state of Maryland. It concluded that the commission, lacking jurisdiction to try Mudd, "denied him his due process rights, particularly his right to trial by a jury of his peers," and that this denial "constituted such a gross infringement of his constitutionally protected rights, that his conviction should be set aside. To fail to do so would be unjust."[191]

A federal district court in 1998 ruled that the Johnson pardon did not make the Mudd case moot and that the rejection by the Secretary of the Army of the board's recommendation was unsupported by substantial evidence in the record.[192] In a subsequent decision, the court held that the military commission had jurisdiction to try Mudd for violations of laws of war.[193] Mudd's grandson died on May 21, 2002.[194] Later that year, the D.C. Circuit dismissed the suit because the descendants of Dr. Mudd who attempted to clear his name lacked standing.[195]

The widespread use of military tribunals throughout the Civil War marked a turning point in America's experience. Hundreds of tribunals operated with little supervision by Congress or the courts. Few examples of tribunals emerged after the end of the war and Reconstruction to World War II. What prevailed over this period of more than 70 years was an effort to develop codes of modern warfare that would cover both civil wars and military conflicts between states. Congress also tackled the need to revise the Articles of War, which had remained largely unchanged since 1806.

191. Mudd v. Caldera, 26 F.Supp.2d 113, 117 (D.D.C. 1998).

192. Id. at 119–23 .

193. Mudd v. Caldera, 134 F.Supp.2d 138 (D.D.C. 2001). See John Paul Jones, ed., Dr. Mudd and the Lincoln Assassination: The Case Reopened (1995).

194. "Richard D. Mudd, 101; Grandson of Booth Doctor," Washington Post, May 22, 2002, at B7.

195. Mudd v. White, 309 F.3d 819 (D.C. Cir. 2002); Neil A. Lewis, "Suit to Clear Doctor Who Treated Booth Is Dismissed," New York Times, November 9, 2002, at A13.

4

CODES OF MODERN WARFARE

The rapid rise and erratic use of military tribunals during the Civil War called for uniform standards of warfare, especially to clarify the rights of citizens in occupied territories. Most of the officers who served on the tribunals were volunteers, with little knowledge of the laws and usages of war. Out of the conflicting practices in different regions of the country came the efforts of Dr. Francis Lieber to develop rules of conduct for modern war. His work had great impact on other countries and led to both national and international standards. Lieber's code was considered at the Conference of Brussels of 1874 and later heavily influenced the Hague and Geneva Conventions. All of these developments placed new constraints on the creation and operation of military tribunals.

Lieber's Code

Francis Lieber, born in Berlin in 1800, received his doctor of philosophy degree from the University of Jena in 1820. To these scholarly pursuits he added a personal commitment to political freedom. At age 15, serving with Prussian troops against Napoleon, he found himself on the battlefield at Waterloo. Twice wounded, during one battle he was shot in the neck and chest and left on the field to die. Later, for political activities found disagreeable to authorities, he was held in preventive detention for five months.[1] In 1821, Lieber volunteered to fight in the Greek war of independence. He visited London for a short stay and then emigrated to the United States in 1827, first settling in Boston. After spending time in New York and Philadelphia, he moved south to accept the Chair of History and Political Economy at South Carolina College in 1835 and taught there for 22 years. In 1857, he joined Columbia College in New York as Professor

---

1. Ernest Nys, "Francis Lieber—His Life and His Work" (Part I), 5 Am. J. Int'l L. 84, 91–93, 97 (1911); James F. Childress, "Francis Lieber's Interpretation of the Laws of War: General Orders No. 100 in the Context of His Life and Thought," 21 Am. J. Jurisprudence 34, 42 (1976).

of Modern History, Political Science, and International, Civil, and Common Law.

On the eve of the Civil War, Lieber was uniquely positioned to bring clarity, consistency, and humanity to modern warfare. He had given close study to public law, international law, and the laws of war. All three of his sons wound up fighting in the war, two for the North and one for the South. His son Hamilton lost an arm while fighting for the Union army. Oscar, who had joined the Confederates, died in battle in Williamsburg, Virginia. Lieber said he had known war as a soldier and a wounded man in the hospital, "but I had yet to learn it in the phase of a father searching for his wounded son, walking through the hospitals, peering in the ambulances."[2]

In 1859, Lieber tried to introduce a course on the rules of war at West Point. The commandant rejected the proposal on the grounds that the curriculum was already overcrowded.[3] As a result, even officers trained at West Point lacked an understanding of the laws of war and the rights of citizens in occupied territories. Years later, long after the Civil War, West Pointers were drilled on the military code that Lieber completed in 1863. The instructor who ensured that this information would be front and center was his son, Norman.[4]

On August 19, 1861, Lieber sent a letter to Henry Wager Halleck, General in Chief of the Union Armies, saying that he wanted to write "a little book on the Law and Usages of War, affecting the combatants."[5] Halleck had established his own credentials as a scholar, having authored the 900-page treatise *International Law* in 1861. The alternative title shows how much he and Lieber had in common: *Rules Regulating the Intercourse of States in Peace and War.* Overwhelmed with military details, Halleck did not give Lieber immediate directions to proceed with the project. Lieber spent the winter of 1861–62 delivering a set of lectures on "The Laws and Usages of War" at the law school of Columbia College. Halleck took an interest in these lectures and requested Lieber to send copies or a syllabus of them.[6] After receiving the materials, Halleck told Lieber to order 5,000 copies and even recommended a publisher that specialized in books on military subjects.[7]

---

2. Frank Freidel, Francis Lieber: Nineteenth-Century Liberal 325 (1947).

3. Frank Freidel, "General Orders 100 and Military Government," 32 Miss. Valley Hist. Rev. 541, 542–43 (1946).

4. Id. at 555–56.

5. Richard Shelly Hartigan, Lieber's Code and the Law of War 2 (1983).

6. Freidel, Francis Lieber, at 324; Hartigan, Lieber's Code and the Law of War, at 74, 78.

7. Hartigan, Lieber's Code and the Law of War, at 78.

Halleck asked Lieber on August 6, 1862, to submit his views on guerrilla war. The problem, Halleck explained, was that rebel authorities claimed the right to send men "in the garb of peaceful civilians, to waylay and attack our troops, to burn bridges and houses, and to destroy property and persons within our lines." Should such guerrilla forces, he inquired, be treated as ordinary belligerents and be given the same rights as prisoners of war if captured?[8]

Lieber submitted to Halleck a paper on "Guerrilla parties considered with reference to the laws and usages of war." Lieber began by distinguishing among guerrillas, partisans, and regular troops. He regarded a guerrilla party as "an irregular band of armed men, carrying on an irregular war, not being able, according to their character as a guerrilla party, to carry on what the law terms a regular war."[9] Guerrilla parties formed "no integral part of the organized army, do not stand on the regular pay-roll of the army, or are not paid at all, take up arms and lay them down at intervals, and carry on petty war (guerrilla) chiefly by raids, extortion, destruction, and massacres."[10] Lieber's definitions of rebel, partisan, brigand, and guerrilla were picked up by the Army and published on April 22, 1863, as General Orders No. 30.[11]

To Lieber, it was not decisive whether guerrillas wore a uniform. The absence of a uniform might be taken "as very serious prima facie evidence against an armed prowler or marauder," but in some cases, regular soldiers did not have a uniform and were treated as prisoners of war.[12] It was more important, however, if the absence of a uniform was used "for the purpose of concealment or disguise, in order to get by stealth within the lines of the invader, for destruction of life or property, or for pillage, and whether the parties have no organization at all, and are so small that they cannot act otherwise than by stealth."[13] If captured "in fair fight and open warfare," guerrillas should be treated in the same manner as a regular partisan, but no army or society could allow "unpunished assassination, robbery, and devastation without the deepest injury to itself and disastrous consequences which might change the very issue of the war."[14] Necessar-

8. 3:2 The War of the Rebellion: A Compilation of the Official Records of the Union and Confederate Armies 301 (1894) (hereafter "War of the Rebellion"). 2:1 stands for Series 2, vol. 1.
9. Id. at 302.
10. Id. at 307–8.
11. 1:22 (Part 2) War of the Rebellion 237–39.
12. 3:2 War of the Rebellion 306.
13. Id. at 307.
14. Id. at 308–9.

ily, Lieber spoke at a high level of abstraction and left to Halleck the application of these principles to specific cases.

On November 13, 1862, Lieber wrote again to Halleck: "Ever since the beginning of our present War, it has appeared clearer and clearer to me, that the President ought to issue a set of rules and definitions providing for the most urgent cases, occurring under the Laws and Usages of War, and on which our Articles of War are silent." Lieber suggested that Lincoln, through the Secretary of War, appoint a committee to draw up a code in which "certain acts and offences (under the Law of War) ought to be defined and, where necessary, the punishment be stated."[15] Not hearing from Halleck, Lieber continued to inquire about the status of the committee. He wrote to Halleck on November 25, expressing the hope that "you will take the suggestion out of the pigeon hole of your mind."[16]

Finally, on December 17, a special order by the Secretary of War created a committee of five people, including Lieber, "to propose amendments or changes in the Rules and Articles of War, and a code of regulations for the government of armies in the field, as authorized by the laws and usages of war."[17] Lieber was the only civilian selected for the committee, which included three major generals and one brigadier general.

The special order seemed to contemplate a bill that would be placed before Congress and enacted as part of the Rules and Articles of War. In fact, the code that Lieber and his colleagues presented the following year amounted to an executive decree without statutory support. Lieber wrote to Halleck on February 20, 1863, including a draft copy of the code. For two or three of the paragraphs, he said, there was need for congressional action but "that is now too late." On the complexity of the task, he wrote colorfully and somewhat extravagantly about the drafting process:

> I had no guide, no ground-work, no text-book. I can assure you, as a friend, that no counselor of Justinian sat down to his task of the Digest with a deeper feeling of the gravity of his labor, than filled my breast in the laying down for the first time such a code, where nearly everything was floating. Usage, history, reason, and conscientiousness, a sincere love of truth, justice, and civilization have been my guides; but of course the whole must be still very imperfect.[18]

15. Hartigan, Lieber's Code and the Law of War, at 79.
16. Id. at 83.
17. 3:2 War of the Rebellion 951.
18. George B. Davis, "Doctor Francis Lieber's Instructions for the Government of Armies in the Field," 1 Am. J. Int'l L. 13, 20 (1907).

Of course Lieber did not labor in such a wasteland. He had his own publications and lecture notes to turn to, as well as Halleck's highly detailed treatise and the writings of August W. Heffter, Hugo Grotius, Cornelius van Bynkershoek, Samuel Pufendorf, and other authorities.[19] Lieber could also look profitably at Gen. Winfield Scott's General Orders No. 20, issued at Tampico on February 19, 1847, for guidance on martial law and the rights of citizens in occupied territories.[20]

General Orders No. 100

Lieber's comprehensive code was released on April 24, 1863, as General Orders No. 100, called "Instructions for the Government of Armies of the United States in the Field."[21] He wanted the document called a "Code," but it was changed to "Instructions." There may have been apprehension that President Lincoln had no constitutional authority to issue a code, and that any document implying a code or statute required action by Congress. Lieber noted: "Congress adjourned, and we could not wait; nor did the general of the Board want the word 'Code.'"[22]

The instructions consist of 157 articles organized under ten sections. The first section is called "Martial law—Military jurisdiction—Military necessity—Retaliation." Other sections dealt with public and private property of the enemy, deserters and prisoners of war, definitions of partisans and rebels, spies, exchange of prisoners, the release (or parole) of POWs, armistice and capitulation, assassination, and a final section on insurrection, civil war, and rebellion.

Lieber drafted the code to introduce humane standards to combat while at the same time recognizing that military commanders required flexibility to win wars. Neither he nor the other members of the committee intended to write a code so abstract and impractical that it could not be applied. In addressing these competing values, the code carried inevitable contradictions and was open to wide interpretations. Upon reading it through, one contemporary remarked: "I am aware it gives a license for a man to be

19. Freidel, Francis Lieber, at 333, n. 38.
20. R. R. Baxter, "The First Modern Codification of the Law of War: Francis Lieber and General Orders No. 100 (Part II)," 26 Int. Rev. Red Cross 240 (May 1963).
21. Lieber's code is reproduced in many places, including 3:3 War of the Rebellion 148–64; Hartigan, Lieber's Code and the Law of War, at 45–71; and 1 Leon Friedman, ed., The Law of War 158–86 (1972).
22. R. R. Baxter, "The First Modern Codification of the Law of War: Francis Lieber and General Orders No. 100 (Part I)," 25 Int. Rev. Red Cross 185 (April 1963).

either a fiend or a gentleman. He can find abundant authority for either role in the order."[23]

Parts of the code are quite clear in repudiating military oppression and cruelty. Article 11 states that the law of war disclaims "all cruelty and bad faith concerning engagements concluded with the enemy during the war." Article 16 counsels that military necessity "does not admit of cruelty—that is, the infliction of suffering for the sake of suffering or for revenge, nor of maiming or wounding except in fight, nor of torture to extort confessions."

Military necessity, as defined in Article 16, does not permit the use of poison "in any way, nor of the wanton devastation of a district." Article 70 prohibits the use of poison "in any manner, be it to poison wells, or food, or arms," for such actions are "wholly excluded from modern warfare." Whoever used poison "put himself out of the pale of the law and usages of war." Military necessity does not include any act of hostility "which makes the return to peace unnecessarily difficult."

Lieber sought to place constraints on martial law, which Article 4 describes as "simply military authority exercised in accordance with the laws and usages of war." Laws and the usages of war were meant to place limits on military operations. Military oppression, said the code, was "not martial law; it is the abuse of the power which that law confers." Those who administer martial law are "to be strictly guided by the principles of justice, honor, and humanity—virtues adorning a soldier even more than other men, for the very reason that he possesses the power of his arms against the unarmed." In this way, Lieber rejected the notion that might makes right.

Still, it was left unclear how martial law would be restrained by laws, the usages of war, and the principles of justice, honor, and humanity. Were those just general values operating in the mind of a commander, to be applied as each officer decided? Throughout the code, the principle of military necessity seemed to be the overriding value. Article 5 ends with: "To save the country is paramount to all other considerations." Article 14 defines military necessity as "those measures which are indispensable for securing the ends of the war, and which are lawful according to the modern law and usages of war." Article 23 refers to "the overruling demands of a vigorous war."

Article 15 speaks further of military necessity, saying that it "admits of all direct destruction of life or limb of armed enemies, and of other persons whose destruction is incidentally unavoidable in the armed contests

---

23. 2:5 War of the Rebellion 744 (letter of June 5, 1863, from Robert Ould to Lt. Col. William H. Ludlow).

of the war." Military necessity allowed for "all destruction of property, and obstruction of the ways and channels of traffic, travel, or communication, and of all withholding of sustenance or means of life from the enemy." Military commanders could appropriate from the enemy whatever was necessary for the subsistence and safety of the army. Yet Article 15 ends with this admonition: "Men who take up arms against one another in public war do not cease on this account to be moral beings, responsible to one another and to God."

Article 19 advises commanders, "whenever admissible," to inform the enemy of an intention to bombard a place, "so that the non-combatants, and especially the women and children, may be removed before the bombardment commences." This article then adds a qualifier: "But it is no infraction of the common law of war to omit thus to inform the enemy. Surprise may be a necessity." Article 23 claims that in modern wars private citizens "are no longer murdered," and yet under Article 19 they might be. .

Section II introduces some constraints on the seizure of public and private property. It begins with Article 31, which permits a victorious army to appropriate all public money and to seize all public movable property. Article 34, however, states that as "a general rule" the property belonging to churches, hospitals, or other establishments "of an exclusively charitable character," and to establishments of education, public schools, universities, museums of the fine arts, or of a scientific character, should not be appropriated or seized. In Article 35, classical works of art, libraries, scientific collections, precious instruments (such as astronomical telescopes), and hospitals should be secured "against all avoidable injury." If these artistic and scientific collections can be removed without injury, that should be done for the benefit of the occupied country.

Military Tribunals

As with other parts of Lieber's code, it was uncertain as to the extent to which military tribunals could supplant civil courts. Article 3 defines martial law in a hostile country as "the suspension by the occupying military authority of the criminal and civil law," but added the qualification "as far as military necessity requires this suspension, substitution, or dictation." The implication is that civil courts could continue to operate in some capacity. Thus, the commander "may proclaim that the administration of all civil and penal law shall continue either wholly or in part, as in times of peace, unless otherwise ordered by the military authority."

Article 13 refers to two kinds of military jurisdiction: that which is "conferred and defined by statute," and a second that is derived from "the

common law of war." The first is controlled by Congress, the second by
the executive. Military offenses under statutory law must be tried in the
manner as directed by Congress, "but military offenses which do not come
within the statute must be tried and punished under the common law of
war." In the United States, the first type of military jurisdiction is exercised
by courts-martial, "while cases which do not come within the Rules and
Articles of War, or the jurisdiction conferred by statute on courts-martial,
are tried by military commission."

Lieber distinguished between the treatment of enemies in uniform, captured as prisoners of war, and enemies captured without a uniform. This
issue arose with the German saboteurs who entered the United States in
1942 and 1944, initially with portions of a uniform but then switched to
civilian dress after they were safely in the country. A prisoner of war, as
noted in Article 56, "is subject to no punishment for being a public enemy,
nor is any revenge wreaked upon him by the intentional infliction or any
suffering, or disgrace, by cruel imprisonment, want of food, by mutilation,
death, or any other barbarity." However, troops who fight "in the uniform
of their enemies, without any plain, striking, and uniform mark of distinction of their own, can expect no quarter" (Article 63). Section IV elaborates
on these distinctions. Partisans who wear the enemy's uniform are entitled
to all the privileges of the prisoner of war, but men who conduct themselves as highway robbers, armed prowlers, or "war-rebels" and lack a uniform are not entitled to the privileges of prisoners of war. If someone in
civilian dress, or in the uniform of the army hostile to their own, is found
lurking behind enemy lines, he is treated as a spy and put to death.

Lieber's Legacy

General Orders No. 100 has had a continuing impact both within the
United States and beyond its borders. When the Supreme Court decided in
Ex parte Vallandigham (1864) that it had no jurisdiction to review the proceedings of a military commission, Justice Wayne began his opinion by
noting that military commanders had acted in conformity with the instructions issued to the armies, "approved by the President of the United States,
and published by the Assistant Adjutant-General, by order of the Secretary
of War, on the 24th of April, 1863." A footnote explains: "They were prepared by Francis Leiber [*sic*], LL.D., and were revised by a board of officers, of which Major-General E. A. Hitchcock was president."[24]

24. 1 Wall. (68 U.S.) 243, 248 (1864).

In 1863 and 1864, Congress made an effort to revise the Articles of War. On February 23, 1863, Senator Henry Wilson, who would later serve as Vice President under Ulysses S. Grant, introduced a bill for "establishing rules and articles for the government of the armies of the United States." The 35-page bill, introduced before the publication of General Orders No. 100, does not reflect Lieber's influence. Instead, the list of 105 Articles builds on previous statutory efforts. Article 23 provides that in "time of war or public danger military commissions may be constituted, and shall have jurisdiction over all offences and offenders against the common laws of war not cognizable by courts-martial."[25] As with other statutes on the Articles of War, the bill concentrates on military conduct, court-martial procedures, and punishments, not the broad law of war that preoccupied Lieber.

This bill was referred to the Senate Committee on Military Affairs and the Militia. Four days later, the committee reported the bill, with several amendments, and asked the Senate to concur in the amendments "without taking up time by reading them." The objective was to have the bill, as amended, printed for Senate action on the following day. The Senate agreed to this procedural step, but there was no action on the bill.[26] Senator Wilson reintroduced the bill in the 38th Congress. There was no further legislative action.[27]

When Germany prepared for war against France in 1870, it adopted General Orders No. 100 to guide the conduct of its armies in the field.[28] At the Brussels Conference of 1874, convened for the purpose of codifying the laws and customs of war, the president of the conference announced that the idea of calling an international convention had its origin in the General Orders No. 100. In 1880, the Institute of International Law issued a manual on the laws of war upon land, relying on the work of the Brussels Conference and the code devised by Lieber. The Hague Conferences of 1899 and 1907 looked extensively to General Orders No. 100 for guidance and inspiration.[29] When the War Department released the *Rules*

25. S. 563, 37th Cong., 3d Sess. (1863). The introduction of this bill is cited at Cong. Globe, 37th Cong., 3d Sess. 1179 (1863).

26. Cong. Globe, 37th Cong., 2d Sess. 1323 (1863).

27. S. 67, 38th Cong., 1st Sess. (1864); Cong. Globe, 38th Cong., 1st Sess. 262 (1864).

28. Elihu Root, "Francis Lieber," 7 Am. J. Int'l L. 453, 456 (1913); Davis, "Doctor Francis Lieber's Instructions for the Government of Armies in the Field," at 22.

29. Root, "Francis Lieber," at 457; Davis, "Doctor Francis Lieber's Instructions for the Government of Armies in the Field," at 22.

of Land Warfare in 1914, the influence of General Orders No. 100 was seen throughout.[30]

Johann Kaspar Bluntschli, a scholar of international law, acknowledged the world's debt to Lieber, whose code "was a deed of great moment in the history of international law and of civilization." Lieber's "legal injunctions rest upon the foundation of moral precepts. The former are not always sharply distinguished from moral injunctions, but nevertheless, through a union with the same, are ennobled and exalted." Embodied in the code is "the spirit of humanity, which spirit recognizes as fellow-beings, with lawful rights, our very enemies, and which forbids our visiting upon them unnecessary injury, cruelty, or destruction." Bluntschli noted that Lieber remained "fully aware that, in time of war, it is absolutely necessary to provide for the safety of armies and for the successful conduct of a campaign; that, to those engaged in it, the harshest measures and most reckless exactions cannot be denied; and that tender-hearted sentimentality is here all the more out of place, because the greater the energy employed in carrying on the war, the sooner will it be brought to an end, and the normal condition of peace restored."[31]

Occupation of the Philippines

Lieber's effort to introduce humanity into warfare had little application once the United States decided, as part of the Spanish-American War, to pacify and occupy the Philippines. The U.S. government did not adopt Gen. Scott's policy in Mexico by relying on a display of justice and evenhandedness to avert guerrilla warfare. Instead, the United States regarded Filipinos as barbarian and unfit for self-government.[32] American military actions against inhabitants triggered an outbreak of guerrilla warfare and led to atrocities by both sides.[33] Gen. Arthur MacArthur placed the Philippines under martial law and relied on a mix of military commissions and Army provost courts to discipline the local population.[34]

---

30. U.S. War Department, Rules of Land Warfare, Doc. No. 467 (1914).

31. Davis, "Doctor Francis Lieber's Instructions for the Government of Armies in the Field," at 22–23. See also Burrus M. Carnahan, "Lincoln, Lieber and the Laws of War: The Origins and Limits of the Principle of Military Necessity," 92 Am. J. Int'l L. 213 (1998).

32. Peter Maguire, Law and War: An American Story 53 (2001).

33. Id. at 55.

34. Brian McAllister Linn, The U.S. Army and Counterinsurgency in the Philippine War, 1899–1902, at 23–25, 55–56 (1989).

American atrocities in the Philippines prompted the Senate, in 1902, to conduct hearings as part of a legislative investigation into U.S. military conduct. William Howard Taft, the civil governor of the Philippine Islands, explained why the Lieber Code, designed to minimize the harshness of war between white and white, would have little practical use in a war marked by racism. Senator Thomas Patterson put the question: "When a war is conducted by a superior race against those whom they consider inferior in the scale of civilization, is it not the experience of the world that the superior race will almost involuntarily practice inhuman conduct?" Taft responded: "There is much greater danger in such a case than in dealing with whites. There is no doubt about that."[35] One senator pointed out that the American practice of burning and destroying the homes and shacks put the punishment "mainly upon the women and little children." When he asked whether that conduct was within the ordinary rules of civilized warfare, an American general chillingly replied: "These people are not civilized."[36]

The Hague Treaties

The Hague treaty of July 29, 1899, signed by the United States, a number of countries in Europe, and Scandinavia, Russia, and other nations, agreed to a set of laws and customs of war on land. Fedor de Martens of Russia credited Lieber and General Orders No. 100 for providing the basis for subsequent efforts to humanize war.[37] Lieber's general approach prevailed. The purpose of the treaty, expressed in the opening paragraphs, was "inspired by the desire to diminish the evils of war so far as military necessities permit."[38]

As with Lieber, Article III of the Hague treaty recognized that the armed forces of the belligerent parties "may consist of combatants and non-combatants." Both categories, if captured by the enemy, "have a right to be treated as prisoners of war."[39] Article IV stated that POWs "must be humanely treated" and that all their personal belongings, "except arms, horses, and military papers remain their property." Unless there is a spe-

35. "Affairs in the Philippine Islands," hearings before the Senate Committee on the Philippines, 57th Cong., 1st Sess. 77 (1902).
36. Id. at 559. See Richard E. Welch Jr., "American Atrocities in the Philippines: The Indictment and the Response," 43 Pac. Hist. Rev. 233 (1974).
37. Frederick W. Holls, The Peace Conference at the Hague 151 (1900).
38. 32 Stat. 1804 (1899).
39. Id. at 1812.

cial agreement between the belligerents, POWs "shall be treated as regards food, quarters, and clothing, on the same footing as the troops of the Government which has captured them" (Article VII). POWs could not be brought before the courts unless, upon release, they were recaptured bearing arms against the "Government to whom he had pledged his honor, or against the allies of that Government" (Article XII).

Article 50 of Lieber's Code provided that "citizens who accompany an army for whatever purpose, such as sutlers, editors, or reporters of journals, or contractors, if captured, may be made prisoners of war and be detained as such." Article XIII of the Hague treaty has a comparable provision. Individuals who follow an army without belonging to it, such as newspaper correspondents and reporters, sutlers, and contractors, and who fall into the enemy's hands and are detained, have a right to be treated as POWs if they can produce a certificate from the military authorities of the army they were accompanying. Thus, they are not subject to trial, either civilian or military. The Hague treaty grants POWs the right to exercise their religion (Article XVIII). The section on the means of injuring the enemy carries provisions similar to Lieber's Code, including a prohibition on the use of poisons or poisoned arms and efforts to spare, as far as possible, buildings devoted to religion, art, science, and charity, and hospitals (Article XVII).

The Hague treaty picks up Lieber's definition of a spy[40]: "An individual can only be considered a spy if, acting clandestinely, or on false pretenses, he obtains, or seeks to obtain information in the zone of operations of a belligerent, with the intention of communicating it to the hostile party." However, "soldiers not in disguise who have penetrated into the zone of operations of a hostile army to obtain information are not considered spies" (Article XXIX). These definitions track what appears in General Orders No. 30, which itself was based on the paper Lieber submitted to Halleck on guerrilla parties. The Hague treaty of 1899 was revised and supplemented in 1907.[41]

Revising the Articles of War

After enacting the Articles of War in 1806, Congress did not subject the Articles to comprehensive revision for more than a century. They were

40. 1:22 (Part 2) War of the Rebellion 237; 3:2 War of the Rebellion 301–9.
41. 36 Stat. 2259, 2277 (1907). For further comparisons between Lieber's Code and the Hague treaty of 1899, see Root, "Francis Lieber," at 466–69.

reenacted in 1874, as part of a codification effort, but the revisers were not allowed "to go beyond the reconciling of contradictions, the supplying of obvious omissions, and the curing of imperfections in form and language."[42] The task of revisers is generally to look for redundant or obsolete material. The reenactment in 1874 therefore does not represent a revision. During the nineteenth century, Congress at times enacted new Articles or revised some, but never attempted a full-fledged revision. For example, a statute in 1890 amended one of the Articles of War.[43]

The process of bringing the Articles up to date began in 1912 when the House Committee on Military Affairs held hearings to consider a bill designed to revise the Articles of War. Secretary of War Henry L. Stimson advised the committee that in 1888 and 1903 the War Department had made efforts to revise the Articles, but nothing materialized. He called the existing Articles "notoriously unsystematic and unscientific."[44] At these hearings, Judge Advocate General E. H. Crowder drew attention to an "entirely new" Article on military commissions, a type of court that had never been "formally authorized by statute" but was an institution "of the greatest importance in a period of war and should be preserved."[45] Asked what he meant by this tribunal, he described it as a "common law of war court" never regulated by statute.[46] As he put it at subsequent hearings, these war courts grew out of "usage and necessity."[47]

A piecemeal revision of the Articles of War in 1913 seems to challenge the unique jurisdiction of military tribunals to handle disputes over the law of war. New language gave general courts-martial the power to try any person subject to military law for any crime punishable by the Articles of War, but also jurisdiction over "any other person who by statute or by the law of war is subject to trial by military tribunals."[48] That language would reappear in the Articles of War enacted in 1916 and 1920.[49] Did this statutory provision eliminate the need for military tribunals?

To forestall that interpretation, Crowder fashioned language to assure

42. S. Rept. No. 229, 63d Cong., 2d Sess. 20 (1914).
43. 26 Stat. 491 (1890).
44. "Revision of the Articles of War," hearing before the House Committee on Military Affairs, 62d Cong., 2d Sess. 3 (1912).
45. Id. at 29.
46. Id. at 35.
47. S. Rept. No. 130, 64th Cong., 1st Sess. 41 (1916). This report includes the transcript of the hearings.
48. 37 Stat. 722 (1913).
49. 39 Stat. 652, Art. 12 (1916); 41 Stat. 789, Art. 12 (1920).

that conferring jurisdiction on general courts-martial over the law of war did not deprive military tribunals of concurrent jurisdiction. Because he expected the jurisdictions of courts-martial and tribunals to frequently overlap, and questions would naturally arise as to whether congressional action in vesting jurisdiction by statute in courts-martial would eliminate the need for tribunals, he wanted to make "it perfectly plain by the new article that in such cases the jurisdiction of the war court is concurrent."[50]

The Senate Committee on Military Affairs reported legislation in 1914 to revise the Articles of War.[51] During floor action the following year, the Articles were added as an amendment to an army appropriations bill.[52] As enacted in 1916, Crowder's Article 15 read:

> ART. 15. NOT EXCLUSIVE.—The provisions of these articles conferring jurisdiction upon courts-martial shall not be construed as depriving military commissions, provost courts, or other military tribunals of concurrent jurisdiction in respect of offenders or offenses that by the law of war may be lawfully triable by such military commissions, provost courts, or other military tribunals.[53]

New controversies erupted in 1917 because of charges that military law lacked adequate procedures and opportunities for proper review. Also, several sensational cases were brought forward to highlight excessive punishment of American soldiers during World War I.[54] In 1920, Congress decided to put the new Articles of War not in an appropriations bill but in an authorization measure called National Defense Act Amendments. As reported by the House Committee on Military Affairs, the National Defense Act did not contain the new Articles.[55] However, the Senate included the

50. "Revision of the Articles of War," hearing before the House Committee on Military Affairs, 62d Cong., 2d Sess. at 29.

51. S. Rept. No. 229, 63d Cong., 2d Sess. (1914).

52. 52 Cong. Rec. 4290, 4296–303 (1915). See also S. Rept. No. 130, 64th Cong., 1st Sess. (1916) and 53 Cong. Rec. 11474, 11504–13 (1916).

53. 39 Stat. 653 (1916). An earlier appropriations bill, also containing the Articles of War, was vetoed by President Wilson because of a dispute over language concerning the treatment of retired officers. H. Doc. No. 1334, 64th Cong., 1st Sess. (1916). Congress did not challenge the veto of this bill (H.R. 16460).

54. Herbert F. Margulies, "The Articles of War, 1920: The History of a Forgotten Reform," 43 Military Affairs 85 (1979).

55. H. Rept. No. 680, 66th Cong., 2d Sess. (1920).

Articles in the bill, as did the conferees.[56] The wording of Article 15 was changed slightly. Instead of restricting the Article to offenses under "the law of war," the new Article covered offenses both by statute and the law of war:

> ART. 15. JURISDICTION NOT EXCLUSIVE.—The provisions of these articles conferring jurisdiction upon courts-martial shall not be construed as depriving military commissions, provost courts, or other military tribunals of concurrent jurisdiction in respect of offenders or offenses that by statute or by the law of war may be triable by such military commissions, provost courts, or other military tribunals.[57]

The 1920 statute refers to military tribunals at several other places, such as provisions dealing with self-incrimination, depositions, courts of inquiry, contempts, presidential authority to prescribe procedural rules, captured or abandoned property, assisting the enemy, spies, and the appointment of reporters and interpreters.[58]

Despite sharing concurrent jurisdiction over the law of war, it appeared that military tribunals held an edge over general courts-martial. Under Article 43 of the 1916 statute, no person convicted of an offense punishable by death could be executed "except by the concurrence of two thirds" of the general court-martial, and only for "an offense in these articles expressly made punishable by death."[59] When this Article appeared in the 1920 statute, the two-thirds majority was replaced by "the concurrence of all the members of said court-martial," while retaining the language "an offense in these articles expressly made punishable by death."[60] A military tribunal created by the President might not be subject to these statutory limitations.

---

56. H. Rept. No. 1049, 66th Cong., 2d Sess. 66 (1920); 59 Cong. Rec. 7834 (1920). An earlier committee on conference was unable to reach agreement because of a dispute over the National Guard; H. Rept. No. 1000, 66th Cong., 2d Sess. 2 (1920). For Senate hearings in 1919 on the Articles of War, see "Establishment of Military Justice," hearings before a Subcommittee of the Senate Committee on Military Affairs, 66th Cong., 1st Sess. (1919).

57. 41 Stat. 790 (1920).

58. Articles 24–27 (41 Stat. 792), Article 32 (id. at 793), Article 38 (id. at 794), Articles 80–82 (id. at 804), and Article 115 (id. at 810).

59. 39 Stat. 657 (1916).

60. 41 Stat. 796 (1920). For detailed analysis of the 1916–20 legislative action on the Articles of War, see Jonathan Lurie, Arming Military Justice: The Origins of the United States Court of Appeals for the Armed Forces, 1775–1980, at 46–126 (1992).

During Senate hearings in 1916, Crowder discussed the option of using courts-martial and tribunals, explaining that Article 15 "just saves to these war courts [tribunals] the jurisdiction they now have and makes it a concurrent jurisdiction with courts-martial, so that the military commander in the field in time of war will be at liberty to employ either form of court that happens to be convenient."[61] He then added: "Both classes of courts have the same procedure."[62] That has not been the case. The procedures for courts-martial have been spelled out in statutory Articles of War and in the *Manual for Courts-Martial*. Military tribunals have been relatively free in adopting whatever procedures they like, even adopting them after a trial is underway. The scope of that freedom is discussed later, particularly in the chapter of the Nazi saboteurs in 1942.

Part of the Articles of War in 1920 appeared to restrict what a President may do in adopting procedures for military tribunals. Article 38 authorized the President to prescribe, by regulations, "which he may modify from time to time," the rules for cases before courts-martial, courts of inquiry, military commissions, and other military tribunals. Congress directed that these regulations "shall, in so far as he shall deem practicable, apply the rules of evidence generally recognized in the trial of criminal cases in the district courts of the United States." Moreover, "nothing contrary to or inconsistent with these articles shall be so prescribed." All rules made pursuant to Article 38 were to be placed before Congress each year.[63] Those provisions imposed certain rules and standards on the President. In subsequent military tribunals, including the trial of the German saboteurs in 1942 and the Yamashita case in 1945, Presidents and military commanders devised rules and procedures that departed widely from these earlier statutory standards.

Military Trials for Civilians?

On April 16, 1918, Senator George Chamberlain (D-Ore.) introduced a bill to punish sedition by military trial instead of by the criminal courts. His bill was designed to subject to trial by court-martial or military commission persons who endangered the "good discipline, order, movements, health, safety, or successful operations" of U.S. land or naval forces by acting as

---

61. S. Rept. No. 130, 64th Cong., 1st Sess. 40 (1916).
62. Id.
63. 41 Stat. 794 (1920).

spies in time of war in the United States.[64] After the bill's referral to the Committee on Military Affairs, chaired by Chamberlain, a motion was made to request the Judiciary Committee to report whether any of the provisions of the bill were in violation of the Constitution.[65] The sponsor of the motion, Senator Frank Brandegee (R-Conn.), charged that the bill "simply bristles with constitutional questions and in my opinion is absolutely violative of every guaranty contained in the Constitution as to trial by jury and individual liberty."[66]

Four days after the bill's introduction, President Woodrow Wilson wrote to Senator Lee Slater Overman (D-N.C.), stating that he was "wholly and unalterably opposed to such legislation" because it was "not only unconstitutional, but that in character it would put us nearly upon the level of the very people we are fighting and affecting to despise."[67] After Wilson's action, Chamberlain recognized that "it would seem to be a work of supererogation to undertake to press a bill when the Chief Executive opposes it."[68]

Attorney General Thomas W. Gregory disclosed that Chamberlain's bill had been prepared by Charles Warren, Assistant Attorney General, without Gregory's knowledge. The general policies in the bill, Gregory said, "are exactly contrary to those approved by the Assistant to the Attorney General in charge of the problems involved and by the Attorney General himself." Gregory expressed his disapproval of Warren's action, "and it would not have been permitted if I had known that it was contemplated."[69] Warren resigned from the Justice Department on April 19.[70]

Lothar Witzke Crosses the Border

During World War I, Lothar Witzke entered the United States at the Mexican border. Although he had a Russian passport, he was a German spy using

---

64. 56 Cong. Rec. 5120 (1918); "Court-Martial for Spies," New York Times, April 17, 1918, at 12.

65. 56 Cong. Rec. 5401 (1918).

66. Id. at 5402.

67. 47 The Papers of Woodrow Wilson 381 (1984). See also "Wilson Opposes New Spy Bill," New York Times, April 23, 1918, at 6.

68. 56 Cong. Rec. 5472 (1918).

69. "Gregory Repudiates Warren," New York Times, April 23, 1918, at 6.

70. 47 The Papers of Woodrow Wilson 382 (1984). See also Charles Warren, "Spies, and the Power of Congress to Subject Certain Classes of Civilians to Trial by Military Tribunal," 53 Am. L. Rev. 195 (1919), and Arthur Krock, "When Martial Law Was Proposed for Everybody," New York Times, July 14, 1942, at 18.

the alias Pablo Waberski on a mission to commit sabotage against certain American targets. He was picked up by Army officials in Nogales, Arizona, and brought to Fort Sam Houston in San Antonio, Texas, where he faced a military tribunal of two brigadier generals and three colonels. He was charged with violating Article of War 82: "Any person who in time of war shall be found lurking or acting as a spy in or about any of the fortifications, posts, quarters, or encampments of any of the armies of the United States, or elsewhere, shall be tried by a general court-martial or by a military commission, and shall, on conviction thereof, suffer death." Two-thirds of the tribunal—a sufficient number at that time—found him guilty.[71]

An opinion by Attorney General Thomas W. Gregory in 1918 understood Waberski to be a Russian national sent to the United States by the German ambassador to Mexico to function as a German agent or spy. It was believed that he intended to explode and wreck munition barges, powder magazines, and other war utilities in the United States. The moment he touched foot on U.S. territory, he was apprehended by military authorities and had not entered any camp, fortification, or other U.S. military facility. Martial law had not been declared at Nogales or anywhere else in the United States, and the regular federal civilian courts were functioning in that district.

Relying in part on *Ex parte Milligan*, Gregory concluded that Witzke could not be tried by a military tribunal because he had been apprehended in U.S. territory not under martial law, and had not entered any camp, fortification, or other U.S. military premise.[72] Even without *Milligan*, Gregory said, the provisions of the Constitution

would themselves plainly bring us to the same conclusions as those set forth in the opinion of the court in that case, namely, that in this country, military tribunals, whether courts-martial or military commissions, can not constitutionally be granted jurisdiction to try persons charged with acts or offenses committed outside of the field of military operations or territory under martial law or other peculiarly military territory, except members of the military or naval forces or those immediately attached to the forces such as camp followers.[73]

71. Captain Henry Landau, The Enemy Within: The Inside Story of German Sabotage in America 112–27 (1937).

72. 31 Op. Att'y Gen. 356 (1918).

73. Id. at 361.

Gregory also pointed to Article 29 of the Hague Convention: "A person can only be considered a spy when acting clandestinely or on false pretences obtains or endeavors to obtain information *in the zone of operations* of a belligerent with the intention of communicating it to a hostile party."[74] Gregory added: "Obviously Waberski does not fit into these definitions."[75]

In the Nazi saboteur case of 1942, defense counsel seized upon Gregory's opinion to argue that the eight Germans could not be charged with spying if their activities were not in a theater of operations. Gregory had said that in this country, military tribunals could not try persons charged with offenses committed outside the field of military operations, except members of the military or naval forces and those immediately attached to the forces such as camp followers.[76]

To minimize the damage done by Gregory's language, the Justice Department on July 29, 1942—in the midst of the Nazi saboteur trial—released a previously unpublished Attorney General opinion, dated December 24, 1919, taking the opposite position. Attorney General A. Mitchell Palmer reversed Gregory on the basis of new facts. Witzke was a German citizen, not a Russian national, and it was now determined that he was found "lurking or acting as a spy." The military commission therefore had jurisdiction to try him under Article 82.[77] What the defense had relied on in the Nazi saboteur case was now without value. A few days after the release of the 1919 opinion, Oscar Cox from the Solicitor General's office drafted a memo for Attorney General Francis Biddle, giving further details on why the Justice Department decided to repudiate Gregory's opinion and to do so without public admission.[78]

On May 27, 1920, President Wilson commuted Witzke's sentence to confinement at hard labor for the rest of his life. He was transferred to Leavenworth Prison. Germany pressed for his release, as with other prisoners of war. The Judge Advocate General recommended his release on September 26, 1923, and he returned to Germany.[79]

---

74. Id. at 363. Gregory said the Hague Convention of 1917, but he must have meant 1907; 36 Stat. 2303 (1907).

75. 31 Op. Att'y Gen. at 363.

76. Id. at 361. For the defense attorney's position, see RG 153, Records of the Office of the Judge Advocate General (Army), Court-Martial Case Files, CM 334178, 1942 German Saboteur Case, National Archives, College Park, Md., at 2796.

77. 40 Op. Att'y Gen. 561 (1919), released for publication July 29, 1942.

78. Memo from Cox to Biddle, July 2, 1942, and from Biddle to Alexander Holtzoff, July 2, 1942, Papers of Oscar Cox, Box 61, Franklin D. Roosevelt Library.

79. Landau, The Enemy Within, at 127–28.

The period from the Civil War to the 1930s contains few experiences with military tribunals. Lieber explored the extent to which these tribunals could supplant civilian courts and offered guidelines on how to decide which belligerents were entitled to be treated as prisoners of war. The only examples of the military holding trials of civilians were in the Philippines and with Lothar Witzke. When Congress revised the Articles of War in 1916 and 1920, it made only glancing reference to tribunals. A proposal in 1918 to use military trials to punish American spies was thoroughly repudiated by Congress and President Wilson. However, America's interest in tribunals would be quickly reawakened in 1942 with the case of the Nazi saboteurs.

5

NAZI SABOTEURS

In June 1942, eight German saboteurs reached the United States by submarine, intent on using explosives against railroads, factories, bridges, and other strategic targets. One of the Germans turned himself in to the FBI and helped the agency quickly round up the others. President Roosevelt issued a proclamation to create a military tribunal, which a month later found the eight men guilty. Before the tribunal could issue its verdict, the Germans sought a writ of habeas corpus from the civil courts. That avenue was blocked when the Supreme Court, in *Ex parte Quirin* (1942), upheld the jurisdiction of the tribunal. Late in 1944 the Roosevelt administration captured two more German spies, but this time it decided that the tribunal of 1942 was fundamentally flawed and selected another type of military proceeding.

Training for Terrorism

The eight Germans recruited for sabotage had all lived in America and spoke English fairly well. They underwent training at a school located on the Quenz farm near Brandenburg, about 35 miles west of Berlin. Over a period of three weeks, the men learned about explosives, fuses, and timing devices. Lectures instructed them on American railroad systems and identified the main terminal points and vulnerable targets, such as bottlenecks and weak spots on boxcars and switching devices. Practical exercises required the men to use explosives on wooden posts buried in sand and on iron tracks laid on the ground. The explosives they took to the United States included lumps of TNT that looked like pieces of coal. The lumps could be put in the furnaces of railroad locomotives or in coal-burning furnaces to crack and ruin the boilers. Other techniques of sabotage included putting sand or emery dust in the bearings and machinery of trains and factories. The men studied U.S. maps to learn the locations of aluminum and magnesium plants, bridges, tunnels, and waterways.[1]

1. For further details on the training, see Louis Fisher, Nazi Saboteurs on Trial: A Military Tribunal and American Law 1–21 (2003).

The eight finalists were divided into two groups. One, led by George John Dasch, included Ernest Peter Burger, Heinrich Harm Heinck, and Richard Quirin. The second, under the direction of Edward John Kerling, consisted of Herbert Haupt, Hermann Neubauer, and Werner Thiel. After finishing classes and taking a short vacation, the men returned to Berlin and spent three days visiting aluminum plants, railroad yards, and canal locks. They learned that aluminum plants work on electrical power and can be disabled by striking the high-tension poles carrying power to the plants. By interrupting power for eight hours, the contents of the stove and bath would congeal, rendering them useless.

The men took an express train to Paris and went from there to Lorient, on the French coast, to board two submarines. Kerling's group left first, on May 26, 1942, and Dasch's group left two days later. They were instructed to wear German uniforms when they landed on the shores of America because, if caught immediately, they would be treated as prisoners of war rather than spies. They understood that captured spies faced a likely death sentence. Once they reached the beach safely and undetected, they were to change into civilian clothes and put their uniforms in a sack to be returned to the submarine.

Dasch's submarine reached the coast of Long Island on the evening of June 12. Shortly after midnight, the four men came up on deck and got in a rubber boat that contained four boxes of explosives. Two members of the crew paddled them to shore. When they began to unload the raft and change clothes, they encountered an unarmed coastguardsman, John C. Cullen. Dasch used threatening language while at the same time offering Cullen money to keep quiet. Dasch refused to follow Cullen's instructions to follow him back to the station house. After Cullen left, the men carried the boxes to the back of the beach and buried them in the sand. They also buried their German uniforms that should have been sent back to the submarine. Eventually they found a railroad station at Amagansett and took the train first to Jamaica and then on to Manhattan.[2]

Cullen returned to the station house and showed the cash ($260) he had been given. Several people from the station and two members of Coast Guard Intelligence returned to the beach and had little difficulty finding the buried boxes and a duffel bag with the uniforms. Three FBI agents arrived to inventory the materials. The government now knew that German saboteurs had entered the country but had no idea where they had gone or whether others had landed elsewhere. In the meantime, Kerling's group

2. Id. at 25–28.

reached Ponte Vedra, near Jacksonville, Florida, and made it to the beach without incident. They returned their uniforms to the sub and buried the boxes. Thiel and Haupt went to Cincinnati, with Haupt continuing on to Chicago, where he had family members. Kerling and Neubauer took a train to Cincinnati and split up, Kerling proceeding to New York City and Neubauer traveling to Chicago.

The FBI was able to round up the men rapidly because Dasch decided to turn himself in. He first made an anonymous call to the FBI office in New York City and then took a train to Washington, D.C., where he called the FBI and disclosed the plan for sabotage. With Dasch's help, FBI agents had little difficulty in picking up the three members of his team in New York City.[3] Haupt made the mistake of stopping by the FBI office in Chicago to inform the bureau that he had returned from Mexico. The FBI found his visit suspicious and put a tail on him, eventually leading the agents to Neubauer. Kerling and Thiel were picked up in New York City.[4]

The press reported their dramatic capture, giving full credit to the FBI. *The New York Times* reported: "before the men could begin carrying out their orders the FBI was on their trail and the roundup began. One after another they fell into the special agents' net."[5] Other newspaper accounts gloried in the FBI's detection abilities: "Almost from the moment the first group set foot on United States soil the special agents of the Federal Bureau of Investigation were on their trail."[6] According to another account, the FBI seized the men "almost as they landed on the sandy beaches."[7] A *Washington Post* editorial praised the FBI's "brilliant job of detection."[8]

Very little was known about Dasch's role in helping the FBI find the other seven saboteurs. Lewis Wood of the *New York Times* wrote a lengthy story about Cullen's encounter with Dasch and provided verbatim details of their conversation.[9] Some reporters were getting close to understanding the extent of Dasch's assistance. On July 5, the *Washington Post* reported that one of the Germans had "lost his nerve" and gave a coastguardsman "hot money" that made it easier for federal agents to stay on their

3. Id. at 40–41.

4. Id. at 35–38, 41–42.

5. Will Lissner, "Invaders Confess," New York Times, June 28, 1942, at 1, 30.

6. Id. at 30.

7. Lewis Wood, "Nazi Saboteurs Face Stern Army Justice," New York Times, July 5, 1942, at 6E.

8. "FBI's Master Stroke," Washington Post, June 29, 1942, at 6.

9. Lewis Wood, "Lone Coast Guardsman Put FBI on Trail of Saboteurs," New York Times, July 16, 1942, at 1, 38.

trail.[10] This particular incident was not yet linked to Dasch. A day later, however, the *Post* learned that Dasch might stand a chance of clemency because he had cooperated with U.S. officials "in procuring evidence against the others."[11] Another *Post* story on July 8 reported that Dasch would have his own counsel and was likely to escape the death penalty.[12] On July 16, the *Post* stated that the military trial had consumed an entire day reading the confession of one of the men identified as an "informer."[13] The reporter connected that person to Dasch.

Why a Tribunal?

At the time that FBI agents interrogated Dasch and the other seven, they planned to arraign them before a district judge and try them in civil court. The agents never considered the prospect of a military tribunal. They told Dasch that if he agreed to plead guilty, they would set the wheels in motion for a presidential pardon. At the military trial, Dasch's attorney asked one of the agents: "Was it stated as a part of that proposal that after his plea of guilty he should be sentenced and that during the trial he should not divulge anything with respect to the agreement that was made, and that after the case had died down and for about, say, three to six months, the F.B.I., would get a Presidential pardon for him?" The agent replied: "That, in substance, is true."[14] The FBI warned Dasch that if he appeared in open court to testify about his cooperation with the government, it might endanger his family in Germany.[15] Any such testimony from Dasch, of course, would eliminate the chance of a pardon.

On Saturday afternoon, June 27, the FBI told Dasch that he would be indicted and tried before a civil court. In testimony before the military tribunal, Dasch said that he agreed to plead guilty with the understanding

---

10. "German Spy's Loss of Nerve Led to Capture," Washington Post, July 5, 1942, at 11.

11. "Saboteurs' Trial to Start in Washington Wednesday," Washington Post, July 6, 1942, at 1.

12. Dillard Stokes, "One Spy Gets Separate Counsel, Hinting at Leniency for Him," Washington Post, July 8, 1942, at 1.

13. Dillard Stokes, "Confession of Spy Who Told All Read to Military Commission," Washington Post, July 16, 1942, at 7.

14. RG 153, Records of the Office of the Judge Advocate General (Army), Court-Martial Case Files, CM 334178, 1942 German Saboteur Case, National Archives, College Park, Md., at 542 (hereafter "Military Trial").

15. Id. at 541, 548.

that everything would be kept quiet. Yet the following morning, when he looked through the slit in his cell door and saw an agent reading the Sunday newspaper, Dasch's photo was prominently "in front."[16] Feeling betrayed, Dasch withdrew his offer to plead guilty. He now wanted to go into civil court and make a full explanation, even if it put his family at risk.[17] FBI agents knew what Dasch meant by "full explanation." He was primed to talk for hours, if not days.

The administration now realized that a civil trial was out of the question. The public had the impression that uncanny FBI organizational skills had quickly exposed the plot. FBI Director J. Edgar Hoover, after being praised for discovering the saboteurs, did not want it known that one of them had turned himself in and fingered the others. Neither did President Roosevelt and other top officials. The government did not want to broadcast how easily German U-boats had reached American shores undetected. By sending a message that the executive branch had vast capacity to intercept enemy saboteurs, the United States wanted to discourage future attempts by Germany or any other country.

There was a second reason for a military tribunal. The statute on sabotage carried a maximum 30-year penalty, and even on that charge, the government had little confidence that it could prevail. The men had not actually committed sabotage. In his memoirs, Attorney General Francis Biddle concluded that an indictment for attempted sabotage probably would not have been sustained in a civil court "on the ground that the preparations and landings were not close enough to the planned act of sabotage to constitute attempt." He pointed out that if a man bought a pistol with the intent to murder someone, "that is not an attempt at murder."[18]

Federal prosecutors could add the charge of conspiracy to commit crimes, but the maximum penalty was only three years.[19] A military tribunal offered many advantages: it could act in secret, move swiftly, adopt rules that favored the prosecution, and mete out the ultimate penalty. There was some debate within the administration whether Burger and Haupt, as naturalized U.S. citizens, would have to be tried in civil court, but plans were soon underway to prosecute all eight before a military tribunal.

Maj. Gen. Myron C. Cramer, Judge Advocate General of the Army, had similar concerns about the relatively light penalties available in civil pro-

---

16. Id. at 2546.
17. Id. at 677.
18. Francis Biddle, In Brief Authority 328 (1962).
19. Id.

ceedings. In a memo of June 28, he said that a district court "would be unable to impose an adequate sentence." It could impose a sentence of two years and a fine of $10,000 for conspiracy to commit a crime. The government could also punish the Germans for violating immigration laws by entering the country clandestinely and for violating customs laws by bringing the articles they had carried ashore. However, Cramer concluded that the "maximum permissible punishment for these offenses would be less than it is desirable to impose."[20] Oscar Cox, in the Solicitor General's office, knew of Cramer's estimate that what the Germans had done was "only a two-year offense at most."[21]

On late Sunday afternoon, June 28, Secretary of War Henry L. Stimson received a phone call from Biddle, scheduling a meeting the next day to decide whether to prosecute the saboteurs in civil court or military court.[22] At about noon on Monday, Biddle told Stimson the result of conferences that Biddle had been having with Cramer. To Stimson's surprise, Biddle, "instead of straining every nerve to retain civil jurisdiction of these saboteurs, was quite ready to turn them over to a military court." Biddle suggested that instead of a court-martial the government should appoint a special military commission, with Stimson serving as chairman. Stimson thought it was not "seemly" for him to both appoint the commission and chair it, so he recommended that a civilian chair the commission. The person he had in mind, Robert Patterson (Assistant Secretary of War), preferred that the court be wholly military.[23]

The press learned of these meetings. On June 29, Biddle indicated that the eight Germans might be prosecuted by the War Department and that Biddle had been consulting with Stimson and Cramer.[24] A press release by the Justice Department on June 30 disclosed that Biddle and his staff "have been in constant consultation throughout the day with the Secretary

20. Memorandum for the Assistant Chief of Staff, G-2, June 28, 1942, by Maj. Gen. Myron C. Cramer, at 4, in "German Saboteurs" file, RG 107, Office of the Secretary of War, Stimson "Safe File," National Archives, College Park, Md. (hereafter "Stimson's Safe File").

21. Memo of June 29, 1942, Sunday, "German Saboteurs," Papers of Oscar Cox, Diaries and Related Material, Box 146, Franklin D. Roosevelt Library, Hyde Park, N.Y.

22. Diary of Henry L. Stimson, June 28, 1942, Roll 7, at 128–29, Manuscript Room, Library of Congress, Washington, D.C. (hereafter "Stimson Diary").

23. Id. at 131, June 29, 1942.

24. "Saboteurs Face Military Justice; Inquiry Widens," New York Times, June 30, 1942, at 1.

of War, the Judge Advocate General, and other War Department officials."[25]

Oscar Cox sent a memo to Biddle on June 29, concluding that the men could be tried by either a court-martial or a military tribunal. *Milligan,* Cox said, did not require a civil trial for enemy aliens who came through the lines out of uniform for the purpose of committing sabotage. In comparing the merits of the two types of military courts, he emphasized that a general court-martial "must follow statutory procedures presented in the Articles of War," whereas the procedures of a military commission were not necessarily governed by statutes. Yet he added this qualification: "it has been the practice for military commissions to follow the composition and procedure of courts-martial."[26] That is not how the military tribunal for the saboteurs would function. It departed from court-martial practice whenever it felt like it.

By June 30, journalists learned that the basic decision to proceed by military trial had been made.[27] Stimson spent that day selecting military officers to serve on the commission.[28] Biddle received a note from Roosevelt on June 30, referring to the death penalty as "almost obligatory."[29] Roosevelt said that "without splitting hairs" he could see no difference between this case and the hanging of Major André. He ended with this warning: "i.e., don't split hairs, Mr. Attorney General."[30] All that remained was the official announcement. On July 1, newspapers learned that Roosevelt would appoint a seven-member military commission to try the eight men and that Biddle would share prosecutorial duties with Cramer.[31] That procedure was highly irregular. The Judge Advocate General belongs at the end of a prosecution, in a reviewing function, not at the beginning. Stimson objected to Biddle taking the time to perform as prosecutor, at the cost of more important duties at the Justice Department. Stimson noted in his diary on July 1 that Biddle "seemed to have the bug of publicity in his mind."[32]

---

25. Press Release, Department of Justice, June 30, 1942, "German Saboteurs, Trial of (I)," Papers of Oscar Cox, Box 61, FDR Library.

26. Id. at 3, memo from Cox to Biddle, June 29, 1942.

27. "Army to Try 8 Saboteurs Landed by Sub," Washington Post, June 30, 1942, at 1.

28. Stimson Diary, June 30, 1942, at 133.

29. Memo from Roosevelt to Biddle, June 30, 1942, PSF, "Departmental File, Justice, 1940–44," Box 56, FDR Library.

30. Biddle, In Brief Authority, at 330.

31. "Death to Be Sought for 8 Saboteurs," Washington Post, July 2, 1942, at 12.

32. Stimson Diary, July 1, 1942, at 136.

Roosevelt's Proclamation

A memo from Biddle to Roosevelt on June 30 reviewed the advantages of proceeding by military commission. Espionage laws and treason carried the death penalty, but Biddle thought it would be difficult to prove either in civil court. In fact, Biddle wanted to make sure that the operation of a military commission would not be subjected to second-guessing by civil courts. He recommended language that would deny the eight Germans any access to civil courts. He believed that his proposed language would not represent a suspension of the writ of habeas corpus, although the wording "should produce the same practical result for such enemies." By confining the language to the eight men, he thought the administration "would not raise the broad policy questions which would follow a 'suspension' of the writ." It had "long been traditional," he told Roosevelt, "to deny our enemies access to the courts in time of war."[33]

On July 2, less than a week after the eight men had been apprehended, Roosevelt issued Proclamation 2561 to create a military tribunal. The proclamation carried this title: "Denying Certain Enemies Access to the Courts of the United States."[34] The initial paragraph began by stating that the "safety of the United States demands that all enemies who have entered upon the territory of the United States as part of an invasion or predatory incursion, or who have entered in order to commit sabotage, espionage, or other hostile or warlike acts, should be promptly tried in accordance with the law of war."

Reference to "law of war" was crucial. Had Roosevelt cited the Articles of War, he would have triggered the statutory procedures established by Congress for courts-martial. The category "law of war," undefined by statute, represented a more diffuse collection of principles and customs developed in the field of international law. Dating back to Article of War 15 crafted by Judge Advocate General Crowder, Congress took note of the law of war in this manner: "The provisions of this chapter conferring jurisdiction upon courts-martial do not deprive military commissions, provost courts, or other military tribunals of concurrent jurisdiction with respect to offenders or offenses that by statute or by the law of war may be tried by military

---

33. Memo from Biddle to Roosevelt, June 30, 1942, OF 5036, Box 4, FDR Library. A memo by the Justice Department on July 1 explored the risk of the eight saboteurs seeking a writ of habeas corpus. Memo from Ernest W. Jennes to Oscar Cox, July 1, 1942, "German Saboteurs, Trial of (I)," Papers of Oscar Cox, Box 61, FDR Library.

34. 7 Fed. Reg. 5101 (1942).

commissions, provost courts, or other military tribunals."[35] Statutory law is fixed; with the "law of war," a military tribunal could pick and choose among the principles and procedures it found compatible with the overall theme of Roosevelt's proclamation.

The second paragraph of the proclamation described Roosevelt acting as "President of the United States of America and Commander in Chief of the Army and Navy of the United States, by virtue of the authority vested in me by the Constitution and the statutes of the United States." Thus, Roosevelt was not claiming inherent or exclusive constitutional authority. He acted under a mix of constitutional authority accorded to the President and statutory authority granted by Congress. The proclamation goes on to proclaim "that all persons who are subjects, citizens or residents of any nation at war with the United States or who give obedience to or act under the direction of any such nation, and who during time of war enter or attempt to enter the United States or any territory or possession thereof, through coastal or boundary defenses, and are charged with committing or attempting or preparing to commit sabotage, espionage, hostile or warlike acts, or violations of the law of war, shall be subject to the law of war and to the jurisdiction of military tribunals."

The second paragraph contained a controversial provision that attempted to deny the eight men access to any civil court: "such persons shall not be privileged to seek any remedy or maintain any proceeding directly or indirectly, or to have any such remedy or proceeding sought on their behalf, in the courts of the United States, or of its States, territories, and possessions, except under such regulations as the Attorney General, with the approval of the Secretary of War, may from time to time prescribe." The denial was not total; it could be lifted by specified executive officials.

Roosevelt felt strongly about denying judicial review to the saboteurs. He told Biddle: "I won't give them up. . . . I won't hand them over to any United States marshal armed with a writ of habeas corpus. Understand?"[36] Biddle understood. Late in the proceedings of the military tribunal, seven of the saboteurs would probe the civilian courts for relief.

Also on July 2, 1942, Roosevelt issued a military order appointing the members of the tribunal, the prosecutors, and the defense counsel.[37] Acting under Article of War 38, he appointed Maj. Gen. Frank R. McCoy to

35. 10 U.S.C. § 821 (2000).
36. Biddle, In Brief Authority, at 331.
37. 7 Fed. Reg. 5103 (1942).

serve as president of the tribunal and selected three major generals and three brigadier generals to complete the seven-member court. The military order directed Biddle and Cramer to conduct the prosecution and assigned two colonels, Cassius M. Dowell and Kenneth Royall, to serve as defense counsel. Dowell had 40 years of military service, and Royall could call upon extensive experience as a trial lawyer. On July 7, Col. Carl L. Ristine was appointed to represent Dasch, leaving Dowell and Royall to defend the other seven.

In directing the tribunal to meet on July 8, "or as soon thereafter as is practicable," Roosevelt's order referred to the trying of offenses against both the "law of war and the Articles of War." However, the order clearly liberated the tribunal from some of the restrictions established by Congress in the Articles of War. The tribunal would "have power to and shall, as occasion requires, make such rules for the conduct of the proceeding, consistent with the powers of military commissions under the Articles of War, as it shall deem necessary for a full and fair trial of the matters before it." This language freed the tribunal from the specific procedures enacted by Congress and the *Manual for Courts-Martial*. It could admit evidence "as would, in the opinion of the President of the Commission, have probative value to a reasonable man." The meaning of the reasonable-man test would be worked out over the course of the trial as the tribunal issued its rulings.

Roosevelt's military order departed from the Articles of War with regard to the votes needed for sentencing. The order stated that the concurrence of "at least two-thirds of the members of the Commission present shall be necessary for a conviction or sentence." Two-thirds of the commission could convict and sentence the men to death. Under a court-martial, however, a death penalty required a unanimous vote.

Finally, Roosevelt's order directed that the trial record, including any judgment or sentence, be transmitted "directly to me for my action thereon." This, too, marked a significant departure from military trials. Under Articles of War 46 and 50½, any conviction or sentence by a military court was subject to review within the military system, including the Judge Advocate General's office. That avenue was closed because Cramer participated as co-prosecutor. The July 2 order vested "final reviewing authority" in Roosevelt.

Tribunal Proceedings

Rules adopted by the tribunal on July 7 flatly stated that "sessions shall not be open to the public."[38] An announcement followed the next day: "The sessions will be closed, necessarily so, due to the nature of the testimony, which involves the security of the United States and the lives of its soldiers, sailors, and citizens."[39] National security interests were less important than making sure that the public did not learn of Dasch's cooperation with the Justice Department. With the permission of General McCoy, Biddle and Cramer drafted a private statement on "the reasons for employing a military commission and the reasons for secrecy" in the trial of the eight Germans. It was "of the utmost importance that no information be permitted to reach the enemy on any of these matters." Seven items followed, the first of which read: "How the saboteurs were so swiftly apprehended."[40] The Biddle-Cramer statement further notes: "We do not propose to tell our enemies the answers to the questions which are puzzling them." Certainly one of the puzzles in the minds of Nazi authorities was how the American government could round up the eight men so quickly. To top officials in the Roosevelt administration, the reason was clear: Dasch had turned himself (and the others) in. Biddle did not want that information made public.

By the time the trial began, the defense team of Dowell and Royall had been augmented with two other officers: Maj. Lauson H. Stone and Capt. William G. Hummell. One might assume that these defense attorneys would cooperate with Dasch's attorney, Ristine, but frequently the strategy of one defense team interfered with and jeopardized the work of the other. Dowell and Royall even found it difficult to defend one of the seven men they represented without prejudicing the interests of the others. Praising one defendant implicitly cast a shadow over the others.

The military tribunal met from July 8 to August 1. Unlike the detailed rules that apply to courts-martial, the tribunal on July 7 adopted some sketchy rules, including this provision: "(a) No peremptory challenge shall be allowed. (b) Challenge of members of the Commission for cause may be permitted. The Commission, by a two-thirds vote of those voting—the

38. "Rule Established by the Military Commission Appointed by Order of the President of July 2, 1942," at 1, Papers of Frank Ross McCoy, Box 79, Library of Congress (hereafter "McCoy Papers").

39. July 8, 1942, Statement, Court Room, Department of Justice, McCoy Papers.

40. Untitled, undated three-page statement, at 3, McCoy Papers. The same language appears in "Proposed Statement for Elmer Davis," who was the director of Office of War Information, id.

challenged member not voting—may pass on any challenge."[41] If defense counsel raised objections under the Articles of War, the tribunal could simply vote to overrule. It was at liberty to jettison procedures from the Articles or the *Manual for Courts-Martial* whenever it wanted to. As Cramer told the tribunal, it had discretion "to do anything it pleases; there is no dispute about that."[42] Consequently, defense counsel did not know the rules in advance. They discovered them as the trial progressed.

Even before the tribunal could swear itself in, Royall rose to state his belief that Roosevelt's order creating the tribunal "is invalid and unconstitutional." Drawing on the principles established in *Ex parte Milligan,* he stated that the civil courts in the District of Columbia were open and questioned the jurisdiction of any court to try the case except a civil court. Moreover, he charged that Roosevelt's order "violates in several specific particulars congressional enactments as reflected in the Articles of War."[43] Royall also questioned the competence of the members of the tribunal to try a case when they served directly under the President as Commander in Chief. He posed the question delicately by asking whether any of the generals had "to any degree the feeling that the circumstances under which the commission is appointed would make it difficult or embarrassing for him to reach a judgment in favor of the defendants in the event the evidence should so indicate."[44] The generals answered no.

Biddle stumbled on the role to be played by civil courts. After hearing Royall challenge the competence of the tribunal to sit, he first said that "the question of law involved is a question, of course, to be determined by the civil courts should it be presented to the civil courts." Having implied that some questions might be addressed by civil courts, he tried to slam the door shut: "this is not a trial of offenses of law of the civil courts but is a trial of the offenses of the law of war, which is not cognizable to the civil courts."[45]

After the tribunal was sworn in, the prosecutors and defense counsel were asked whether they would faithfully and impartially perform their duties and "not divulge the findings or sentence of this Military Commission to any but the proper authority until they shall be duly disclosed." Biddle

41. "Rules Established by the Military Commission Appointed by Order of the President of July 2, 1942," at 3, McCoy Papers.
42. Military Trial, at 991.
43. Id. at 5.
44. Id. at 14.
45. Id.

and Cramer agreed to the oath, understanding that it enabled them to speak to President Roosevelt and other high officials. Royall expressed his misgivings about the oath. He told the commission that "it is possible that some limited disclosure would have to be made if someone sought to assert the civil rights of these defendants; and we conceive it our duty not to take an oath that would prevent us from so doing."[46] Royall knew that he might have to go to a civil court or designate someone from the private sector to do that. The defense counsel agreed to the oath with that understanding.

The government charged the eight Germans with four crimes: one against the "law of war," two against the Articles of War (81st and 82d), and one involving conspiracy. The first charge under the law of war consisted of two specifications:

SPECIFICATION 1. In that, during the month of June 1942, Edward John Kerling (and others) being enemies of the United States and acting for and on behalf of the German Reich, a belligerent enemy nation, secretly and covertly passed, in civilian dress, contrary to the law of war, through the military and naval lines and defenses of the United States, along the Atlantic Coast, and went behind such lines and defenses in civilian dress within zones of military operations and elsewhere, for the purpose of committing acts of sabotage, espionage, and other hostile acts, and, in particular, to destroy certain war industries, war utilities, and war materials within the United States.

SPECIFICATION 2. In that, during the month of June 1942, Edward John Kerling (and others), being enemies of the United States and acting for and on behalf of the German Reich, a belligerent enemy nation, appeared, contrary to the law of war, behind the military and naval defenses and lines of the United States, within the zones of military operations and elsewhere, for the purpose of committing or attempting to commit sabotage, espionage, and other hostile acts, without being in the uniform of the armed forces of the German Reich, and planned and attempted to destroy and sabotage war industries, war utilities, and war materials within the United States, and assembled together within the United States explosives, money, and other supplies in order to accomplish said purposes.

There is much duplication between the two specifications. Both emphasize wearing civilian dress and not being in uniform. The second tracks

---

46. Id. at 19–20.

much of the first, but speaks more broadly of not merely "committing" acts but "committing or attempting" to commit them. It also mentions the availability of explosives, money, and other supplies to be used to accomplish those objectives. Those activities could have been—and were—addressed in the charges under the Articles of War.

Charge II relies on this language from Article 81: "Whoever relieves or attempts to relieve the enemy with arms, ammunition, supplies, money, or other things, or knowingly harbors or protects or holds correspondence with or gives intelligence to the enemy, either directly or indirectly, shall suffer death or such other punishment as a court-martial or military commission may direct."[47] The verb relieve was used in the legal sense of "to assist." The government fleshed out Charge II with this specification:

> In that, during the month of June 1942, Edward John Kerling (and others), being enemies of the United States and acting for and on behalf of the German Reich, a belligerent enemy nation, and without being in the uniform of the armed forces of that nation, relieved or attempted to relieve enemies of the United States with arms, ammunition, supplies, money and other things, and knowingly harbored, protected and held correspondence with and gave intelligence to enemies of the United States by entering the territorial limits of the United States, in the company of other enemies of the United States, with explosives, money and other supplies with which they relieved each other and relieved the German Reich, for the purpose of destroying and sabotaging war industries, transportation facilities, or war materials of the United States, and by harboring, communicating with, and giving intelligence to each other and to other enemies of the United States in the course of such activities.

This charge went beyond sabotage efforts to the communicating of intelligence with one another and to enemies of the United States. Charge III was based on this language in Article 82: "Any person who in time of war shall be found lurking or acting as a spy in or about any of the fortifications, posts, quarters, or encampments of any of the armies of the United States, or elsewhere, shall be tried by a general court-martial or by a military commission, and shall, on conviction thereof, suffer death."[48] The specification in Charge III read:

47. 41 Stat. 804 (1920).
48. Id.

In that, during the month of June 1942, Edward John Kerling (and others), being enemies of the United States and acting for and on behalf of the German Reich, a belligerent enemy nation, were, in time of war, found lurking or acting as spies in or about the fortifications, posts, and encampments of the armies of the United States and elsewhere, and secretly and covertly passed through the military and naval lines and defenses of the United States, along the Atlantic Coast, and went about, through, and behind said lines and defenses and about the fortifications, posts, and encampments of the armies of the United States, in zones of military operations and elsewhere, disguised in civilian clothes and under false names, for the purpose of committing sabotage and other hostile acts against the United States, and for the purpose of communicating intelligence relating to such sabotage and other hostile acts to each other, to the German Reich, and to other enemies of the United States, during the course of such activities and thereafter.

This charge focuses on spying and repeats language in the second charge about attempting to communicate information with one another and to the enemy. The language "under false names" refers to the efforts of the eight men to create code names for use in the United States.[49] Charge IV covered conspiracy:

SPECIFICATION: In that, during the year 1942, Edward John Kerling (and others), being enemies of the United States, and acting for and on behalf of the German Reich, a belligerent enemy nation, did plot, plan, and conspire with each other, with the German Reich, and with other enemies of the United States, to commit each and every one of the above-enumerated charges and specifications.

Charges I and III claimed that the eight Germans were "within zones of military operations," behind the military and naval defense lines of the United States, or "about the fortifications, posts, and encampments" of U.S. military forces. Royall and Ristine denied that the men had been in those locations. As to encountering the coastguardsman at Amagansett, Royall argued that because Cullen had not been armed, the patrol was not a zone of military operations.[50] Royall pursued that point in later stages of the tri-

---

49. Fisher, Nazi Saboteurs on Trial, at 18–19, 31, 35.
50. Military Trial, at 119.

bunal proceedings, but first he decided it was necessary to go to civil court to test the constitutionality of Roosevelt's proclamation and military order.

Appeal to the Civil Courts

On July 6, before the trial began, Royall and Dowell wrote to President Roosevelt that "there is a serious legal doubt" as to the constitutionality of the proclamation and the order. As military officers, they were unsure whether they could act in a manner contrary to the wishes of the Commander in Chief. Their request for a meeting with Roosevelt was refused. In the end, all they got was a call from a Roosevelt aide, Marvin McIntyre, that they should act in accordance with their own judgment.[51]

By July 21, day 12 of the trial, Royall decided it was time to test the civil courts. He told the tribunal that he had been unable to secure civilian counsel to carry out that task and that it was his plan to present an application for a writ of habeas corpus to the federal district court in the District of Columbia. Dowell and Ristine announced their opposition to this appeal to a civilian court, although Dowell ended up working with Royall on the brief to the Supreme Court. The tribunal refused to pass on the question whether Royall could go to civil court.[52]

With time running out, Royall met ex parte with Justice Hugo Black at the Justice's home in Alexandria, Virginia. When Black said he didn't want to have anything to do with the case, Royall responded: "Mr. Justice, you shock me. That's all I can say to you."[53] Turned down by Black, Royall tried unsuccessfully to reach Justice Frankfurter in Massachusetts. The following morning, he learned that Justice Owen Roberts was in Washington, D.C., to attend the funeral of Justice George Sutherland. Royall went to Roberts's office and waited for him to return. After listening to Royall outline the case, Roberts said: "I think you've got something here that ought to be reviewed" and suggested that they meet the following day, July 23, at Justice Roberts's farm outside Philadelphia.[54] Dowell, Biddle, and Cramer joined them. After discussing the matter, Roberts phoned Chief Justice Stone and got the go-ahead for holding oral argument on Wednes-

51. Fisher, Nazi Saboteurs on Trial, at 64–66.
52. Id. at 66–67.
53. "The Reminiscences of Kenneth Clairborne Royall," Oral History Research Office, Columbia University, New York, N.Y., 1964, at 35.
54. Id. at 36.

day, July 29. Roberts was able to reach all the Justices except two (Douglas and Murphy).[55]

What was extraordinary, of course, was that nothing had yet been done to take the matter to a lower court: the district court or the appellate court (the D.C. Circuit). Royall managed to get papers to the district court for a petition for a writ of habeas corpus, but he was turned down on July 28, at 8 PM, with oral argument before the Supreme Court scheduled for the next day. District Judge James W. Morris issued a brief statement denying permission, stating that the defendants came within a category—subjects, citizens, or residents of a nation at war with the United States—that, under Roosevelt's proclamation, is "not privileged to seek any remedy or maintain any proceedings in the courts of the United States." Judge Morris did not consider *Ex parte Milligan* controlling in the circumstances of the Germans.[56]

Oral argument began at noon the next day, with the Justices poorly prepared to decide questions they rarely considered, including the Articles of War and the law of war. The briefs submitted by the two sides are dated July 29, the same day that oral argument began. Chief Justice Stone decided to waive the Court's rule limiting each side to one hour. Over a two-day period, oral argument proceeded for a remarkable nine hours. The extra time was needed for the prosecution and defense to present their case and for the Justices to get up to speed.

The first difficulty for Royall was to explain how he could be before the Supreme Court without action by the appellate court. In their petition for a writ of certiorari, Royall and Dowell asked the Court to bring up the case pending in the D.C. Circuit "before judgment is given in that court."[57] Pressed by Justice Frankfurter on how the Court could take a case directly from Judge Morris, Royall was unable to give a persuasive answer. He could only suggest that the Court agree to continue with the oral argument, and that he would take the procedural steps necessary to get the paperwork to the D.C. Circuit.

Another serious problem was whether some of the Justices should recuse themselves because of personal interests. Justice Frank Murphy had already disqualified himself because of his status as an officer in the mili-

55. Id. at 38; Fisher, Nazi Saboteurs on Trial, at 67–68.

56. Ex parte Quirin, 47 F.Supp. 431 (D.D.C. 1942).

57. "Petition for Writ of Certiorari to the Court of Appeals for the District of Columbia," reprinted in 39 Landmark Briefs and Arguments of the Supreme Court of the United States 296 (1975) (hereafter "Landmark Briefs").

tary reserves. Chief Justice Stone's son, Lauson, was part of the defense team. Biddle offered a strained technical argument that Stone could sit because his son did not participate in the habeas corpus proceedings. In what seemed a carefully orchestrated move, Stone asked the defense whether they concurred with that argument and Royall replied: "We do."[58]

Stone was not the only Justice with a cloud over his head. Frankfurter frequently stopped by the White House to share his views with President Roosevelt and other top officials. On June 29, two days after the eight Germans had been rounded up, Frankfurter told Secretary Stimson over dinner that the contemplated military tribunal should be composed entirely of soldiers, with no civilians included.[59] Long before the Court agreed to hear the case, Frankfurter had already staked out a position that favored the government. For months, Justice James F. Byrnes had been serving as a de facto member of the Roosevelt administration, working closely with Roosevelt and Biddle on the war effort. Biddle wrote a series of "Dear Jimmie" letters, asking Byrnes for advice on draft executive orders, a draft of the Second War Powers Bill, and requesting him to intervene to get bills out of committee and onto the floor for passage.[60] Despite their personal involvement, Frankfurter and Byrnes participated in the case.

Dowell and Royall defined the essential legal issue in this manner: "whether the President of the United States may provide for the trial by military commission of offenses which are (with the exception of the charge of spying covered by Article of War 82) cognizable in the district or other appropriate courts of the United States, at a time when such courts of the United States are open and functioning regularly."[61] Their 72-page brief challenged the validity of Roosevelt's proclamation creating the tribunal and his military order appointing the tribunal members. With regard to Charges II and III, claiming a violation of Articles of War 81 and 82, Dowell and Royall said that the defendants had not committed any act in a zone of military operations, and that no proof existed of an effort to obtain military information. As to Charge I (the law of war), they could find nowhere "in the unpublished Rules of Land Warfare any such offense as is described in the specifications in the first Charge."[62] Moreover, they considered the law of war to be a species of international law analogous to common law

58. Id. at 496–97.
59. Stimson Diary, June 29, 1942, at 131.
60. Fisher, Nazi Saboteurs on Trial, at 95–96.
61. Landmark Briefs, at 297.
62. Id. at 333.

and concluded that no principle "is better settled than the principle that there is no common law crime against the United States Government."[63] Crimes, they said, must be covered by a statute enacted by Congress. To the extent a crime existed under the law of war, it would include the offenses of sabotage and espionage, which are treated in the statutes enacted by Congress and are "triable by the civil courts."[64] Charge IV, on conspiracy, was also covered by a congressional statute and "is not triable by a military commission."[65]

Dowell and Royall flagged another issue: the Ex Post Facto Clause. The Constitution expressly prohibits Congress from passing an ex post facto law, which is a law that inflicts punishment on a person for an act that was not illegal at the time committed. Similarly, Congress cannot increase the penalty for a crime committed in the past. Increased penalties may apply only to future transgressions. Yet Roosevelt's proclamation had been issued after the commission of the acts charged against the eight Germans. The proclamation "is, therefore, ex post facto as to them."[66] Without the proclamation, the maximum penalty for sabotage in time of war could not exceed 30 years. In the case of espionage, the death penalty was not mandatory. Roosevelt's proclamation allowed the death penalty if two-thirds of the tribunal agreed, even though Article of War 43 required a unanimous vote for a death sentence. If Congress could not have passed legislation on July 2 increasing the penalty for the acts already committed, on what constitutional grounds could the President act?

Writs of Habeas Corpus

For the prosecutors, Biddle and Cramer insisted that the defendants had "no capacity to sue in this Court or in any other court" because they were enemies of the United States.[67] The Court lacked jurisdiction to interfere with the right of the Provost Marshal (Albert Cox) to hold the eight Germans in lawful custody "by virtue of the laws of war and the lawful orders of his superiors."[68] A 93-page brief submitted by Biddle and Cramer argued that the saboteurs were not entitled to have access to U.S. courts for the purpose of obtaining writs of habeas corpus: "The great bulwarks of our

63. Id. at 333–34.
64. Id. at 334.
65. Id.
66. Id. at 343.
67. Id. at 393.
68. Id.

civil liberties—and the writ of habeas corpus is one of the most important—was never intended to apply in favor of armed invaders sent here by the enemy in time of war."[69]

Biddle and Cramer argued that by "no stretch of interpretation" could *Ex parte Milligan* be applied to the eight Germans.[70] Lambdin Milligan did not wear the uniform of an armed force at war with the United States, he was continuously a resident of Indiana, and he did not cross through military lines and enter into a theater of operations. The Germans, by contrast, arrived on American shores in uniform, were residents of Germany, and "as agents of the German Government crossed our lines secretly in enemy warships for the purpose of committing hostile acts."[71]

The prosecution emphasized the sweeping changes in warfare since 1864: "Wars today are fought on the total front on the battlefields of joined armies, on the battlefields of production, and on the battlefields of transportation and morale, by bombing, the sinking of ships, sabotage, spying, and propaganda."[72] Under his constitutional oath to protect and defend the United States against enemies, President Roosevelt "had the clear duty to meet force with force and to exercise his military authority to provide a speedy, certain and adequate answer, long prescribed by the law of war, to this attack on the safety of the United States by invading belligerent enemies."[73]

Biddle and Cramer pointed out that the Fifth Amendment, requiring presentment or indictment by a grand jury, did not apply to "cases arising in the land or naval forces." Thus, U.S. soldiers charged with military offenses had no right to insist on the protections of grand juries and civil trials. "It would be fantastic," they said, "to extend such privileges to invading soldiers of the enemy."[74]

As for the writ of habeas corpus, they cited British precedents to show that it was intended to protect the subjects of the nation, not subjects of a country "with which we are at war, or who are subject to its orders."[75] Biddle and Cramer conceded that those precedents had been "relaxed in modern times in a very limited class of cases, to permit enemy nationals to have access to the courts in cases of civil litigation for the enforcement of

69. Id. at 409.
70. Id. at 411.
71. Id.
72. Id.
73. Id. at 412.
74. Id. at 413.
75. Id. at 415–16.

pecuniary claims whenever the enemy nationals can be said to have been residing in the country with the license of the sovereign authority."[76]

To Biddle and Cramer, the manner of dealing with the German saboteurs lay exclusively with the President, and neither Congress nor the judiciary could interfere with his decisions: "The President's power over enemies who enter this country in time of war, as armed invaders intending to commit hostile acts, must be absolute."[77] Biddle pressed that point later in oral argument but had to back off. Having argued that the war power is exercised jointly by Congress and the President, he began to assert that in some instances a President as Commander in Chief could act in ways that even Congress could not control. Chief Justice Stone cut him off: "We do not have to come to that?" Biddle agreed: "You do not have to come to that."[78] By the time the Court issued its full decision, it declined to endorse Biddle's broad theory of presidential power.

Several other issues remained. As to the alleged citizenship of Burger and Haupt, Biddle and Cramer argued that they had forfeited any claim to American citizenship by invading the United States as belligerent enemies. By actively aiding an enemy nation, their status had changed from U.S. citizen to enemy of the United States.[79] Dowell and Royall did not actively defend Burger's U.S. citizenship. They seemed to agree that he had lost that citizenship when he returned to Germany and joined its army. Insisting that Haupt was a U.S. citizen, they would lose that argument as well.

Rules of Procedure

The last dispute centered on the extent to which Roosevelt had violated the Articles of War and thus congressional policy established by statute. Royall insisted that Congress possessed the constitutional authority to legislate on military courts and military tribunals, and that any action by the President contrary to statutory standards would be invalid. He first pointed to language in Article 38 that authorized the President, by regulation, to prescribe the procedure for cases before courts-martial, courts of inquiry, military commissions, and other military tribunals, but "nothing contrary to or inconsistent with these Articles shall be so prescribed."[80] Royall charged that Article 38 directed *the President* to prescribe the rules of procedure.

---

76. Id. at 416–17.
77. Id. at 423.
78. Id. at 608.
79. Id. at 426–27.
80. Id. at 550.

Instead, Roosevelt had transferred that function to the military tribunal. On July 7, the day before the trial began, the tribunal adopted a three-and-a-half page, double-spaced statement of rules, dealing primarily with the sessions being closed to the public, the taking of oaths of secrecy, the identification of counsel for the defendants and the prosecution, and the keeping of a record. Only eight lines referred to rules of procedure: disallowing peremptory challenges, allowing one challenge for cause, and then this concluding language: "In general, wherever applicable to a trial by Military Commission, the procedure of the Commission shall be governed by the Articles of War, but the Commission shall determine the application of such Articles to any particular question."[81] Thus, the commission could make up the rules as the trial went along.

The Articles of War required unanimity for a death penalty. Roosevelt's proclamation allowed a two-thirds majority. Royall pointed to the review procedure in Article 46, directing that the trial record of a general court-martial or a military tribunal be referred to a staff judge advocate or the Judge Advocate General for review. Article 50½ called for examination by a board of review. Yet Roosevelt's proclamation provided that the trial record of the military tribunal come directly to him as the final reviewing authority.[82]

As to possible conflicts between Roosevelt's actions and the Articles of War, Biddle said that Article 46 "is the only case whether there is doubt."[83] The Justices entered into a diffuse discussion about Articles 38, 46, 48, and 50½. They would have to focus on those issues again in writing the full decision, released in October. Royall made one of the few concrete points by insisting that the "law of war" could not create offenses punishable in the courts, whether military or civil. No one, he said, "can create an offense in the absence of express Congressional enactment. The Constitution requires that." On the same point: "I say there is no Law of War in absence of a statute."[84]

The Per Curiam

After oral argument concluded on July 30, the Justices met in conference to discuss the best course of action.[85] Which issues had to be dealt with quick-

81. "Rules Established by the Military Commission Appointed by Order of the President of July 2, 1942," at 3–4, McCoy papers.

82. Landmark Briefs, at 557–61.

83. Id. at 637.

84. Id. at 652, 658.

85. Frankfurter's "Notes taken at conference," July 30, 1942, Felix Frankfurter Papers, Part III, Reel 43, Library of Congress (hereafter "Frankfurter Papers").

ly, and which could be postponed until the Court released a full opinion? At noon the following day, with reporters present, Chief Justice Stone read a short per curiam that upheld the jurisdiction of the military tribunal. Defense lawyers carried the papers from the D.C. Circuit to the Supreme Court only a few minutes before Stone spoke. The petition for certiorari was not filed in the Court until 11:59 AM on July 31. One minute later, the Court convened, granted cert, and issued its per curiam decision.[86] Through these procedural niceties, the Court was able to act on "writs of certiorari to the United States Court of Appeals for the District of Columbia." In granting cert, the Court denied motions for leave to file petitions for writs of habeas corpus and affirmed the decision of the district court.

In announcing its decision, the Court said that it was acting "in advance of the preparation of a full opinion which necessarily will require a considerable period of time for its preparation and which, when prepared, will be filed with the Clerk."[87] A quick per curiam was necessary because the work of the tribunal had been put on hold. It could now move forward, but the legal reasoning behind the Court's decision would have to wait for the Justices to hammer out a full opinion. It took the Court three months to craft a decision that would avoid any concurrences or dissents, even though the Justices were well aware that Roosevelt had violated several Articles of War.[88]

Finishing Up

The tribunal now had the Court's blessing to complete its work. Royall cautioned the tribunal members to act in a manner that would protect Americans brought up before foreign tribunals. The United States was moving into the zone of military operations on other continents, "and the chances are that American soldiers will have to face this situation much more frequently than will the enemy agents." The tribunal's decision "may establish a criterion which will be applicable, ten to one, to our own boys who are going overseas."[89] Because the United States was fighting World War II "to preserve our own system of government," it was important to administer

86. General Myron C. Cramer, "Military Commissions: Trial of the Eight Saboteurs," 17 Wash. L. Rev. State Bar. J. 247, 253 (1942).
87. Ex parte Quirin, 63 S.Ct. 1–2 (1942). The per curiam also appears as a footnote in Ex parte Quirin, 317 U.S. 1, 18–19 (1942).
88. Fisher, Nazi Saboteurs on Trial, at 109–21.
89. Military Tribunal, at 2775–77.

procedures "with equity and justice in times of stress as well as in times of peace and quiet." He urged the tribunal not to be a "fair-weather government."[90] The United States, he predicted, would win the war, but it should not "want to win it by throwing away everything we are fighting for, because we will have a mighty empty victory if we destroy the genuineness and the truth of democratic government and fair administration of law." The real test of a system of justice "is not when the sun is shining but is when the weather is stormy."[91]

Six Executions

After the military trial concluded on August 1, the members of the tribunal deliberated and decided that all eight men were guilty and deserved the death penalty. Roosevelt approved the death penalty for six but chose prison sentences for Dasch and Burger. The six were electrocuted on August 8. With six of the saboteurs dead, the Court's full opinion could hardly imply that its per curiam rested on shaky legal grounds or that the administration had not acted with adequate authority. Drafting the decision from his summer home in Franconia, New Hampshire, Chief Justice Stone told his law clerk, Bennett Boskey: "We may also come finally to the question whether we or the Commission & President should construe articles 46 & 50½ etc."[92] For six of the saboteurs, "coming to that question" would be a little late.

Stone wrote to Frankfurter on September 10 that he found it "very difficult to support the Government's construction of the articles [of war]." He was concerned that it "seems almost brutal to announce this ground of decision for the first time after six of the petitioners have been executed and it is too late for them to raise the question if in fact the articles as they construe them have been violated." Only after the war, he said, would the facts be known, with release of the trial transcripts and other documents to the public. By that time, Dasch and Burger could challenge the proceedings successfully, which "would not place the present Court in a very happy light."[93]

90. Id. at 2784–85.

91. Id. at 2785. For other arguments by Royall, Dowell, Ristine, Biddle, and Cramer in the final week of the trial, see Fisher, Nazi Saboteurs on Trial, at 69–77.

92. Letter from Stone to Boskey, August 5, 1942, Papers of Harlan Fiske Stone, Box 69, Library of Congress (hereafter "Stone Papers").

93. Letter from Stone to Frankfurter, September 10, 1942, Frankfurter Papers.

Stone had earlier expressed concern about possible violations of the Articles of War. When he prepared the per curiam, he included a paragraph stating that the Court did not pass upon the construction of Articles 46 and 50½ in the absence of a decision by the military tribunal or action by the President requiring their construction.[94] The Court decided to strike that paragraph from the per curiam. For the Court to duck a crucial issue in the per curiam and address it later in the full opinion was, Stone knew, highly unappealing. If Dasch and Burger prevailed, after all the facts were known, this "would leave the present Court in the unenviable position of having stood by and allowed six to go to their death without making it plain to all concerned—including the President—that it had left undecided a question on which counsel strongly relied to secure petitioners' liberty."[95]

Drafting the Full Opinion

To present the issues fully to the Justices, Stone prepared a memo opinion with alternative endings designated Memorandum A and Memorandum B. The first declined to pass upon the construction of the Articles; the second ventured an interpretation. Memorandum B troubled him because he could find no basis in the record to write an opinion on the subject, and he was "reluctant" to see the Court write what would be fairly called an advisory opinion.[96] The full opinion, released on October 29, concluded that the secrecy surrounding the trial made it impossible for the Court to judge whether Roosevelt's proclamation and order violated or were in conflict with the Articles of War.[97] In the words of Alpheus Thomas Mason, the involvement of the Justices in the trial "through their decision in the July hearing practically compelled them to cover up or excuse the President's departures from customary practice."[98]

Institutionally, it was important for the Court to issue a unanimous opinion and avoid any concurrences that might raise doubts about the per curiam, the full opinion, or the execution of the six men. Stone wanted to stick to fundamental points and discouraged his colleagues from offering sup-

---

94. "Memorandum re Saboteur Cases," September 25, 1942, at 1, Stone Papers.
95. Id. at 2.
96. Id.
97. Ex parte Quirin, 317 U.S. 1, 46–47 (1942).
98. Alpheus Thomas Mason, "Inter Arma Silent Leges: Chief Justice Stone's Views," 69 Harv. L. Rev. 806, 826 (1956).

plemental views. When Robert Jackson prepared a draft of a concurring opinion, Stone and other Justices intervened to convince Jackson to withdraw it.[99] Hugo Black told Stone that he was troubled by the argument that "every violation of every rule of the Laws of War" would subject every person living in the United States to the jurisdiction of military tribunals.[100]

In one of his memos, Frankfurter offered the view that "there can be no doubt that the President did not follow" Articles of War 46 through 53. He had "not a shadow of doubt" that Roosevelt "did not comply with Article 46 *et seq.*" He then fudged the issue by saying that "either he did comply or he did not."[101] Stone had to stay on the alert to keep memos of this quality from being published.

At some point in October, when it looked like the Court might fragment with separate statements, Frankfurter wrote a bizarre document he called "F. F.'s Soliloquy." Perhaps it was his attempt to inject some humor, but it revealed a total lack of judicial objectivity and balance. To Frankfurter, Roosevelt had the unquestioned power to create the tribunal and any challenges represented needless talk injurious to the country. The soliloquy represented a conversation between Frankfurter and the saboteurs, six of whom were now dead. After listening to their legal claim, he called them "damned scoundrels [who] have a helluva cheek to ask for a writ that would take you out of the hands of the Military Commission." He referred to them as "just low-down, ordinary, enemy spies," and that there was no cause to create "a bitter conflict" among the three branches "after your bodies will be rotting in lime."[102]

The Court's full opinion chose not to address certain questions. Did Haupt lose his U.S. citizenship because he "elected to maintain German allegiance and citizenship"?[103] The Court found it unnecessary to decide that issue. It also made it clear that it was not concerned "with any question of guilt or innocence of petitioners."[104] Their detention and trial could

---

99. Fisher, Nazi Saboteurs on Trial, at 114–16.

100. Memo from Black to Stone, October 2, 1942, Papers of Hugo Lafayette Black, Box 269, Library of Congress.

101. "Memorandum of Mr. Justice Frankfurter, In re Saboteur Cases," Papers of William O. Douglas, Box 77, Library of Congress (emphasis in original).

102. Fisher, Nazi Saboteurs on Trial, at 118–20. See also G. Edward White, "Felix Frankfurter's 'Soliloquy' in Ex parte Quirin," 5 Green Bag 2D 423 (2002), and Michal Belknap, "Frankfurter and the Nazi Saboteurs," Yearbook 1982: Sup. Ct. Hist. Soc., at 66–71.

103. Ex parte Quirin, 317 U.S. at 20.

104. Id. at 25.

not be set aside by courts "without the clear conviction that they are in conflict with the Constitution or laws of Congress constitutionally enacted."[105]

The Court began with some fundamentals: "Congress and the President, like the courts, possess no power not derived from the Constitution."[106] It itemized the war powers conferred upon Congress and the President and discussed the Articles of War enacted by Congress, including the Articles that recognize military tribunals to punish offenses "against the law of war not ordinarily tried by court-martial."[107] These statutes reflected the constitutional authority of Congress under Article I to "define and punish . . . Offences against the Law of Nations."[108] With this approach, the Court could decide that President Roosevelt had exercised authority "conferred upon him by Congress," as well as whatever authority the Constitution granted the President.[109]

Could the President act independently under his interpretation of inherent or implied power, even to the extent of acting contrary to congressional policy as expressed in statute? The Court blocked that inquiry: "It is unnecessary for present purposes to determine to what extent the president as Commander in Chief has constitutional power to create military commissions without the support of Congressional legislation."[110] While accepting the great power of Congress to define the law of war, the Court also recognized that Congress might not decide to enact specific rules for every occasion: "Congress has the choice of crystallizing in permanent form and in minute detail every offence against the law of war, or of adopting the system of common law applied by military tribunals so far as it should be recognized and deemed applicable by the courts. It chose the latter course."[111]

The Court distinguished between "lawful combatants" (uniformed soldiers) and "unlawful combatants" (enemies who enter the country in civilian dress). The former, when captured, are detained as prisoners of war. The latter, said the Court, are subject to trial and punishment by military tribunal.[112] Although the Court declined to address Haupt's status as a U.S. citizen, it made it clear that U.S. citizenship of an enemy belligerent "does

---

105. Id.
106. Id.
107. Id. at 27.
108. Id. at 28.
109. Id.
110. Id. at 29.
111. Id. at 30.
112. Id. at 30–31.

not relieve him from the consequences of a belligerency which is unlawful because in violation of the law of war."[113] A U.S. citizen who associates himself with the military arm of an enemy government, and enters the United States for the purpose of committing hostile acts, is an "enemy belligerent" within the meaning of the Hague Convention and "the law of war."[114] Such U.S. citizens are subject to the jurisdiction of a military tribunal.

As for *Ex parte Milligan,* the Court drew a distinction between the facts of that case and the Nazi saboteurs. Milligan was a U.S. citizen who had resided in Indiana for 20 years; he did not reside in any of the rebellious states and was not an enemy combatant entitled to POW status or subject to the penalties imposed on unlawful belligerents.[115] He was a "non-belligerent, not subject to the law of war."[116] The Court declined to define with "meticulous care" the "ultimate boundaries" of military tribunals to try persons charged with violating the law of war. It was enough for the Court to say that the defendants were "plainly within these boundaries."[117]

Did Roosevelt's proclamation and military order conflict with Articles of War 38, 43, 46, 50½, and 70? The Court held that the secrecy surrounding the trial and proceedings before the tribunal "will preclude a later opportunity to test the lawfulness of the detention."[118] Secrecy denied the Justices essential information, but over time the record of the tribunal would become available and cast doubt on the Court's performance. Other questions were left unaddressed. "We need not inquire whether Congress may restrict the power of the Commander in Chief to deal with enemy belligerents."[119] The Court was unanimous in deciding that the Articles in question "could not at any stage of the proceedings afford any basis for issuing the writ."[120] Although of one mind on that point, the Justices divided on the legal reasoning: "a majority of the full Court are not agreed on the appropriate grounds for decision." Some Justices believed that Congress did not intend the Articles of War to govern a presidential military tribunal convened to try enemy invaders. Others concluded that the military tribu-

---

113. Id. at 37.
114. Id. at 37–38.
115. Id. at 45.
116. Id.
117. Id. at 46.
118. Id. at 47.
119. Id.
120. Id.

nal was governed by the Articles of War, but that the Articles in question did not foreclose the option selected by President Roosevelt.[121]

Evaluating the Decision

The decision in *Quirin* drew praise in many quarters as an impressive display of military justice. For those who wondered why the men were tried instead of being placed against a wall and shot, the *New York Times* took the high ground: "We had to try them because a fair trial for any person accused of crime, however apparent his guilt, is one of the things we defend in this war."[122] That judgment would have been sound had the eight saboteurs been tried in civil court, with all the procedural safeguards, rather than before a military tribunal handpicked by the President. Also, the proceedings before the Supreme Court had nothing to do with judging guilt; it was to determine the jurisdiction of the tribunal.

One of the few to express skepticism about the trial was Norman Cousins of the *Saturday Review of Literature.* Just as there was no need for a summary execution, there was "similarly no need to make a farce out of justice, when everyone knew at the very start of the trial what the outcome would be. If the saboteurs *actually had a chance,* it would be different, but they didn't; we knew it, and they knew it."[123] Writing in 1947, constitutional scholar Edward S. Corwin viewed *Quirin* as "little more than a ceremonious detour to a predetermined end."[124] John P. Frank, who clerked for Justice Black in 1942, remarked years later that the Court "sent the defendants to their deaths some months before Chief Justice Stone was able to get out an opinion telling why."[125]

The articles that first appeared in law journals were generally brief descriptions of *Quirin,* offering little in the way of analysis, judgment, or

---

121. Id.

122. "They That Take the Sword" (editorial), New York Times, August 9, 1942, at 8. For other positive editorials, see "The Saboteurs and the Court," New Republic, August 10, 1942, at 159; "Justice Is Done," Washington Post, August 9, 1942, at 6; "Habeas Corpus," Washington Post, July 31, 1942, at 12; "Motions Denied," New York Times, August 1, 1942, at 10.

123. "The Saboteurs," Saturday Review of Literature, August 8, 1942, at 8 (emphasis in original).

124. Edward S. Corwin, Total War and the Constitution 118 (1947).

125. John P. Frank, The Marble Palace: The Supreme Court in American Life 249 (1972).

evaluation.[126] Other articles, somewhat more perceptive, were written quickly and without access to many of the facts that would become public within a few years.[127] Other short treatments were published during the first year, offering little more than description.[128] An article in the *Harvard Law Review* noted that as a result of "certain powers vested exclusively in Congress by the Constitution, it would seem that Congress has the basic power to create military commissions."[129]

A more extensive treatment, written after the full opinion, appeared in an article by Cyrus Bernstein. He highlighted the ex post facto issue in Roosevelt's proclamation, which increased the maximum penalty of sabotage from 30 years to death: "Congress could not have passed an ex post facto law of that tenor; Congress could not have authorized the President to issue such a proclamation."[130] Bernstein also pointed to a conflict of interest for Biddle. The proclamation authorized the Attorney General, with the approval of the Secretary of War, to make exceptions to the prohibition against remedies or proceedings in the civil courts, yet Biddle also served as prosecutor.[131] Similarly, Bernstein noted that Cramer's participation as co-prosecutor eliminated the customary JAG review role of a military court's decision.[132]

By far the most shallow, error-ridden account appears in Biddle's memoirs. He said that Dasch "forced $350" into Cullen's hand.[133] The figure is either $300 (Dasch's intent) or $260 (what Cullen received). Biddle identified defense counsel Dowell as "McDowell."[134] In an error of stunning proportions, Biddle said that *Ex parte Milligan* had been decided "in 1876."[135]

---

126. E.g., "Note: Jurisdiction of Military Tribunals," 37 Ill. L. Rev. 265 (1942); George T. Schilling, "Saboteurs and the Jurisdiction of Military Commissions," 41 Mich. L. Rev. 481 (1942).

127. Robert E. Cushman, "Ex parte Quirin et al.—The Nazi Saboteur Case," 28 Corn. L. Q. 54 (1942); Robert E. Cushman, "The Case of the Nazi Saboteurs," 36 Am. Pol. Sci. Rev. 1082 (1942); Cramer, "Military Commissions," at 247; F. Granville Munson, "The Arguments in the Saboteur Trial," 91 U. Pa. L. Rev. 239 (1942).

128. Charles Cheney Hyde, "Aspects of the Saboteur Cases," 37 Am. J. Int'l L. 88 (1943).

129. "Note: Federal Military Commissions: Procedure and 'Wartime Base' of Jurisdiction," 56 Harv. L. Rev. 631, 639 (1943).

130. Cyrus Bernstein, "The Saboteur Trial: A Case History," 11 G.W. L. Rev. 131, 157 (1943).

131. Id.

132. Id. at 158–59.

133. Biddle, In Brief Authority, at 326.

134. Id. at 331.

135. Id. at 328.

An unfortunate typo? Not really. According to Biddle, *Milligan* was issued "a decade after the Civil War."[136]

Alpheus Thomas Mason, in his book on Chief Justice Stone and in a law review article, explained Stone's dilemma of having to draft an opinion that would do the least damage to the judiciary. The Court could do little other than uphold the jurisdiction of the tribunal, being "somewhat in the position of a private on sentry duty accosting a commanding general without his pass."[137] Stone was well aware that the judiciary was "in danger of becoming part of an executive juggernaut."[138]

Frederick Bernays Wiener

The most penetrating critique of *Quirin* was prepared by Frederick Bernays Wiener, Frankfurter's former student at Harvard Law School. The Court's decision sufficiently troubled Frankfurter that he asked Wiener, by now an expert on military law, to share his thoughts about the ruling. Wiener prepared three analyses, dated November 5, 1942, January 13, 1943, and August 1, 1943. Each letter found serious deficiencies with the Court's work.

The first letter credits the Court for taking "the narrowest—and soundest—ground" by holding that the eight saboteurs were "war criminals (or unlawful belligerents) as that term is understood in international law" and that, "under established American precedents extending back through the Revolution, violators of the laws of war are not entitled, as a matter of constitutional right, to a jury trial."[139] At the same time, he criticized the Court for creating "a good deal of confusion as to the proper scope of the Articles of War insofar as they relate to military commissions." Weaknesses in the decision flowed "in large measure" from the administration's disregard for "almost every precedent in the books" when it established the military tribunal.[140]

Wiener complimented the Court for confronting some of the "extravagant dicta" in the majority's opinion in *Milligan*, and agreed with the Court that Haupt's citizenship was irrelevant in deciding the tribunal's jurisdiction to try him.[141] Yet he "parted company" with the Court's "careless or unin-

---

136. Id. For other Biddle errors, see Fisher, Nazi Saboteurs on Trial, at 136–37.

137. Mason, "Inter Arma Silent Leges," 69 Harv. L. Rev. at 830.

138. Id. at 831. These views would also appear in Mason's book, Harlan Fiske Stone: Pillar of the Law 665–66 (1956).

139. "Observations of Ex parte Quirin," at 1, signed "F.B.W." Frankfurter Papers.

140. Id.

141. Id.

formed handling" of the Articles of War. The Court said that Article 15 saved the concurrent jurisdiction of military commissions.[142] Wiener argued that the legislative history of Article 15 demonstrated that it was intended as a *restriction* on military commissions, which had extended their authority to offenses punishable by courts-martial. During the Civil War, he said, tribunals had repeatedly and improperly assumed jurisdiction over offenses better handled by courts-martial.[143]

The fact that Roosevelt had appointed the commission did not give it a free charter. If the President appointed a general court-martial, Wiener said, it would still be subject to the provisions of the Articles of War. Presidential appointment did not make a tribunal "immune from judicial scrutiny."[144] Passages from the *Digest of Judge Advocate General's Opinions* showed that military tribunals were subject to restrictions just like courts-martial: "the rules which apply in these particulars to general courts-martial have almost uniformly been applied to military commissions."[145]

To Wiener, it seemed "too plain for argument" that Article 46 required "legal review of a record of trial by military commission before action thereon by the reviewing authority; that the President's power to prescribe rules of procedure did not permit him to waive or override this requirement; that he did in fact do so; and that he disabled his principal legal advisers [the Judge Advocate General] by assigning to them the task of prosecution." It would be difficult to craft a more sweeping condemnation.

Wiener denied that Roosevelt's actions could be justified under his powers as Commander in Chief or by invoking implied or inherent executive authority: "I do not think any form of language, or any talk about the President's inherent powers as Commander in Chief, is sufficient to justify that portion of the precept, which, in my considered judgment, was palpably illegal."[146] Having identified these statutory and constitutional violations, Wiener nevertheless concluded that "not even this flagrant disregard of AW 46 was sufficient to justify issuance of the writ" of habeas corpus. The issue before the Court was whether the saboteurs were in lawful custody, not whether they could be sentenced "without benefit of the advice of staff judge advocate."[147]

---

142. Ex parte Quirin, 317 U.S. at 28.
143. "Observations of Ex parte Quirin," at 3–4.
144. Id. at 4.
145. Id. at 5.
146. Id. at 8.
147. Id. at 9.

Wiener flagged other problems. Military commissions were normally appointed by War Department Special Orders, not by presidential proclamation or military order. He found only one precedent of using the Judge Advocate General of the Army as prosecutor, and it was one "that no self-respecting military lawyer will look straight in the eye: the trial of the Lincoln conspirators." Even in that sorry precedent, "the Attorney General did not assume to assist the prosecution."[148]

Notwithstanding Wiener's conclusion that there was no justification for issuing the writ of habeas corpus or moving the trial from the tribunal to a civil court, he thought the saboteurs could have been better tried either by commissions appointed by the commanding generals of New York and Florida, or by a military commission operating under the limitations of a general court-martial. When two more German saboteurs arrived in November 1944 and were apprehended, they were tried along the lines suggested here by Wiener.

In the second letter, Wiener told Frankfurter that the conclusion seemed "inescapable that AW 46 and ¶ 2 of AW 50½ read together require that the record of trial by a military commission appointed by the President must go to the B/R [Board of Review] and the JAG." There was no basis to contend that a presidential military commission is subject to procedures that vary from ordinary military commissions "except where statute makes it so." The Constitution vested authority in Congress, not the President, to "define and punish . . . Offences against the Law of Nations." Both Article 46 and paragraph 2 of Article 50½ "imposed such limitations" on the President.[149]

Writing a third time, on August 1, 1943, Wiener again addressed the issue whether Article 15 supported the administration's use of a military tribunal. He referred to Judge Advocate General Crowder's testimony before Congress in 1916, where he said that Article 15 gave military tribunals "the jurisdiction they now have and makes it a concurrent jurisdiction with courts-martial, so that the military commander in the field in time of war will be at liberty to employ either form of court that happens to be convenient."[150] Wiener omitted Crowder's concluding sentence: "Both classes of courts have the same procedure." Congress did not intend military tribunals to dream up their own rules and regulations. However, Roosevelt's

---

148. Id.
149. Letter from Wiener to Frankfurter, January 13, 1943, at 1, Frankfurter Papers.
150. Letter from Wiener to Frankfurter, August 1, 1943, at 1–2, citing S. Rept. No. 130, 64th Cong., 1st Sess. 40 (1916), Frankfurter Papers.

proclamation authorized the military tribunal to depart from those procedural safeguards whenever it decided it was appropriate or necessary.

Later Assessments

These letters from Wiener must have had an impact on Frankfurter. In 1953, when the Court was considering whether to sit in summer session to hear the espionage case of Ethel and Julius Rosenberg, someone recalled that the Court had sat in summer session in 1942 to hear the saboteur case. Frankfurter wrote: "We then discussed whether, as in *Ex parte Quirin,* 317 U.S. 1, we might not announce our judgment shortly after the argument, and file opinions later, in the fall. Jackson opposed this suggestion also, and I added that the *Quirin* experience was not a happy precedent."[151] In an interview on June 9, 1962, Justice Douglas made a similar observation: "The experience with *Ex parte Quirin* indicated, I think, to all of us that it is extremely undesirable to announce a decision on the merits without an opinion accompanying it. Because once the search for the grounds, the examination of the grounds that had been advanced is made, sometimes those grounds crumble."[152]

Some of the deficiencies of the 1942 process would be corrected three years later by the Roosevelt administration when it faced another trial of German saboteurs. It was a mistake to have the Judge Advocate General share prosecutorial duties with the Attorney General. The Judge Advocate General adds integrity to the system of military justice by serving as a reviewing authority, not as a prosecutor. Whatever the military tribunal decided should have come for review to the Judge Advocate General and his staff, acting in an independent capacity, and then to the President for possible clemency. The trial record of 3,000 pages should never have gone directly to Roosevelt. Neither Roosevelt nor any other President is in a position to read a transcript of that length with the requisite care, independence, and legal judgment.

The saboteur case of 1942 represented an unwise and ill-conceived concentration of power in the executive branch. Roosevelt appointed the tri-

---

151. "Memorandum Re: Rosenberg v. United States, Nos. 111 and 687, October Term 1952," June 4, 1953, at 8, Frankfurter Papers, Harvard Law School, Part I, Reel 70, Library of Congress.

152. Conversation between Justice William O. Douglas and Professor Walter F. Murphy, June 9, 1962, at 204–5, Seeley G. Mudd Manuscript Library, Princeton University.

bunal, selected the judges, prosecutors, and defense counsel, and served as the final reviewing authority. The generals on the tribunal, the colonels serving as defense counsel, and the two prosecutors were all subordinates of the President. "Crimes" related to the law of war came not from the legislative branch, enacted by statute, but from executive interpretations of the "law of war." Throughout the six weeks of the trial and the habeas corpus petition to the Supreme Court, Congress was not a participant in helping to define the jurisdiction and procedures of the tribunal. The judiciary was largely shut out as well. The two days of oral argument before the Court were dramatic and newsworthy but hardly represented a check on presidential power. There was little expectation that the Court would do anything other than what it did: Deny the petition for a writ of habeas corpus.

The purpose of trying the eight Germans in secret was not to protect military secrets or to safeguard national security. The need for secrecy was driven by two reasons: to conceal the fact that Dasch had turned himself (and the others) in, and to mete out heavier penalties. In civilian court, the maximum penalty would have been about three years. Roosevelt was determined to have the Germans put to death. Most of the trial could have been conducted openly, with the public and the press invited, without sacrificing any legitimate national interests. On the rare occasions when sensitive data might have been revealed, the courtroom could have been cleared for that part of the testimony.

It was error to authorize the tribunal to "make such rules for the conduct of the proceeding, consistent with the powers of military commissions under the Articles of War, as it shall deem necessary for a full and fair trial of the matters before it." Procedural rules need to be agreed to before a trial begins, not after. No confidence can be placed in rules created on the spot, particularly when done in secret by generals who serve under the President. It would have been better for the military tribunal to operate under the procedures set forth in the Articles of War and the *Manual for Courts-Martial*. Those procedures were in place and represented the product of mature thought and careful study over a long period of time. With their statutory base, they would have given legitimacy to the process and removed the impression of executive arbitrariness.

Assembling the Court in the middle of the summer in emergency session, with briefs hurriedly prepared and read, sent a message of haste and inconsiderateness, not careful judicial deliberation. Nine hours of oral argument highlighted the lack of preparation. Taking the case directly from the district court, without intervening review by the D.C. Circuit, further underscored the rush to judgment. The reasons and analysis that eventually found their way into the full opinion, strained and uninformed in many places, were compromised by the political situation the Court found itself in. It had to make a decision without knowing how the secret trial was being conducted or how it would turn out. The Justices knew that information unavailable to them would be released later, putting the Court's reputation at risk. Nothing in the decision could imply, in any way, that there had been a miscarriage of justice, but precisely that judgment would be reached once experts in military law began to evaluate the Court's work.

The Fate of Confederates

Having acted through a military tribunal for the eight saboteurs, the administration decided to rely on the civilian courts when prosecuting those who had provided assistance to Haupt and others. Initially, 14 people were arrested, eight in Chicago and six in New York City. They included Haupt's parents, Hans Haupt and his wife; Haupt's aunt and uncle, Lucille and Walter Froehling; and two close friends of the Haupts, Otto and Kate Wergin. Harry and Emma Jaques were arrested for hiding the money given to them by Neubauer. Hermann Heinrich Faje pleaded guilty to harboring Heinck and Quirin. Helmut Leiner had met with Kerling and agreed to change some of the $50 bills to other currency. Kerling's girlfriend, Hedwig Engemann, also agreed to change some of his larger bills. Ernst Herman Kerkhof was arrested because of his close contact with Kerling's wife, Marie. His citizenship was revoked. She lost hers and was ordered interned. Anthony Cramer was convicted for assisting Thiel and Kerling.[153]

In addition to these 14, others paid a price. William Wernecke, who tried to help Herbert Haupt, was convicted of violating the Selective Service Act by assuming the role of a minister to evade the draft. Although Pastor Emil Ludwig Krepper never met with the Nazi saboteurs, he was indicted for conspiring with Walter Kappe (who had recruited the eight saboteurs), sending coded messages to Germany, violating the Trading with the Enemy Act, and receiving a salary from the German government without notifying the Secretary of State that he was acting as a German agent. Krepper was sentenced to 12 years in prison.[154]

---

153. For details on the civil trials of these 14, see Fisher, Nazi Saboteurs on Trial, at 80–83.

154. Id. at 84.

Another Submarine in 1944

In 1944, Nazi Germany brought two more saboteurs to the United States by submarine, this time calling on the talents of Erich Gimpel, a native of Germany, and William Colepaugh, a Connecticut-born U.S. citizen.[155] They reached the coast of Maine on November 29, 1944, took a train to Portland and Boston, where they stayed a night before continuing on to New York City. Unlike the 1942 saboteurs, they brought no explosives with them. Their primary mission was to purchase a shortwave radio and transmit intelligence back to Germany. Gimpel's book reveals that he was primarily interested in obtaining information about America's atomic bomb project. He hoped to recruit agents from South America to use explosive devices on the buildings associated with the Manhattan Project.[156] Like the earlier eight, Gimpel and Colepaugh had a falling-out and were picked up by the FBI in New York City, Colepaugh on December 26 and Gimpel four days later.

Initially, it appeared that the two would be tried in the same manner as the eight Nazi agents in 1942: by a military tribunal sitting on the fifth floor of the Justice Department in Washington, D.C. Biddle, along with Cramer, was ready to conduct the prosecution. However, Secretary of War Stimson, who thought it had made no sense for Biddle and Cramer to act as prosecutors in 1942, this time intervened forcefully to block their participation. Stimson told Roosevelt that the men should be tried either by court-martial or military tribunal, with the appointment authority placed in the Army Commander in Boston or in New York.[157] In his diary, Stimson expressed contempt for Biddle's grandstanding: "It is a petty thing. That little man is such a small little man and so anxious for publicity that he is trying to make an enormous show out of this performance—the trial of two miserable spies. The President was all on my side but he may be pulled over."[158]

Stimson prevailed. On January 12, 1945, Roosevelt issued a military order to try the two German spies. Unlike his order of July 2, 1942, this one did not name the members of the tribunal or the counsel for the pros-

---

155. For further details on this incident, see Fisher, Nazi Saboteurs on Trial, at 138–44. Gimpel wrote a book on his experience. First published in Great Britain under the title Spy for Germany, it was published in the United States in 2003 and retitled Agent 146: The True Story of a Nazi Spy in America.

156. Erich Gimpel, Agent 146, at 89, 136, 144, 150–51, 166–67 (2003).

157. Letter from Stimson to Roosevelt, January 7, 1945, at 1–2, RG 107, "Stimson's Safe File."

158. Stimson Diary, January 5, 1945, at 18–19.

ecution and defense. Instead, he empowered the commanding generals, under the supervision of the Secretary of War, "to appoint military commissions for the trial of such persons." Moreover, the trial record would not go directly to the President, as in 1942. The review would be processed within the Judge Advocate General's office: "The record of the trial, including any judgment or sentence, shall be promptly reviewed under the procedures established in Article 50½ of the Articles of War."[159]

Appointments to the seven-man tribunal were made by Maj. Gen. Thomas A. Terry, commander of the Second Service Command. He also selected the officers to serve as prosecutors and defense counsel. In addition to the military personnel, two lawyers from the Justice Department assisted with the prosecution.[160] Biddle had no role as prosecutor and Cramer was limited to his review function within the JAG office. The trial took place not in Washington, D.C., but at Governors Island, New York City.[161]

On February 14, 1945, the tribunal sentenced Colepaugh and Gimpel to death by hanging. They had been found guilty of three counts: violation of the law of war by passing through military lines, violation of Article of War 82 for spying, and conspiracy. The tribunal deliberated for three hours. The verdicts and sentencing went to General Terry, as the appointing officer, and from there to the Judge Advocate General's office.[162] President Roosevelt died on April 12, before the executions could be carried out. On May 8, President Harry Truman announced the end of the war in Europe, and the following month he commuted the death sentences to life imprisonment.[163] In 1955, the U.S. government released Gimpel and deported him to Germany.[164] Colepaugh, without success, initiated a habeas corpus action from prison, arguing that he should not have been tried by a military tribunal.[165] He was not paroled until 1960.[166]

159. 10 Fed. Reg. 548 (1945).

160. "2 Spy Suspects Given to Army for Trial," New York Times, January 19, 1945, at 14.

161. "Spy Trials Open Today," New York Times, February 6, 1945, at 5.

162. "2 Spies Sentenced to Die by Hanging," New York Times, February 15, 1945, at 1.

163. "Truman Commutes to Life Terms Death Sentences of Two Spies," New York Times, June 24, 1945, at 1.

164. "'44 Nazi Spy Landed in U-boat Is Deported to West Germany," New York Times, August 13, 1955, at 15.

165. Colepaugh v. Looney, 235 F.2d 429 (10th Cir. 1956), cert. denied, 352 U.S. 1014 (1957).

166. Richard Willing, "An American Was the Nazi Spy Next Door," USA Today, February 28, 2002, at 2A.

The Roosevelt administration learned several lessons from the Nazi saboteur trials in 1942 and 1945. Military tribunals should not be spectacular
show trials in the nation's capital, the prosecution should not be conducted by the Attorney General and the Judge Advocate General, the President
should not be the appointing official, and he should not receive the trial
record directly from the tribunal. Instead, review of the trial record should
be performed by trained and experienced legal experts within the Office
of Judge Advocate General. However, in other military actions during
World War II and in the years immediately following, the U.S. government
gave little thought to procedural safeguards or principles of fundamental
justice.

6

OTHER WORLD WAR II TRIBUNALS

Throughout World War II and for more than a decade after, federal courts largely deferred to executive and military authorities. Martial law operated in Hawaii. Japanese Americans (most of them natural-born U.S. citizens) were placed in detention centers. Traditional constitutional privileges, including the writ of habeas corpus and the right to be tried in civil court, were set aside in some communities. Only after the war did a hesitant judiciary begin to recapture lost territory and defend citizen rights against military rule. Ever so slowly, courts imposed restrictions on martial law, military tribunals, and courts-martial, and began to enforce constitutional principles that deny executive officials the right to simultaneously legislate, prosecute, and adjudicate. The concentration of such powers in a single branch violates the American system of limited government, separation of powers, and checks and balances.

Martial Law in Hawaii

Before the December 7, 1941, attack on Pearl Harbor by Japan, Hawaii enacted emergency legislation to place extraordinary powers in the Governor in the event of war. Governor Joseph B. Poindexter urged the legislature to enact a measure that would provide for a delegation of power to the executive that in normal times would be impermissible. The Hawaii Defense Act, approved on October 3, 1941, vested in the executive unprecedented powers to respond to an emergency.[1]

After the December 7 attack, Poindexter decided against exercising the emergency powers granted him by the Hawaii Defense Act. Instead, he issued a proclamation transferring all governmental functions (including judicial) to the Commanding General of the Hawaiian Department. He called upon the Commanding General, Lt. Gen. Walter C. Short, to prevent an invasion and to suspend the privilege of the writ of habeas corpus.[2] On

1. J. Garner Anthony, Hawaii Under Army Rule 4 (1955).
2. J. Garner Anthony, "Martial Law in Hawaii," 30 Cal. L. Rev. 371, 371–72, 392–93 (1942).

that same day, Short assumed the role of "Military Governor" and created two forms of military tribunal to try any case involving an offense against federal law, Hawaiian law, "or the rules, regulations, orders or policies of the military authorities." These military courts included provost courts, which were authorized to impose fines up to $5,000 and imprisonment for up to five years, and a military tribunal empowered to decide more severe sentences, including the death penalty.[3] Pursuant to the Hawaiian Organic Act, Short cabled Roosevelt about the declaration of martial law and the suspension of the writ of habeas corpus and received Roosevelt's approval.[4]

The Organic Act, passed by Congress in 1900, established a government in Hawaii with three branches, subject to the U.S. Constitution, "and, except as herein otherwise provided, all the laws of the United States which are not locally inapplicable."[5] Although the statute appeared to embody separation of powers and checks and balances, one feature of the Governor's power stood apart. Section 67 provided that in case of rebellion or invasion, "or imminent danger thereof, when the public safety requires it," the Governor may "suspend the privilege of the writ of habeas corpus, or place the Territory, or any part thereof, under martial law, until communication can be had with the President and his decision thereon made known."[6]

Martial law under Gen. Short covered not only 159,000 civilians of Japanese ancestry but also the territory's entire population of 465,000.[7] After the surprise attack on Pearl Harbor, Short was removed from command because he had ordered inadequate defensive preparations. He was succeeded by Gen. Delos C. Emmons and later by Gen. Robert C. Richardson Jr. They continued to exercise martial law in Hawaii. In August 1942, Ingram M. Stainback replaced Poindexter as Governor.

Hans Zimmerman

Several challenges to martial law and the suspension of the writ of habeas corpus reached the federal courts. One involved a petition for a writ filed on February 19, 1942, by Clara Zimmerman, who claimed that her hus-

---

3. Id. at 393–94.
4. J. Garner Anthony, "Martial Law, Military Government and the Writ of Habeas Corpus in Hawaii," 31 Cal. L. Rev. 477, 478 (1943).
5. 31 Stat. 141–42, Sec. 5 (1900).
6. Id. at 153, Sec. 67.
7. Harry N. Scheiber and Jane L. Scheiber, "Constitutional Liberty in World War II: Army Rule and Martial Law in Hawaii, 1941–1946," 3 West. Leg. Hist. 341, 342 (1990).

band, Hans, had been unlawfully detained and imprisoned by military authorities. Both were U.S. citizens. District Judge Delbert E. Metzger denied the writ on the ground that military orders had forbidden its issuance. He remarked: "I feel that the court is under duress by reason of the order and not free to carry on the function of the court in a manner in which the court conceives to be its duty."[8]

On December 14, 1942, the Ninth Circuit affirmed the denial of the petition, holding that the Governor of Hawaii was authorized to suspend until further notice the privilege of the writ of habeas corpus. The court relied on Section 67 of the Organic Act.[9] Although no charges had been filed against Zimmerman, the military kept him in prison. The Ninth Circuit said that civil courts, "in circumstances like the present, ought to be careful to avoid idle or captious interference."[10] The Hawaiian Islands, it said, were "peculiarly exposed to fifth-column activities."[11] Under these conditions, executive officials were entitled to "detain without interference persons suspected of harboring designs harmful to the public safety."[12] Mere suspicion was sufficient, and there could be no second-guessing or review by the judiciary. Civil courts "are ill adapted to cope with an emergency of this kind. As a rule they proceed only upon formal charges."[13] Under this reasoning, so long as the government pressed no charges, it could hold Zimmerman indefinitely, or at least to the end of martial law. Similar claims would be made by the Bush administration after 9/11 in holding "enemy combatants" incommunicado.

In a dissent to the Ninth Circuit ruling, Judge Bert Emory Haney said that military government "is not expressly recognized in the Constitution and is wholly and entirely contrary to the form of government provided for therein."[14] Government by a commanding officer, he noted, "is of course not government by executive, legislative and judicial branches, the kind of government provided for in the Constitution."[15] In reviewing the express powers in Articles I and II of the Constitution, he could find nothing that

---

8. Anthony, "Martial Law, Military Government and the Writ of Habeas Corpus in Hawaii," at 485.

9. Ex parte Zimmerman, 132 F.2d 442, 444 (9th Cir. 1942).

10. Id. at 446.

11. Id.

12. Id.

13. Id. at 446.

14. Id. at 449.

15. Id.

authorized either the President or Congress to establish a "military government anywhere."[16]

To the extent that a military government could exist by reason of "necessity," constitutional support had to come, Haney said, from congressional authority to "provide for calling forth the Militia to execute the Laws of the Union, suppress Insurrections and repel Invasions," and the responsibility of the national government in Article IV to protect each state "against Invasion." But whether a particular military action is "necessary" is a "question of fact" that courts are competent to judge, "depending on the existence of facts in the territory."[17] Without judicial and legislative checks, "it would be simple for a tyrannical executive to declare martial law, and then under a pretext of necessity, take in custody, the members of Congress, as well as the courts, thus effectually abolishing the Constitution."[18]

Judge Haney recalled that the government admitted during oral argument that there were no charges against Zimmerman for violating "the Constitution, a statute of the United States, a statute of the Territory of Hawaii, the Articles of War, the Law of War, any order of the President, the Secretary of War, the Military Governor or any other commanding officer."[19] In view of this record, Haney concluded that the district court should have issued the writ or an order to the government to show cause why it would not release Zimmerman.[20] Later, the Supreme Court denied cert on the ground that the case was moot, "it appearing that Hans Zimmerman . . . has been released from the respondent's custody."[21]

Restoring Some Civil Functions

In taking office in August 1942, Governor Stainback was intent on shifting political power from martial law to civilian authority.[22] The United States had carried off the very successful Battle of Midway in June 1942, inflicting such heavy damage on the Japanese fleet that it was commonly understood that the danger of a land invasion of Hawaii no longer existed. Shortly after Stainback's inauguration, military authorities issued a general order on

16. Id.
17. Id. at 450.
18. Id.
19. Id. at 452.
20. Id. at 453.
21. Zimmerman v. Walker, 319 U.S. 744 (1943).
22. Anthony, Hawaii Under Army Rule, at 22.

August 31, returning to the Hawaiian courts "criminal prosecutions and civil litigation to the extent that war conditions permit." The privilege of habeas corpus remained suspended, however, and martial law still prevailed. The general order specified the type of criminal proceeding and civil suit that would remain within the jurisdiction of the military.[23] Stainback released a proclamation several days later, on September 2, stating that the Commanding General had determined that "it is no longer impossible for the judicial officers and employees of this Territory and of the counties and cities therein to function, within limits set forth in various orders."[24]

Stainback went to Washington, D.C., to discuss with the Interior and Justice Departments the possibility of having military government removed and civilian government restored. War Department officials insisted that military government continue. A compromise shifted a number of functions to the civil government.[25] In a confidential memo to President Roosevelt on December 17, 1942, Attorney General Biddle spoke about the need to turn civilian government in Hawaii "back to Stainback, but leaving the military job (including martial law, suspension of *habeas corpus,* and special emergency powers) in the military." The transfer would be difficult, he said, because "the military, who are now running Hawaii lock, stock and barrel, don't want to give an inch." Biddle urged that the military give up certain functions like "food supply and distribution, commerce, communications, traffic, hospitals and health, O.P.A., civilian defense, liquor, gasoline rationing, and fiscal matters."[26]

Proclamations on February 8, 1943, signed by both the Governor and the Commanding General, restored much of civil authority to Hawaii. With regard to violations of territorial law and federal law, trial by jury and indictment by grand jury in the civil courts replaced the provost courts and military tribunals. Nevertheless, Stainback's proclamation included language that "a state of martial law remains in effect and the privilege of the writ of habeas corpus remains suspended."[27] Judicial proceedings were restored, both criminal and civil, except (1) criminal prosecutions against

---

23. Id. at 159–60.

24. Id. at 129.

25. Id. at 22–23; Fred L. Israel, "Military Justice in Hawaii, 1941–1944," 36 Pac. Hist. Rev. 243 (1967).

26. Confidential Memorandum for the President re: Hawaii, from Biddle to Roosevelt, December 17, 1942, at 1; PSF, "Departmental File, Justice, Biddle, Francis: 1941–43, Box 56, Franklin D. Roosevelt Library, Hyde Park, N.Y.

27. Anthony, "Martial Law, Military Government and the Writ of Habeas Corpus in Hawaii," at 482, 508–11.

members of the armed forces, (2) civil suits against members of the armed forces, and (3) criminal prosecutions for violations of military orders. The Commanding General could waive the last exception for a particular prosecution or suit.[28]

Glockner and Seifer

After federal courts acquiesced in the Zimmerman case, Judge Metzger confronted the military's detention of two other men in Hawaii. Walter Glockner and Erwin R. Seifer, Americans of German descent, had been held by the military for some time. When petitions for writs of habeas corpus were filed on their behalf, the U.S. Attorney argued that the petitions should be dismissed. Metzger denied the government's motion partly on the ground that the proclamation issued by Stainback on February 8, 1943, had restored both civil government and the writ.[29] In July 1943, Metzger issued a writ of habeas corpus to have the two men produced in court. When the military refused, he fined Gen. Richardson $5,000 for contempt. The contempt citation found Richardson in "open and notorious defiance of the mandate of the court."[30] The face-off recalls the confrontation between Judge Hall and Andrew Jackson.

Richardson upped the ante by issuing an order that prohibited habeas corpus proceedings, directed Metzger to purge the court's records of the contempt citation, and threatened to punish him either through the provost courts or the military tribunal. Penalties by the provost court could amount to confinement for up to five years and a fine not to exceed $5,000, while the military commission could select whatever punishment it wanted.[31] As the dispute escalated, Richardson set Glockner and Seifer free on the condition that they leave Hawaii.[32] The Justice Department rushed in and convinced Richardson to rescind his order, which was done, and asked Metzger to expunge the contempt judgment and remit the fine. He declined to do that, but did reduce the fine to $100, which President Roosevelt later canceled through a pardon.[33]

---

28. Id. at 509 (section (i)) and 510 (section (j)).

29. Walter P. Armstrong, "Martial Law in Hawaii," 29 Am. Bar Ass'n J. 698, 698 (1943).

30. Anthony, "Martial Law, Military Government and the Writ of Habeas Corpus in Hawaii," at 488.

31. Id. at 511–14.

32. Id. at 490.

33. Claude McColloch, "Now It Can Be Told: Judge Metzger and the Military," 35 Am. Bar. Ass'n J. 365 (1949).

Metzger paid a price for asserting an independent voice. As a territorial judge, he was appointed to the Hawaiian trial court in 1934 for a term of four years and was reappointed in 1938. The following year he received a six-year appointment to the U.S. District Court. In 1945 he was returned to that seat but failed to be reappointed at the end of the Truman administration.[34]

White, Spurlock, and Duncan

Other cases of civilians tried by military courts followed. Harry E. White, a U.S. citizen, was arrested by the military and brought before the provost court on a charge of embezzlement. His attorney challenged the jurisdiction of the court and demanded a trial by jury. Found guilty, White was sentenced to five years in prison. Although no appeal from a provost court judgment was allowed, the sentence was later reduced to four years. The trial was speedy. It began and ended on the afternoon of August 25, 1942.[35] White's trial took place after the Battle of Midway, which removed the threat of a Japanese invasion.[36] Several judges of the Hawaiian territorial courts stipulated that their courts were open and fully capable of taking and deciding cases.[37] Midway helped strengthen the effort to restore civil authority.

U.S. District Judge J. Frank McLaughlin ruled that even if a valid state of martial law existed in Hawaii in August 1942, White had been deprived of his constitutional rights under the Fifth and Sixth Amendments. In holding that the provost court lacked jurisdiction either over White or the subject matter of his case, McLaughlin relied on both *Milligan* and *Quirin* to insist that courts in time of war or peace have an obligation to preserve the safeguards of civil liberty.[38] He also denied that Poindexter had any authority on December 7, 1941, to transfer or delegate the judicial power to the military.[39] Building on those positions, McLaughlin granted the habeas writ and discharged White.

34. Delbert Metzger, "No Longer a Judge: An Ex-Jurist Tells Why," The Nation, July 18, 1953, at 52.
35. The specifics of the provost court action are described in Ex parte White, 66 F.Supp. 982, 984 (D. Haw. 1944).
36. Id. at 984–85.
37. Id. at 985.
38. Id. at 986–87.
39. Id. at 987.

Judge McLaughlin also handled the case of Fred Spurlock, a black American brought before a provost court and charged with assaulting a civilian policeman. The court found him guilty and sentenced him to five years in prison. After he pleaded for leniency, the court placed him on probation. When he got in trouble again, the provost court sentenced him to five years at hard labor. That time was later reduced by the Military Governor to two and a half years. Even though Spurlock's problems preceded the Battle of Midway, McLaughlin ruled that the provost court lacked jurisdiction either over Spurlock or the charge brought against him, and that the conviction was thus null and void.[40]

Although Spurlock's conduct occurred in 1942, McLaughlin did not issue his decision until June 23, 1944. In a brief per curiam, the Ninth Circuit reversed the district court, basing its decision on the Duncan case, discussed next.[41] After other Hawaiian martial law cases had been accepted by the Supreme Court, Gen. Richardson intervened to grant Spurlock a pardon.[42]

Lloyd Duncan, a civilian shipfitter employed at the Navy Yard at Honolulu, was tried and sentenced to imprisonment by a provost court for assaulting two Marine sentries on duty at the Navy Yard. By the time the case reached Judge Metzger, Governor Stainback had issued his proclamation of February 8, 1943, restoring some powers and functions to civilian agencies, including civil and criminal courts.[43] After the decisive U.S. defeat of the Japanese navy at Midway, both Gen. Richardson and Adm. Chester Nimitz agreed that a Japanese invasion of Hawaii was now practically impossible.[44] Metzger refused to allow martial law to override civilian institutions unless Congress passed specific authorizing legislation:

> If the present laws do not give the Nation the fullest desirable protection against subversive or suspicious Japanese aliens, or even native-born persons of alien parentage, and such fact is known to the Army or Navy organizations, clearly it is the duty of such organizations to ask for legislative curb and procedure, instead of insisting upon holding by force of arms an entire population under a form of helpless and unappealable subjugation called martial law or military

---

40. Ex parte Spurlock, 66 F.Supp. 997, 1003 (D. Haw. 1944).
41. Steer v. Spurlock, 146 F.2d 652 (9th Cir. 1944).
42. 92 Cong. Rec. A4673 (1946).
43. Ex parte Duncan, 66 F.Supp. 976, 979 (D. Haw. 1944).
44. Id.

government, under the reasoning of Army or Navy officers that such form of government is required, or is convenient to them, in local and national protection and safety.[45]

Judge Metzger held that the Organic Act of Hawaii gave Governor Poindexter no power to transfer or abdicate his authority to military officials,[46] and that martial law did not lawfully exist in Hawaii in 1943, particularly after March 10, 1943 (the effective date of Stainback's proclamation).[47] Therefore, the Military Governor possessed no lawful authority over civilian affairs or persons, and the provost court lacked authority to try, find guilty, or sentence civilians.[48]

On November 1, 1944, the Ninth Circuit reversed this decision and also the ruling by Judge McLaughlin in Harry White's case.[49] It held that the proclamation of February 8, 1943, did not have the effect of terminating the suspension of the privilege of the writ of habeas corpus. Moreover, to the extent that military orders had restored some power to local courts, it would be "a perversion of the truth to say that the courts were 'open' during this period—certainly they did not function as a coordinate or independent branch of the government. So far as they were permitted to operate they did so 'as agents of the Military Governor.'"[50] The Ninth Circuit further argued that for the civilian courts to function in criminal matters, they had to assemble juries "and citizens of Japanese extraction could not lawfully be excluded from jury panels on the score of race—even in cases of offenses involving the military security of the Territory."

On February 12, 1945, the Supreme Court granted cert to hear the Duncan and White cases.[51] It did not issue a decision until a year later, after the war was over. Thus, the wartime legal scrutiny of martial law in Hawaii occurred entirely at the level of district courts and the Ninth Circuit. During time of war, the Supreme Court did not participate at all in the constitutional debate over the use of provost courts and military commissions in Hawaii.

In 1946, the Supreme Court held that Section 67 of the Organic Act authorized the Governor of Hawaii, with the approval of the President, to

45. Id. at 980.
46. Id. at 981.
47. Id.
48. Id. at 981–82.
49. Ex parte Duncan, 146 F.2d 576 (9th Cir. 1944).
50. Id. at 579.
51. Duncan v. Kahanamoku; White v. Steer, 324 U.S. 833 (1945).

"invoke military aid under certain circumstances," but Congress "did not specifically state to what extent the army could be used or what power it could exercise. It certainly did not explicitly declare that the Governor in conjunction with the military could for days, months or years close all the courts and supplant them with military tribunals."[52] The term "martial law" in Section 67 "carries no precise meaning."[53] The Court rejected the argument of the Justice Department that the legislative history of Section 67 revealed congressional intent "to give the armed forces extraordinarily broad powers to try civilians before military tribunals."[54] Military trials of civilians charged with crimes, "especially when not made subject to judicial review, are so obviously contrary to our political traditions and our institution of jury trials in courts of law, that the tenuous circumstances offered by the Government can hardly suffice to persuade us that Congress was willing to enact a Hawaiian supreme court decision [from 1895] permitting such a radical departure from our steadfast beliefs."[55]

Rather than read Section 67 broadly, the Court said it would be a "mistaken premise" to maintain that Hawaiian inhabitants are less entitled to constitutional protection than the citizens in the 48 states.[56] The Court reviewed the development of governmental institutions in America to press home the fundamental principle that courts "and their procedural safeguards are indispensable to our system of government," and that the framers "were opposed to governments that placed in the hands of one man the power to make, interpret and enforce the laws."[57] Through such reasoning the Court held that both Duncan and White were entitled to be released from custody. The Court's interpretation on matters of military law came late, as it often does in time of war. Whatever judicial resistance to military government that does emerge is more likely to come from the lower courts.

Treatment of Japanese Americans

The greatest wartime deprivation of individual rights in the United States fell on Japanese Americans. Two decisions by the Supreme Court uphold-

---

52. Duncan v. Kahanamoku, 327 U.S. 304, 315 (1946).
53. Id.
54. Id. at 316.
55. Id. at 317.
56. Id. at 318–19.
57. Id. at 322.

ing the government's policy do not directly concern military tribunals. However, they speak volumes about the unwillingness of the judiciary to exercise constitutional independence in times of emergency. The decisions reveal what appears to be an ingrained instinct of Justices to defer to wartime executive and military judgments. The Japanese American cases unleashed a series of withering critiques, both within the Court and outside, warning the judiciary that continued submissive conduct would come at the cost of institutional respect and integrity. The cases also shed light on the capacity of the executive branch to misinform and deliberately mislead the courts in time of war.

In the first of the two cases, handed down in 1943, the Court unanimously upheld a curfew order directed against more than 110,000 Japanese Americans, about two-thirds of them natural-born U.S. citizens.[58] The nighttime curfew, which applied to "all persons of Japanese ancestry," had been supported by Executive Order 9066, promulgated by President Roosevelt on February 19, 1942, and by legislation enacted by Congress on March 21, 1942. A concurring opinion by Justice Douglas cautioned that "we cannot sit in judgment on the military requirements of that hour."[59]

Another concurrence, by Justice Murphy, was far more critical. He said that the "broad guaranties of the Bill of Rights and other provisions of the Constitution protecting essential liberties" are not suspended by "the mere existence of a state of war." The Court should never forget that "there are constitutional boundaries which it is our duty to uphold." Singling out the Japanese American population disturbed him: "Distinctions based on color and ancestry are utterly inconsistent with our traditions and ideals. They are at variance with the principles for which we are now waging war."[60] The curfew policy toward the Japanese Americans, he said, "bears a melancholy resemblance to the treatment accorded to members of the Jewish race in Germany and in other parts of Europe."[61] Then came this blunt warning: "In my opinion this goes to the very brink of constitutional power."[62]

A third concurrence by Justice Rutledge also indicated that he might not tolerate heavier sanctions against the Japanese Americans. A military officer required wide discretion, but "it does not follow there may not be

58. Hirabayashi v. United States, 320 U.S. 81 (1943).
59. Id. at 106.
60. Id. at 110.
61. Id. at 111.
62. Id.

bounds beyond which he cannot go and, if he oversteps them, that the courts may not have power to protect the civilian citizen."[63]

A year later, the Court split 6 to 3 in upholding the placement of Japanese Americans in detention camps.[64] In the first of the dissents, Justice Roberts distinguished this case from the previous one "of keeping people off the streets at night."[65] Instead, it was a case of "convicting a citizen as a punishment for not submitting to imprisonment in a concentration camp, based on his ancestry, and solely because of his ancestry, without evidence or inquiry concerning his loyalty and good disposition towards the United States."[66] In language unusually sharp for a Justice, he called assembly centers a "euphemism for a prison" and relocation centers "a euphemism for concentration camps."[67]

True to his warning, Justice Murphy's dissent said that the exclusion of Japanese Americans "goes over 'the brink of constitutional power' and falls into the ugly abyss of racism."[68] He did not deny that there were disloyal persons of Japanese descent on the Pacific Coast, but the same could be said of Germans and Italians in other parts of the country.[69] He insisted that under the American system of law, individual guilt—not group guilt— "is the sole basis for deprivation of rights."[70] He pointed out that "not one person of Japanese ancestry was accused or convicted of espionage or sabotage after Pearl Harbor while they were still free."[71] In a stunning repudiation of the decision, he called it a "legalization of racism."[72] This ruling convinced Murphy that it was time to impose judicial checks on the growth of military power.[73]

In the third dissent, Justice Jackson reminded the Court that "if any fundamental assumption underlies our system, it is that guilt is personal and not inheritable."[74] Article III of the Constitution, he said, specifically forbade punishment because of treasonable acts by parents or ancestors: "no Attainder of Treason shall work Corruption of Blood, or Forfeiture except

---

63. Id. at 114.
64. Korematsu v. United States, 323 U.S. 214 (1944).
65. Id. at 225.
66. Id. at 226.
67. Id. at 230.
68. Id. at 233.
69. Id. at 240.
70. Id.
71. Id. at 241.
72. Id. at 242.
73. J. Woodford Howard Jr., Mr. Justice Murphy: A Political Biography 367 (1968).
74. 323 U.S. at 243.

during the Life of the Person attainted." And yet here was an attempt by the government "to make an otherwise innocent act a crime merely because this prisoner is the son of parents as to whom he had no choice, and belongs to a race from which there is no way to resign."[75] He warned of the dangers when the Court lends its endorsement to military orders:

> A military order, however unconstitutional, is not apt to last longer than the military emergency. Even during that period a succeeding commander may revoke it all. But once a judicial opinion rationalizes such an order to show that it conforms to the Constitution, or rather rationalizes the Constitution to show that the Constitution sanctions such an order, the Court for all time has validated the principle of racial discrimination in criminal procedure and of transplanting American citizens. The principle then lies about like a loaded weapon ready for the hand of any authority that can bring forward a plausible claim of an urgent need.[76]

In later years, Jackson wrote more searchingly about the kinds of judicial weaknesses and vulnerabilities that can jeopardize individual freedoms and constitutional rights. The Court "can never quite escape consciousness of its own infirmities, a psychology which may explain its apparent yielding to expediency, especially during war time."[77]

Earl Warren was Attorney General of California during the war years and supported the actions against the Japanese Americans. Once on the Court, as Chief Justice, he regretted what the nation had done and particularly deplored the record of the judiciary. In a law review article in 1962, he made a remarkable statement that decisions in the Japanese American cases "that a given program is constitutional, does not necessarily answer the question whether, in a broader sense, it actually is."[78] No one has ever more effectively shot holes in the claim that the Court has a monopoly (or wisdom) in interpreting the Constitution. The Court's failure to invalidate the government's actions against the Japanese Americans did not mean that constitutional standards had been followed—far from it. In a democratic society, Warren said, "it is still the Legislature and the elected Executive

---

75. Id.

76. 323 U.S. at 246.

77. Robert H. Jackson, The Supreme Court in the American System of Government 25 (1955).

78. Earl Warren, "The Bill of Rights and the Military," 37 N.Y.U. L. Rev. 181, 193 (1962).

who have the primary responsibility for fashioning and executing policy consistent with the Constitution."[79]

Scholarship since Warren's time has highlighted the extent to which the executive branch was willing to deceive the judiciary and withhold vital evidence from the courts. At the time of *Korematsu,* Justice Department attorneys learned that a 618-page document called *Final Report,* prepared by the War Department, contained erroneous claims about espionage efforts by Japanese Americans. Analyses by the FBI and the Federal Communication Commission disproved War Department conclusions that Japanese Americans had sent signals from shore to assist in Japanese submarine attacks along the Pacific coast. Justice Department attorneys drafted a footnote to be included in their brief for *Korematsu,* alerting the Supreme Court to errors and misconceptions in the *Final Report.* The footnote specifically repudiated the claim of shore-to-ship signaling by persons of Japanese ancestry. However, the Justice Department watered down the footnote to the point where the Court could have no understanding of factual conflicts within the administration.[80]

On February 20, 1976, President Gerald Ford issued a proclamation declaring the evacuation of Japanese Americans "wrong" and rescinding Roosevelt's 1942 executive order.[81] In 1982, the Commission on Wartime Relocation and Internment of Civilians issued a scathing report that documented governmental misconduct toward Japanese Americans.[82] Some of the convictions of Japanese Americans were later vacated in the 1980s because the Justice Department had deliberately misled the courts.[83] In 1988, Congress passed legislation to offer the nation's apology for the injustices committed against Japanese Americans and to provide cash reparations to survivors and their families.[84]

Trials of Three Japanese Leaders

After dividing on the Japanese American cases, the Court split again on the use of military tribunals to judge the wartime conduct of two Japanese gen-

79. Id. at 202.

80. Peter Irons, Justice at War 278–92 (1983).

81. 41 Fed. Reg. 7741 (1976).

82. Personal Justice Denied, Commission on Wartime Relocation and Internment of Civilians (1982).

83. Korematsu v. United States, 584 F.Supp. 1406 (N.D. Cal. 1984); Hirabayashi v. United States, 828 F.2d 591 (9th Cir. 1987).

84. 102 Stat. 903 (1988).

erals—Tomoyuki Yamashita and Masaharu Homma—and Foreign Minister
Koki Hirota. Judicial review of military trials during World War II rarely
touched the vast number of allied military tribunals created in the Far East.
Those trials led to the execution of 920 Japanese and prison terms for some
3,000. An International Military Tribunal in Tokyo, sitting from 1946 to
1948, tried and sentenced 25 prominent Japanese war criminals, including
Prime Minister Hideki Tojo.[85]

Yamashita and Homma were charged with permitting atrocities against
civilians and prisoners of war. The magnitude and horror of the atrocities
were never in doubt. Japanese soldiers tossed infants in the air and caught
them on their bayonets. Women were raped, citizens beheaded, and parents burned to death. The question before the tribunal was whether
Yamashita and Homma were responsible for the crimes. Newspapers covering the trial called Yamashita the "Beast of Bataan," even though he was
stationed outside the Philippines at the time of the Bataan Death March.[86]
He was better known as the "Tiger of Malaya" because of his defeat of
British forces in Singapore in 1942. The British surrendered 130,000 troops
to Yamashita's 60,000.[87] Homma had distinguished himself by defeating
Gen. Douglas MacArthur in the Philippines in 1942.[88]

Three years later, MacArthur was in a position to determine the fate of
both men. The Nazi saboteur cases of 1942 and 1945 recognized that theater commanders could set up military tribunals and try those who violate
the law of war. As commander of the Far Eastern theater, MacArthur had
all the leverage he needed.[89] He directed Lt. Gen. Wilhelm D. Styer to
establish the tribunal for Yamashita, and it was Styer who appointed the
prosecutors, defense counsel, and members of the tribunal.[90] Yet MacArthur
retained control over the all-important power to decide the charges against
the accused and the rules that would govern tribunal procedures.[91]

---

85. Philip R. Piccigallo, The Japanese on Trial: Allied War Crimes Operations in the
East, 1945–1951 xi (1979).
86. Id. at 52.
87. Richard L. Lael, The Yamashita Precedent: War Crimes and Command Responsibility 6 (1982).
88. Id. at 26.
89. Id. at 59–77.
90. Id. at 71, 73.
91. Id. at 73.

Yamashita

After his surrender on September 3, 1945, Yamashita was charged as a war criminal on September 25. The tribunal was under great pressure from President Truman to "proceed, without avoidable delay."[92] Prosecutors accused Yamashita in his capacity as commanding general of the Japanese Fourteenth Army Group in the Philippines of failing to prevent his troops from committing atrocities against the civilian population and prisoners of war. Homma faced similar charges. They would be prosecuted not for what they did but for what they failed to do, not for what they knew but what they should have known. MacArthur's aides, tasked with drafting plans for a military tribunal, realized that there was no precedent for charging a field commander "with the negligence of duty in controlling his troops."[93]

In addition to 64 individual charges, the comprehensive charge claimed that between October 9, 1944, and September 2, 1945, Yamashita "unlawfully disregarded and failed to discharge his duty as commander to control the operations of the members of his command, permitting them to commit brutal atrocities and other high crimes" against Americans and allies (particularly Filipinos), all of which constituted violations of the "laws of war."[94] The specific charges referred to the murder and mistreatment of over 32,000 Filipino citizens and captured Americans, the rape of Filipino women, and the destruction of private property. None of the charges established a direct link between Yamashita and the underlying criminal acts.[95] Later, shortly before the trial began, the prosecution submitted a supplemental list of 59 additional charges, including the murder of over 4,500 citizens.[96]

Gen. Styer appointed six U.S. army officers to defend Yamashita. They had only three weeks to prepare for trial, locate witnesses, and conduct research on 123 charges.[97] Five American generals sat on the tribunal, none of them lawyers.[98] One of the generals was designated a "law member" but he was not a lawyer.[99] Only one of the generals had extensive combat com-

---

92. Id. at 67, 89, 91.
93. Id. at 69.
94. George F. Guy, "The Defense of Yamashita," 4 Wyo. L. J. 153, 156 (1950).
95. Lael, The Yamashita Precedent, at 80.
96. Id. at 81–82.
97. Id. at 81.
98. J. Gordon Feldhaus, "The Trial of Yamashita," 15 S. Dak. B. J. 181, 185 (1946).
99. Guy, "The Defense of Yamashita," at 161.

mand experience.[100] They had little understanding of the capacity of a commander in wartime to control troops.

When the trial began on October 29, 1945, a defense counsel for Yamashita argued that the charges set forth "no instance of neglect of duty" by him, no acts of commission or omission that "permitted" the crimes, and that American military jurisprudence did not hold a commanding officer responsible for the criminal acts of subordinates.[101] The prosecution responded that the crimes were so flagrant that "they must have been known" to Yamashita, and that if he did not know "it was simply because he took affirmative action not to know."[102] Two prosecution witnesses attempted to link Yamashita to the atrocities, but the first depended on hearsay and the second's testimony was rebutted by a defense witness. Both prosecution witnesses had much to gain personally and financially by cooperating with U.S. officials.[103] A Japanese colonel admitted that he ordered the suppression of Filipino guerrillas, but insisted that civilians had been killed because they were guerrilla combatants and not innocent noncombatants.[104] Cross-examination of the prosecution's Filipino witnesses revealed that many had engaged in guerrilla activities.[105]

On December 7, 1945, the tribunal found Yamashita guilty as charged and sentenced him to death by hanging. Twelve international correspondents covering the trial voted 12 to 0 that Yamashita should have been acquitted.[106] His counsel filed an unsuccessful appeal to the Philippine Supreme Court, which ruled that it lacked jurisdiction over the U.S. Army. Defense counsel telegraphed a request to the U.S. Supreme Court for a stay of execution, which was granted.[107] The next step was to file a petition for a writ of habeas corpus to the Court, contending that the tribunal was without lawful authority or jurisdiction to place him on trial. The defense counsel offered four grounds for reversing the December 7 verdict: (1) the cessation of hostilities denied MacArthur the authority to create the tribunal, (2) the tribunal failed to charge Yamashita with a violation of the law of war, (3) the procedures followed by the tribunal deprived Yamashita of a

---

100. Stephen B. Ives Jr., "Vengeance Did Not Deliver Justice," Washington Post, December 30, 2001, at B2; Lael, The Yamashita Precedent, at 88.

101. Lael, The Yamashita Precedent, at 82.

102. Id. at 83.

103. Id. at 84–85.

104. Id. at 87.

105. Guy, "The Defense of Yamashita," at 162.

106. Piccigallo, The Japanese on Trial, at 57.

107. Id. at 173.

fair trial, and (4) the tribunal failed to give advance notice of the trial to a neutral power representing the interests of Japan, as required by Article 60 of the Geneva Convention.[108]

The Supreme Court split 6–2 in upholding the tribunal's actions. Writing for the majority was the author of *Quirin,* Chief Justice Harlan Fiske Stone. Before reaching the four questions, he emphasized that the Court was "not here concerned with the power of military commissions to try civilians," citing *Milligan* for authority.[109] Nor did the Court attempt to appraise or weigh the evidence introduced at trial, concluding that such matters were wholly within the competence of the tribunal.[110] When Stone found it impossible to attract a majority of Justices behind certain constitutional principles, he simply struck those sections from his opinion.[111]

On the first point raised by the defense, Stone denied that the executive branch lacked authority to convene a commission after hostilities had ended. It could try individuals who committed violations of the law of war before the cessation, "at least until peace has been officially recognized by treaty or proclamation of the political branch of the Government."[112] On the second point, Stone found that the charges constituted violations of the law of war, and that Yamashita's failure to control his troops deserved inclusion in the law of war. Several provisions of the Fourth Hague Convention of 1907, the Tenth Hague Convention, and the Geneva Red Cross Convention required that troops be "commanded by a person responsible for his subordinates."[113] Language of that breadth, however, does not necessarily mean that a commander is liable for criminal actions by subordinates.

Stone distinguished between violations of the law of war and violations of criminal statutes that are tried in civil court. First: "We do not make the laws of war but we respect them so far as they do not conflict with the commands of Congress or the Constitution."[114] And second: "Obviously charges of violations of the law of war triable before a military tribunal need not be stated with the precision of a common law indictment."[115]

108. In re Yamashita, 327 U.S. 1, 6 (1946).

109. Id. at 9.

110. Id. at 17.

111. John P. Frank, The Marble Palace: The Supreme Court in American Life 136–37 (1972); Mason, Harlan Fiske Stone, at 666–71.

112. In re Yamashita, 327 U.S. at 12.

113. Id. at 15–16. The quoted language comes from Article 1 of the Fourth Hague Convention; 36 Stat. 2295 (1907).

114. Id. at 16.

115. Id. at 17.

Next came Stone's analysis of the procedures followed by the tribunal, including the admission of hearsay as evidence. For example, Article of War 38 provided that the President could prescribe the procedures for courts-martial, courts of inquiry, military commissions, and other military tribunals and shall apply the rules of evidence "generally recognized in the trial of criminal cases in the district courts of the United States." Hearsay is not admissible in federal courts. Yet Stone concluded that Article 38 was not "applicable to the trial of an enemy combatant by a military commission for violations of the law of war."[116] He pointed to other Articles to show that the procedural safeguards were meant to apply to U.S. soldiers and personnel that accompany the U.S. military, not to enemy combatants.[117] By admitting hearsay and other procedures that would not be allowed in federal court, Stone said the tribunal did not violate "any act of Congress, treaty or military command defining the commission's authority."[118]

Finally, Stone examined the charge that the tribunal failed to give notice of the trial to the protecting power, which in this case was Switzerland. Stone concluded that the requirement for notice applies only to persons subjected to judicial proceedings for offenses committed while prisoners of war.[119] It was his judgment that Yamashita's trial did not violate the requirement for notice.

Justices Murphy and Rutledge issued lengthy and biting dissents. Murphy agreed with Stone that the commission had been authorized by the power of Congress to "define and punish . . . Offences against the Law of Nations,"[120] but charged that Yamashita's rights under the Due Process Clause of the Fifth Amendment had been "grossly and openly violated without any justification."[121] The Due Process Clause, Murphy pointed out, applies to "any person" who is accused of a federal crime. No exception "is made as to those who are accused of war crimes or as to those who possess the status of an enemy belligerent."[122]

Murphy said that Yamashita had been "rushed to trial under an improper charge, given insufficient time to prepare an adequate defense, deprived of the benefits of some of the most elementary rules of evidence and summarily sentenced to be hanged."[123] Although "brutal atrocities" had been

116. Id. at 19.
117. Id.
118. Id. at 23.
119. Id. at 24.
120. Id. at 26, 31.
121. Id. at 40.
122. Id. at 26.
123. Id. at 27–28.

inflicted upon the Filipino population by Japanese armed forces under Yamashita's command,[124] there was no evidence that he knew of the atrocities or in any way ordered them. In fact, U.S. forces had done everything possible to disrupt his control over Japanese troops. Murphy objected that to "use the very inefficiency and disorganization created by the victorious forces as the primary basis for condemning officers of the defeated armies bears no resemblance to justice or to military reality."[125]

In a separate dissent, Justice Rutledge concluded that the proceedings and rules of evidence of the Yamashita tribunal violated two Articles of War (25 and 38). Although the majority held that those Articles were not applicable to the proceeding against Yamashita, Rutledge insisted that both Articles applied to all military commissions and tribunals.[126] Article 25 described the process of taking depositions and specified that they may be read in evidence before any military court or tribunal "in any case not capital." Article 38 required the President to prescribe procedures for military courts, with the requirement that the procedures ("insofar as he shall deem practicable") shall apply the rules of evidence generally recognized in the trial of criminal cases in federal court. Article 38 closed with this limitation: "nothing contrary to or inconsistent with these articles shall be so prescribed."

It was not in the American tradition, Rutledge said, "to be charged with crime which is defined after his conduct, alleged to be criminal, has taken place; or in language not sufficient to inform him of the nature of the offense or to enable him to make defense."[127] He distinguished what the Court did in *Quirin*, in the middle of war, with the conditions surrounding Yamashita's trial, after hostilities had ceased.[128] Moreover, in *Quirin* the Court decided that it would not review the evidence, but "it was not there or elsewhere determined that it could not ascertain whether conviction is founded upon evidence expressly excluded by Congress or treaty; nor does the Court purport to do so now."[129] A separate section of Rutledge's dissent concluded that Yamashita's trial was in conflict with the Geneva Convention of 1929.[130] In a private letter, Rutledge said that the Yamashita case "will outrank Dred Scott in the annals of the Court."[131]

Following the Court's decision, defense counsel appealed to President

124. Id. at 29.
125. Id. at 35.
126. Id. at 61.
127. Id. at 43.
128. Id. at 46.
129. Id. at 47.
130. Id. at 72–78.
131. Frank, The Marble Palace, at 137.

Truman for clemency. He declined to act, leaving the matter in the hands of the military.[132] MacArthur confirmed the sentence and on February 23, 1946, in a prison camp 30 miles south of Manila, Yamashita was hanged. A. Frank Reel, a member of the defense team, wrote critically about the conduct of the trial. Regarding the treatment of Yamashita as "unjust, hypocritical, and vindictive," he advised that the United States "must learn that victory without justice is a dead thing, that humanity cannot live without charity," and that "as we judge, so will we be judged; our own rights and privileges are those we grant to the lowliest and most despised of culprits."[133] Reel concluded that Yamashita "was not hanged because he was in command of troops who committed atrocities. He was hanged because he was in command of troops who committed atrocities *on the losing side.*"[134]

Homma

The military tribunal for Gen. Homma began in Manila on January 3, 1946. Charges against him included the bombing of Manila after it was declared an open city, the Bataan Death March of 1942, and POW camp abuses, all of the events occurring during Homma's term as Commander in Chief in the Philippines from December 8, 1941, to August 15, 1942.[135] Similar to the Yamashita trial, prosecutors charged that Homma "knew or should have known" of the commission of atrocities.[136] The tribunal found Homma guilty on February 11, 1946, for failure to control the operations of his troops and sentenced him to be hanged. On the same day, the Supreme Court split 6–2 in denying the motion for a writ of habeas corpus to review the tribunal's action. Murphy and Rutledge were again the dissenters.[137] MacArthur ordered that Homma be shot rather than hanged.[138]

Hirota

Koki Hirota was among 28 defendants tried for war crimes before the International Military Tribunal for the Far East. He served as Prime Minister

132. Guy, "The Defense of Yamashita," at 178.
133. A. Frank Reel, The Case of General Yamashita 247 (1949).
134. Id. at 245 (emphasis in original).
135. Piccigallo, The Japanese on Trial, at 63.
136. Id. at 64.
137. Homma v. Patterson, 327 U.S. 759 (1946).
138. Lawrence Taylor, A Trial of Generals: Homma, Yamashita, MacArthur 218–19 (1981).

from March 9, 1936, to February 2, 1937, and later as Foreign Minister until he retired in 1938. During this last assignment, Japanese forces marched into China and committed the atrocities now known as the Rape of Nanking. During a six-week period, Japanese troops slaughtered more than a quarter million Chinese.[139] Although Hirota was not in charge of the military forces, the issue was whether he knew of the massacres.[140] As with Yamashita and Homma, the Hirota trial illustrates the U.S. doctrine of command responsibility.

In 1948, the Supreme Court reviewed the actions of the International Military Tribunal for the Far East. Although it had been created by MacArthur, a 6–1 majority ruled that it acted as the agent of the Allied Powers rather than of the United States, and that it was therefore not a tribunal of the United States. At the same time, the Court acknowledged that MacArthur "has been selected and is acting as the Supreme Commander for the Allied Powers," and that he had set up the tribunal as the agent of the Allied Powers.[141] The Justices held that U.S. courts had no power or authority to review, affirm, set aside, or annul the judgments and sentences imposed by the tribunal on the residents and citizens of Japan. A concurrence by Justice Douglas expressed uneasiness with the decision: "If no United States court can inquire into the lawfulness of his detention, the military have acquired, contrary to our traditions (see *Ex parte Quirin,* 317 U.S. 1; *In re Yamashita,* 327 U.S. 1), a new and alarming hold on us."[142]

Justice Murphy dissented, but without publishing his views. Justice Rutledge reserved making a decision, allowing him to announce his vote at a later time. Before he could do that, he died on September 10, 1949. Justice Jackson took no part in the decision.

In 1950, Simon Nash, an American citizen, brought an action in federal court on behalf of seven Japanese nationals convicted of war crimes by military tribunals. He petitioned for writs of habeas corpus and for declaratory judgment, attacking the validity of the convictions and the subsequent imprisonments. Nash requested permission to prosecute the case in forma pauperis, citing his poverty as grounds for not paying the costs of an

139. Iris Chang, The Rape of Nanking (1997).

140. John Toland, The Rising Sun 34–35, 42, 48–50 (2003 ed.); Chang, The Rape of Nanking, at 103–4, 148, 174–75; Arnold C. Brackman, The Other Nuremberg: The Untold Story of the Tokyo War Crimes Trials 180–81, 274, 328–29, 380 (1987); Piccigallo, The Japanese on Trial, at 30.

141. Hirota v. MacArthur, 338 U.S. 197, 198 (1948).

142. Id. at 201–2.

appeal. The D.C. Circuit ruled that he had no right to proceed on the basis of an in forma pauperis appeal.[143]

Command Responsibility

Atrocities committed by U.S. forces in Vietnam raised the question whether American generals and commanders could be held responsible under the same test that had been applied to Yamashita, Homma, and Hirota. However, within a few years of those trials, American judges moved away from the standard that a commander "should have known" or "must have known." The test now shifted to whether a commander knew of atrocities or showed a wanton disregard of what his subordinates were doing. In the High Command Case in Nuremberg, in October 1948, a U.S. military tribunal noted that a

> high commander cannot keep completely informed of the details of military operations of subordinates and most assuredly not of every administrative measure. He has the right to assume that details entrusted to responsible subordinates will be legally executed. The President of the United States is Commander in Chief of its military forces. Criminal acts submitted by those forces cannot in themselves be charged to him on the theory of subordination. The same is true of other high commanders in the chain of command. Criminality does not attach to every individual in this chain of command from that fact alone. There must be a personal dereliction. That can occur only where the act is directly traceable to him or where his failure to properly supervise his subordinates constitutes criminal negligence on his part. In the latter case it must be a personal neglect amounting to a wanton, immoral disregard of the action of his subordinates amounting to acquiescence. Any other interpretation of international law would go far beyond the basic principles of criminal law as known to civilized nations.[144]

The court-martial of Capt. Ernest L. Medina in 1971 charged him with responsibility for acts of force and violence while interrogating prisoners of war in Vietnam and a failure to exercise control over subordinates who killed noncombatants. The instructions that the military judge issued to the

---

143. Nash v. MacArthur, 184 F.2d 606 (D.C. Cir. 1950).
144. 2 Leon Friedman, ed., The Law of War: A Documentary History 1450 (1972).

court members differed markedly from the principle of command responsibility applied to Yamashita. The judge stated that a commander is responsible "if he has *actual* knowledge that troops or other persons subject to his control are in the process of committing or are about to commit a war crime and he wrongfully fails to take the necessary and reasonable steps to insure compliance with the law of war." Those legal requirements required a commander to have "actual knowledge plus a wrongful failure to act. Thus mere presence at the scene without knowledge will not suffice. That is, the commander-subordinate relationship alone will not allow an inference of knowledge. While it is not necessary that a commander actually see an atrocity being committed, it is essential that he know that his subordinates are in the process of committing atrocities or are about to commit atrocities."[145]

In summing up his instructions, the judge told court members that in order to find Medina guilty they "must be satisfied by legal and competent evidence beyond reasonable doubt" of four elements.[146] In contrast, Yamashita had not been convicted on the basis of competent evidence. Hearsay, for example, was allowed. And he was not judged by the demanding standard of "beyond reasonable doubt." The second of the four elements for Medina provided: "That their deaths resulted from the omission of the accused in failing to exercise control over subordinates subject to his command *after having gained knowledge* that his subordinates were killing noncombatants, in or at the village of My Lai (4), Quang Ngai Province, Republic of Vietnam, on or about 16 March 1968."[147]

Other studies during the Vietnam period also rejected the principle of command responsibility under which Japanese leaders were tried. Instead of asserting that a commander "must have known" or "should have known," there had to be a showing of actual knowledge of the crime.[148] Studies point out that such trials as the High Command Case were the product of "judicial minds rather than of lay jurors" (as with Yamashita) and that they were prepared "under less emotive circumstances."[149] A division com-

---

145. Id. at 1732 (emphasis in original).

146. Id. at 1733.

147. Id. (emphasis added). For comments by the military judge in the Medina case, see Kenneth A. Howard, "Command Responsibility for War Crimes," 21 J. Pub. L. 7 (1972).

148. Franklin A. Hart, "Yamashita, Nuremberg and Vietnam: Command Responsibility Reappraised," 25 Naval War Coll. Rev. 19, 30 (1972).

149. William H. Parks, "Command Responsibility for War Crimes," 62 Mil. L. Rev. 1, 62 (1973).

mander in Vietnam was reduced in rank, stripped of his distinguished service medal, and censured because the U.S. Army determined that he possessed *information* about atrocities in My Lai.[150]

Gaetano Territo

A 1946 decision by the Ninth Circuit, while not involving a military tribunal, is worth noting because it concerned the capture of an enemy on the battlefield. That issue is addressed in Chapter 8 in the discussion of Yaser Hamdi and the Guantánamo detainees. Gaetano Territo was born in the United States and at all times had been an American citizen. He was captured by the United States in 1943, in Sicily, upon the field of battle while serving in the Italian Army. He was wearing part of the Italian Army uniform and tried to escape from U.S. soldiers. He was taken to California and held as a POW. The question was whether he was being illegally constrained and was entitled to a writ of habeas corpus, requiring the U.S. Army to produce him in court and justify the restraint.

The Ninth Circuit decided that it was immaterial whether Territo was or was not a U.S. citizen. Under the Geneva Convention, his capture as a POW by American military authorities was "valid and legal," as was his detention.[151] Denying his petition for a writ of habeas corpus, the court held: "Those who have written texts upon the subject of prisoners of war agree that all persons who are active in opposing an army in war may be captured and except for spies and other non-uniformed plotters and actors for the enemy are prisoners of war."[152] The court turned to *Quirin* to point out that U.S. citizenship of an enemy belligerent offers no immunity from capture as a POW.[153] The cessation of hostilities between the United States and Italy, and the change from Italy's belligerency to being an ally against the Axis Powers, did not alter Territo's status. No treaty of peace had been negotiated with Italy.[154]

---

150. William V. O'Brien, "The Law of War, Command Responsibility and Vietnam," 60 Geo. L. J. 605, 606 n. 3 (1972). See also Ilias Bantekas, "The Contemporary Law of Superior Responsibility," 93 Am. J. Int'l L. 573 (1999).

151. In re Territo, 156 F.2d 142, 144 (9th Cir. 1946).

152. Id. at 145.

153. Id.

154. Id. at 147–48.

The Eisentrager Decision

In 1950, the Court received another case testing the legality of military tri-bunals, this time raising an issue that would return to the Court in 2004 in the case of the Guantánamo Bay detainees. The basic question: Can the executive branch detain, try, and execute individuals outside the United States without the independent review of federal courts? Did nonresident enemy aliens, tried and convicted in China by an American military tribu-nal for violations of the laws of war, have a right to a writ of habeas cor-pus to U.S. civilian courts? Similar to the situation of martial law in Hawaii, a lower federal court was willing to place limits on the military, while the Supreme Court was not.

The D.C. Circuit held that any person deprived of liberty by U.S. offi-cials, and who can show that his confinement violates a prohibition of the Constitution, has a right to the writ regardless of whether he is a citizen or not. The appellate court noted that the Fifth Amendment applies broadly to "any person."[155] The court denied that its decision created a practical problem of transporting the 21 appellants to the United States for a hear-ing, noting that the Supreme Court had decided *Quirin* without the per-sonal presence of the German saboteurs.[156]

A 6–3 majority of the Supreme Court reversed, pointing to factual differ-ences between the Nazi saboteurs and the 21 appellants. Unlike the eight Germans in *Quirin,* these prisoners had never been in or lived in the United States, were captured outside U.S. territory, were tried and convicted by a military commission sitting outside the United States for offenses against laws of war committed outside the United States, and were at all times imprisoned outside the United States.[157] In denying the writ of habeas cor-pus and refusing review for these petitioners, the Court looked less to the constitutional powers of Congress and the President than it did to the mean-ing of "any person" in the Fifth Amendment. Writing for the Court, Justice Jackson remarked that if the Fifth Amendment "invests enemy aliens in unlawful hostile action against us with immunity from military trial, it puts them in a more protected position than our own soldiers. . . . It would be a paradox indeed if what the Amendment denied to Americans it guaranteed to enemies."[158]

---

155. Eisentrager v. Forrestal, 174 F.2d 961, 963 (D.C. Cir. 1949).
156. Id. at 968.
157. Johnson v. Eisentrager, 339 U.S. 763, 777 (1950).
158. Id. at 783.

The analogy here is misplaced. American soldiers tried by court-martial have more procedural protections than aliens tried by military tribunal. The issue was not whether aliens are entitled to superior rights but what rights they have, if any, before a tribunal. The Court declined to say. As with other tribunal cases during this period, Jackson said that it was "not for us to say whether these prisoners were or were not guilty of a war crime, or whether if we were to retry the case we would agree to the findings of fact or the application of the laws of war made by the Military Commission."[159]

In deciding this type of case, the Court seemed to exclude judicial review of military tribunals if they were located outside the country. A dissent by Justices Black, Douglas, and Burton accused the Court of fashioning a "wholly indefensible" doctrine by permitting the executive branch, "by deciding where its prisoners will be tried and imprisoned, to deprive all federal courts of their power to protect against a federal executive's illegal incarceration."[160] To say that petitioners were denied the privilege of habeas corpus "solely because they were convicted and imprisoned overseas" was to adopt "a broad and dangerous principle."[161] The government had argued that habeas corpus was not available even to U.S. citizens convicted and imprisoned in Germany by American military tribunals.[162]

Placing Limits on Military Courts

From 1952 to 1960, the Supreme Court began to consider and adopt restrictions on military courts, particularly their authority to try U.S. citizens stationed overseas and members of the military who had left the service. These cases illustrate how federal courts in the years following World War II started to awake from their slumbers, rediscovered the principle of judicial independence, and demonstrated a willingness to apply constitutional checks to executive and military judgments.

The first series of cases involved civilian dependents located overseas. The government charged Yvette Madsen, a native-born U.S. citizen, with murdering her husband, an officer of the U.S. Air Force. She was convicted in Germany by a military commission consisting of three U.S. citizens, with review by a military appellate panel of five U.S. citizens. Her sentence

159. Id. at 786.
160. Id. at 795.
161. Id.
162. Id.

was 15 years. In upholding the actions of these military courts, the Court examined the relative powers of the President and Congress and concluded that the President, in the "absence of attempts by Congress to limit the President's power," may in time of war "establish and prescribe the jurisdiction and procedure of military commissions."[163] The Court further noted: "The policy of Congress to refrain from legislating in this uncharted area does not imply its lack of power to legislate."[164]

Black penned the sole dissent, expressing concern that the so-called judicial process was concentrated solely within the executive branch: "Executive officers acting under presidential authority created the system of courts that tried her, promulgated the edicts she was convicted of violating, and appointed the judges who took away her liberty."[165] He said that whatever scope is granted to the President as Commander in Chief of the armed forces, "I think that if American citizens in present-day Germany are to be tried by the American Government, they should be tried under laws passed by Congress and in courts created by Congress under its constitutional authority."[166]

Subsequent decisions began to narrow the broad scope given to military trials. In 1955, the Court reviewed the court-martial of an ex-serviceman after he had served in Korea, been honorably discharged, and returned to the United States. Initially the Justices lined up behind the military, but Black led the dissenters to insist that the case be reargued, particularly after the confirmation of John Marshall Harlan as Associate Justice. After scheduling the rehearing, Chief Justice Earl Warren announced at conference that he had changed his position, thus shifting the majority to Black.[167]

Writing for the Court, Black invoked Article III and the Bill of Rights to place restrictions on what Congress could do under its Article I powers and what Presidents may do as Commander in Chief in asserting military authority over citizens. The Court ruled that ex-servicemen must be tried by federal civil courts.[168] Although the case focused on a court-martial, its reasoning can apply to military tribunals: "We find nothing in the history or constitutional treatment of military tribunals which entitles them to rank along with Article III courts as adjudicators of the guilt or innocence of

---

163. Madsen v. Kinsella, 343 U.S. 341, 348 (1952).
164. Id. at 348–49.
165. Id. at 372.
166. Id.
167. Bernard Schwartz, Super Chief 180–81 (1983).
168. Toth v. Quarles, 350 U.S. 11 (1955).

people charged with offenses for which they can be deprived of their life, liberty or property."[169]

Justices Reed, Burton, and Minton dissented, limiting their analysis to the constitutionality and construction of the Uniform Code of Military Justice, enacted in 1950. In part they objected that the ex-serviceman, under the Court's ruling, "must face a jury far removed from the scene of the alleged crime and before jurors without the understanding of the quality and character of a military crime possessed by those accustomed to administer the Uniform Code of Military Justice."[170] They also accused the majority of judicial activism by interfering with constitutional duties granted to Congress in making rules for the regulation of the armed forces.[171] As to the Uniform Code, they said it "is not for courts to question the wisdom of the legislation."[172]

A series of lawsuits from 1956 to 1960, known as "The Cases of the Murdering Wives," tested the constitutionality of using courts-martial to try civilian dependents of military personnel living overseas. In one case, the wife of an army colonel was tried by a general court-martial in Tokyo for murdering her husband. After she was found guilty and sentenced to life imprisonment, the Court found no constitutional deficiency to the proceeding.[173] This decision came down on June 11, 1956, just as the Court was wrapping up its business for the term. In a section called a "Reservation," Frankfurter delicately referred to some hasty judicial actions: "Doubtless because of the pressure under which the Court works during its closing weeks," several arguments "have been merely adumbrated in its opinion."[174] That was fancy language for saying that the Court had given short shrift to the litigant. A dissent by Warren, Black, and Douglas was more blunt: "The questions raised are complex, the remedy drastic, and the consequences far-reaching upon the lives of civilians. The military is given new powers not hitherto thought consistent with our scheme of government. For these reasons, we need more time than is available in these closing days of the Term in which to write our dissenting views. We will file our dissents during the next Term of Court."[175] There are echoes here of

169. Id. at 17.
170. Id. at 24.
171. Id.
172. Id. at 28.
173. Kinsella v. Krueger, 351 U.S. 470 (1956).
174. Id. at 483.
175. Id. at 485–86.

the *Quirin* Court rushing out a per curiam followed by a full opinion three months later.

On that same day, the Court held that Clarice Covert could be convicted and sentenced to life imprisonment by a court-martial in England for the murder of her husband, an Air Force sergeant. She was brought to the United States and confined in a federal prison for women. The Court distinguished this case from *Toth v. Quarles,* involving the serviceman who had been honorably discharged.[176] The dissent by Warren, Black, and Douglas in the first murdering wife case applied to this case as well.

The unseemly haste in cranking out decisions at the last minute prompted the dissenters to press the Court to rehear these cases.[177] Changes in Court membership helped shift the balance. Sherman Minton stepped down on October 15, 1956, with William Brennan taking his seat. The Court was further liberalized with the retirement of Stanley Reed on February 25, 1957. He was replaced by Charley Whittaker.

After granting a petition for rehearing, the Court on June 10, 1957, reversed both decisions of the murdering wives. Whittaker did not participate in this case. The Court decided that when the United States acts against its citizens abroad, it must act in accordance with all the limitations imposed by the Constitution, including Article III and the Fifth and Sixth Amendments. Citizens must be tried in Article III courts, not military courts.[178] The reasoning is broad enough to cover not only courts-martial but also military tribunals. Dependents of military personnel overseas "could not constitutionally be tried by military authorities."[179]

While acknowledging that the Court had not yet "definitively established to what extent the President, as Commander-in-Chief of the armed forces," can promulgate the procedures of military courts in time of peace or war, and conceding that Congress "has given the President broad discretion to provide the rules governing military trials," Justice Black struck this cautionary note: "If the President can provide rules of substantive law as well as procedure, then he and his military subordinates exercise legislative, executive and judicial powers with respect to those subject to military trials. Such blending of functions in one branch of the Government is the objectionable thing which the draftsmen of the Constitution endeavored to prevent by providing for the separation of governmental powers."[180] That

176. Reid v. Covert, 351 U.S. 487, 491 (1956).
177. Schwartz, Super Chief, at 239–43.
178. Reid v. Covert, 354 U.S. 1 (1957).
179. Id. at 5.
180. Id. at 38–39.

identical principle would return to the Court in 2004 with regard to the treatment of enemy combatants and the detainees at Guantánamo Bay.

Other shifts in Court membership helped bring a more skeptical eye to the scope of courts-martial abroad. The conservative Harold Burton retired on October 13, 1958, replaced by a more moderate Potter Stewart. Three decisions by the Court in 1960 further restricted the use of military courts outside the country, covering civilian dependents of military personnel and civilian employees of the armed forces.[181] In its cautious and labored way, the Court finally began to impose limits on the use of military courts during time of peace. In the Nazi saboteur case, Chief Justice Stone referred to "the duty which rests on the courts, in time of war as well as in time of peace, to preserve unimpaired the constitutional safeguards of civil liberty."[182] Clearly, the Court did not fulfill that duty in the 1942 case or many others. The federal judiciary does relatively little in time of war and takes years, if not decades, to recover its independence in time of peace.

Detlef Tiede

One other case in the post–World War II period deserves mention. It offers powerful insights into the way that American courts operated in occupied territories after the war, the extent to which the U.S. Constitution applied to these courts, and the courage of a federal judge to confront executive authority. Strangely, U.S. District Judge Herbert J. Stern was "appointed" by the U.S. ambassador to the Federal Republic of Germany to sit on the United States Court for Berlin. By accepting this assignment, did he forfeit the independence of an Article III judge and agree to function as a mere agent of the executive branch?

The odd status of the case appears in the opening paragraph of Stern's decision. He called the case a criminal proceeding arising out of the hijacking of a Polish aircraft on August 30, 1978, by two Germans. Instead of a scheduled landing in East Berlin, they forced the plane down in West Berlin. U.S. authorities exercised jurisdiction over the dispute and convened the United States Court for Berlin. Defense counsel moved for a trial by jury. The prosecution objected, "contending that these proceedings are not governed by the United States Constitution, but by the requirements of

---

181. Kinsella v. Singleton, 361 U.S. 234 (1960); McElroy v. Guagliardo, 361 U.S. 281 (1960); Grisham v. Hagan, 361 U.S. 278 (1960).
182. Ex parte Quirin, 317 U.S. 1, 19 (1942).

foreign policy and that the Secretary of State, as interpreter of that policy, has determined that these defendants do not have the right to a jury trial."[183] The United States Court for Berlin, created by the State Department, operated as an Article II court. If Stern decided that the Constitution required a jury trial, the department was in a position to refuse to provide one.[184] Why was an Article III judge presiding in this case?

The two defendants were Hans Detlef Alexander Tiede and Ingrid Ruske. She was released on November 3, 1978, having been kept in custody without formal charge ever since August 30.[185] For a period of over two months she was held incommunicado by order of an American general.[186] Some weeks later, on the basis of information that U.S. authorities were able to obtain from her, she was rearrested and formally charged.[187] Judge Stern held that her two-month detention violated the Fourth, Fifth, and Sixth Amendments, and that the statements elicited from her after November 3 could not be used in evidence because they had been unlawfully and unconstitutionally induced by an American colonel.[188] With the case crumbling, the U.S. government agreed to drop the charges against her.[189] Thereafter the focus fell on Tiede.

Stern inherited the case from two judges who served short stints. On November 30, Dudley B. Bonsal, senior U.S. district judge, was sworn in as United States Judge for Berlin. He limited his participation to the promulgation of rules of criminal procedure and was succeeded by Leo M. Goodman, former judge of the United States Court of the Allied High Commission for Germany. Tiede was brought before Judge Goodman and advised of his rights under the U.S. Constitution. Because of Tiede's indigency, Judge Goodman assigned a member of the Berlin criminal bar to serve as his counsel.

An Occupation Court

On January 11, 1979, Judge Stern replaced Goodman as United States Judge for Berlin. He appointed American counsel for the defendants because it

---

183. United States v. Tiede, 86 F.R.D. 227, 228 (U.S. Court for Berlin 1979).
184. Herbert J. Stern, Judgment in Berlin 97, 117, 129 (1984). This book by Judge Stern illuminates complex personal, political, and legal considerations.
185. Id. at 32.
186. Id. at 181–82, 183.
187. Id. at 41, 49, 59.
188. Id. at 211–12.
189. Id. at 220, 227, 234–35.

was his intention to conduct the trial under American procedural law, "although German substantive law would apply."[190] Stern explained the evolution of occupation courts in Germany after the war. In 1945, Gen. Dwight D. Eisenhower proclaimed that the law applicable within the U.S. zone of occupation in Germany would be "the German law in force at the time of the occupation," subject to modification by U.S. military authorities. A system of "Military Government Courts" was established, and members of those courts could either be military or civilian personnel of the U.S. military government. The jurisdiction of the courts extended to all persons in the occupied zone, "other than military personnel who were subject to military law." The U.S. government allowed for a limited reopening of local German courts, "subject to the direction of the Military Government." In 1948, the judicial structure changed by adopting a system of civilian courts under the military government.[191]

In 1955, the U.S. High Commissioner established the United States Court for Berlin, although it was not convened until the Tiede case. The President had delegated to the U.S. ambassador to the Federal Republic of Germany authority over all governmental functions of the United States in Germany, under the supervision of the Secretary of State. The court thus sat in Berlin as "an instrumentality of the United States, executing the sovereign powers of the United States." As a matter of U.S. law, the court was an Article II tribunal established pursuant to the powers of the President.[192] When Judge Bonsal promulgated the rules of criminal procedure for the court, with one exception he adopted "almost verbatim the Federal Rules of Criminal Procedure and the Federal Rules of Evidence." The exception eliminated jury trials as a constitutional requirement.[193]

No Constitutional Rights?

According to the prosecution, the U.S. Constitution did not apply to the proceedings because Berlin was a territory governed by military conquest. Moreover, everything concerning the conduct of an occupation represented a "political question" and was thus not subject to review by U.S. courts. The occupation courts functioned as an extension of American foreign policy. Whatever rights were available to individuals brought before the United

---

190. United States v. Tiede, 86 F.R.D. at 229.
191. Id. at 236.
192. Id. at 237.
193. Id. at 238.

States Court for Berlin depended entirely on the decisions of the Secretary of State, and he determined, as a matter of foreign policy, that the right to a jury trial was not available to defendants.[194]

Judge Stern found the arguments of the prosecution "entirely without merit."[195] He cited *Ex parte Milligan* for this fundamental principle: "there has never been a time when United States authorities exercised governmental powers in any geographical area—whether at war or in times of peace—without regard for their own Constitution."[196] Constitutional officers, including the Secretary of State, were subject to constitutional limitations when they exercised the powers of their office. The "applicability of any provision of the Constitution is itself a point of constitutional law, to be decided in the last instance by the judiciary, not by the Executive Branch."[197] Stern called attention to this language in *Milligan*:

[The Framers of the American Constitution] foresaw that troublous times would arise, when rulers and people would become restive under restraint, and seek by sharp and decisive measures to accomplish ends deemed just and proper; and that the principles of constitutional liberty would be in peril, unless established by irrepealable law. The history of the world had taught them that what was done in the past might be attempted in the future. *The Constitution of the United States is a law for rulers and people, equally in war and in peace, and covers with the shield of its protection all classes of men, at all times, and under all circumstances.* No doctrine, involving more pernicious consequences, was ever invented by the wit of man than that any of its provisions can be suspended during any of the great exigencies of government. Such a doctrine leads directly to anarchy or despotism, but the theory of necessity on which it is based is false; for the government, within the Constitution, has all the powers granted to it, which are necessary to preserve its existence; as has been happily proved by the result of the great effort to throw off its just authority.[198] [Emphasis added by Judge Stern]

Stern concluded that the position advanced by the prosecution would have "dramatic consequences" not only for Tiede and Ruske but for every

194. Id. at 238–41.
195. Id. at 242.
196. Id.
197. Id.
198. Id.

person within the territorial limits of the U.S. sector of Berlin. Without constitutional limits, no one in the sector would have any protection from the "untrammeled discretion" of occupation authorities. If the Constitution did not apply, there would be no First Amendment, Fifth Amendment, Sixth Amendment, or even the Thirteenth Amendment's prohibition on involuntary servitude. Without the Constitution, the Secretary of State would have the power "to arrest any person without cause, to hold a person incommunicado, to deny an accused the benefit of counsel, to try a person summarily and to impose sentence—all as a part of the unreviewable exercise of foreign policy."[199] With those words, Stern anticipated precisely the kinds of issues that emerged after 9/11, when the Bush administration claimed exclusive authority over the treatment of detainees and enemy combatants.

Insisting on a Jury Trial

Judge Stern had no intention of functioning as an employee of the executive branch, ready to do the bidding of the Secretary of State. The defendants had the right to due process of law, and due process required that the U.S. government come before the United States Court for Berlin "as a litigant and not as a commander." By establishing the court, the Secretary of State delegated his powers to the court and had no authority to "compel that its views be victorious."[200]

In deciding the questions before him, Judge Stern was not concerned with the procedures that might be used by a U.S. military tribunal trying a case in wartime or during the belligerent occupation of enemy territory before war terminates.[201] The Tiede case, he said, did not involve spying or a violation of the laws of war, and he sat not as an international tribunal but as an American court. He placed Tiede and Ruske in the category of "friendly aliens," not as enemy nationals, enemy belligerents, or POWs.[202] Stern concluded that the Constitution required that they be tried by jury, relying extensively on Justice Black's analysis in the 1957 case of Clarice Covert.[203]

Toward the end of the decision, Judge Stern reviewed the prosecution's argument that the United States Court for Berlin "is a type of military commission and defendants tried by a military commission have no right to a

199. Id. at 243.
200. Id. at 244.
201. Id. at 244–45.
202. Id. at 245.
203. Id. at 249–51.

jury trial."[204] To support that contention, the prosecution relied principal-
ly on the cases of the Nazi saboteurs and Yvette Madsen, the U.S. citizen
convicted in Germany by a military commission of murdering her husband.
He pointed out that the Court in *Quirin* found the eight Germans charged
with an offense "against the law of war which the Constitution does not
require to be tried by jury,"[205] but that Tiede and Ruske were not charged
with violations of the laws of war, nor were they enemy aliens or associated with the armed forces of an enemy. As for the Madsen case, Judge
Stern noted that the question of her right to a jury trial was never presented nor considered, she never claimed the right to a jury trial, and had in
fact insisted that she be tried by a general court-martial under the Articles
of War, which did not provide for trial by jury.[206] Moreover, when Yvette
Madsen was tried, the United States and Germany were technically still at
war.[207]

If the State Department refused Judge Stern's ruling for a jury trial, he
announced that the defendants could not be prosecuted in the United States
Court for Berlin. The underlying message: either prepare for a jury trial or
set them free.[208] The call for a jury trial upset delicate political agreements.
West German authorities, unwilling to touch the case, agreed to pay all the
costs of the United States Court for Berlin. But if a jury trial were held,
German citizens would have to participate, exactly what West Germany did
not want.[209] Also, Russian authorities objected that relying on a jury of West
Berliners would be tantamount to acquitting Tiede and Ruske.[210]

The trial began. Out of 400 potential jurors, 80 were selected to under-
go voir dire screening, yielding 12 jurors and 6 alternates. Over a two-week
period, the jurors saw all the elements of an American trial: opening statements, introduction of evidence, questioning of witnesses, and closing
arguments. They heard the judge's detailed instructions of the law. To them
alone was left the issue of whether Tiede's justification for escape to the
West outweighed the crime of hijacking. Beyond the facts, they had to
make ethical and moral judgments. After two days of deliberation, they
reached verdicts on four counts: not guilty of hijacking, guilty of taking a
hostage, not guilty of depriving persons of liberty, and not guilty of doing

---

204. Id. at 253.
205. Id.
206. Id. at 255.
207. Id. at 256.
208. Stern, Judgment in Berlin, at 129–30.
209. Id. at 169.
210. Id. at 194.

bodily injury to the flight attendant on the Polish aircraft. The penalty for taking a hostage was a maximum of 15 years and a mandatory minimum of 3. Taking into account the nine months Tiede had already been confined and his eligibility for parole, he would serve time for seven more months: from May 26, 1979, to January 1, 1980.[211]

A Final Confrontation

One day before Judge Stern was scheduled to take care of Tiede's sentencing, he received a letter from the American ambassador to West Germany. The letter bluntly informed him that his appointment as a judge of the United States Court for Berlin did not extend to a civil suit recently filed with the Court.[212] Once again, Stern bridled at the State Department telling him what he could and could not do. He thought of the German judges who, 40 years before, had followed the orders of the Nazi regime.[213] A lawyer from the Justice Department flew in from Washington, D.C., to tell Stern, in the courtroom, that he was not sitting as an Article III judge, and that he was being directed—appropriately—by the State Department to rule in a certain manner to satisfy foreign policy considerations.[214] From the bench, Stern told the lawyer that he refused to play the role of a judge who was subordinate to political authorities.[215]

     By the time Stern was ready to sentence Tiede, he learned that the prosecutors had passed special legislation and taken other steps to assure that Stern would have no control over the outcome. They first tried to arrange a deal that would impose a minimum sentence if Tiede agreed to forgo a jury trial, which is the procedure that Stern had insisted was a constitutional right, in the face of opposition from the State Department. When that tactic failed, the prosecutors entered into private negotiations, all designed to take from Stern any effective power or authority.[216] In view of the government's actions of bad faith, Stern had no confidence that he could sentence Tiede and entrust him to the custody of the government. Consequently, he sentenced Tiede to time served and announced that he was a free man and could leave the courtroom.[217]

---

211. Id. at 350–51.
212. Id. at 353.
213. Id. at 357.
214. Id. at 360–61.
215. Id. at 362.
216. Id. at 197–204, 344–47, 363–64, 369.
217. Id. at 370.

As for the pending civil case, a lawyer from the Justice Department advised Stern that he could either dismiss the case, without indicating his reasons, or resign. Stern shot back: "Don't come into my court and tell me what to do. And don't come into my court and tell me to resign if I don't like it."[218] On that note he adjourned the court. On the following morning he received a letter from the U.S. ambassador informing him that, with the conclusion of the Tiede case, his appointment as a judge of the United States Court for Berlin was terminated.[219] Judge Stern was sent packing, but not before completing his seminar on judicial independence and sounding the alarm against power concentrated in the executive branch.

The record from martial law in Hawaii to the trials of the Japanese generals shows a federal judiciary largely reluctant to challenge military and executive officials in the midst of war or immediately after. Later examples in this chapter reveal a judiciary willing to place checks on the executive branch when there is no issue of the laws of war, in order to protect the constitutional rights of individuals, both U.S. citizens and aliens. This slow recovery of judicial independence would be severely tested by the terrorist attacks of September 11, 2001, and the aggressive steps taken by the Bush administration to find and detain those who offered assistance to those attacks or who planned future acts of terrorism.

218. Id. at 372.
219. Id. at 374.

7

9/11: A NATION AT WAR

After the September 11 attacks on New York City and the Pentagon, President Bush authorized military tribunals to try noncitizens who provided assistance to the terrorists. His military order closely follows the language in Roosevelt's proclamation and military order of 1942. In response to criticism from a number of quarters, the Defense Department released detailed procedures for the tribunals and continued to make adjustments in the face of new challenges. Although several individuals were arrested for complicity with the 9/11 attacks, they were either tried in civil court or held incommunicado as "enemy combatants." Not until August 2004 were detainees at Guantánamo brought before a tribunal.

Bush's Military Order

In many respects, the Bush order of November 13, 2001, tracked the Roosevelt proclamation and military order of 1942. However, the Bush administration did not take account of the fight between Secretary Stimson and Attorney General Biddle that led to an entirely different military proceeding in 1945 after two more German spies arrived by submarine. Michael Chertoff, head of the Justice Department criminal division, pointed to another key difference. Roosevelt in 1942 addressed "a specific identifiable set of defendants," whereas the Bush order "defines a class of defendants" for future and past crimes.[1]

For Bush's military tribunal, conviction and sentencing would require the vote of only two-thirds of the members of the tribunal, the same fraction used in Roosevelt's order. Bush's tribunal could admit evidence that would have "probative value to a reasonable person," a reworded version of Roosevelt's "probative value to a reasonable man." Bush directed the Secretary of Defense to develop orders and regulations for the conduct of the proceedings and other matters.

---

1. Frank J. Murray, "Justice to Use FDR Precedent for Military Tribunals," Washington Times, December 5, 2001, at A11.

Roosevelt had cautioned his military tribunal to conduct a "full and fair trial." Bush used the same language. Also, Bush adopted Roosevelt's prohibition against judicial review. A defendant "shall not be privileged to seek any remedy or maintain any proceeding, directly or indirectly, or to have any such remedy or proceeding sought on the individual's behalf in (i) any court of the United States, or any State thereof, (ii) any court of any foreign nation, or (iii) any international tribunal."[2] Roosevelt's order denied access to civil courts, except under such regulations as the Attorney General, with the approval of the Secretary of War, prescribed. That exception did not appear in the Bush order.

The Bush order directed that the trial record, including any conviction or sentence, be submitted for review and final decision "by me or by the Secretary of Defense if so designated by me for that purpose." Roosevelt's order of 1942 directed that the trial record, including any judgment or sentence, be transmitted directly to him for final action. The Bush order did not follow the Roosevelt order of 1945, which processed the review first through the office of the Judge Advocate General, although nothing prevented the administration from adopting that procedure.

There are marked differences between the Bush order and the Roosevelt precedents. The latter applied to eight saboteurs in 1942 and two in 1945. Bush's order covers a much larger population: any individual "not a United States citizen" who the President determines that there is "reason to believe" (i) "is or was a member of the organization known as al Qaida," (ii) "has engaged in, aided or abetted, or conspired to commit, acts of international terrorism, or acts in preparation therefor, that have caused, threaten to cause, or have as their aim to cause, injury to or adverse effects on the United States, its citizens, national security, foreign policy, or economy," or (iii) has "knowingly harbored one or more individuals described in subparagraph (i) and (ii)."

By restricting the order to non–U.S. citizens, Bush seemed to respect the *Milligan* principle that U.S. citizens are entitled to be tried in civilian courts when they are open and operating. Yet his group of noncitizens and resident aliens represents a population of an estimated 18 million people. FDR looked backward at a handful of known saboteurs who had confessed. Bush looked forward to a vast population of unknowns, not yet apprehended or charged, from which a subset might be selected for trial by military tribunal. The portion of non–U.S. citizens at risk depends on presidential "determinations" and the definition of such general terms and

2. 66 Fed. Reg. 57835–36, sec. 7 (2001).

phrases as "international terrorism," "have as their aim," and "knowingly harbor." "Aiding or abetting" could involve innocently contributing money to a group that seemed to be a legitimate charitable or humanitarian organization, but one that the U.S. government later claims is a front that provides assistance to al Qaeda or other terrorist bodies.

The Advocates

Vice President Dick Cheney supported Bush's military order by arguing that terrorists, because they are not lawful combatants, "don't deserve to be treated as a prisoner of war." He spoke favorably of the treatment of the German saboteurs in 1942, who had been "executed in relatively rapid order."[3] The concept of a military tribunal had been promoted by William P. Barr, Attorney General in the first Bush administration. His previous position with the Justice Department, as head of the Office of Legal Counsel (OLC), put him in the same space occupied by the 1942 military tribunal. He said that the idea of a tribunal had come to him as one way to try the men charged with blowing up the Pan Am jetliner over Lockerbie, Scotland.[4] Barr regarded the Nazi saboteur case as the "most apt precedent."[5]

Although the administration lined up behind the proposal, one official told a reporter that it was "unlikely" that the tribunals would operate on U.S. territory.[6] That position seemed underscored when Attorney General John Ashcroft justified military tribunals in this manner: "Foreign terrorists who commit war crimes against the United States, in my judgment, are not entitled to and do not deserve the protection of the American Constitution, particularly when there could be very serious and important reasons related to not bringing them back to the United States for justice."[7] To Ashcroft, the issue was clear: constitutional rights are not available to foreign terrorists. The key legal issue, of course, is demonstrating that someone actually *is* a foreign terrorist. Reaching that judgment requires fact-finding and procedural protections, customarily done by an independent court capable

3. Elizabeth Bumiller and Steven Lee Myers, "Senior Administration Officials Defend Military Tribunals for Terrorist Suspects," New York Times, November 15, 2001, at B6.
4. Id.
5. William P. Barr and Andrew G. McBride, "Military Justice for al Qaeda," Washington Post, November 18, 2001, at B7.
6. William Glaberson, "Closer Look at New Plan for Trying Terrorists," New York Times, November 15, 2001, at B6.
7. Robin Toner and Neil A. Lewis, "White House Push on Security Steps Bypasses Congress," New York Times, November 15, 2001, at A1.

of distinguishing between the guilty and the innocent and able to dismiss executive branch assertions that have no basis in fact.

Douglas Kmiec, another former OLC head, defended military tribunals by noting that neither the hearsay rule nor "ill-fitting" exclusionary rules would "derail the admission of evidence obtained under the interrogation authorized by the president." Curiously, he claimed that tribunals "are not primarily for the purposes of punishment."[8] In the past, tribunals have been used as an expeditious way to determine guilt and mete out sentences, including the death penalty.

Among those concerned that a military tribunal might jeopardize individual rights, many acquiesced to presidential power because they feared the kind of televised trial that resulted in the acquittal of O. J. Simpson in civilian court. For example, Stewart A. Baker, a Washington attorney and former general counsel to the National Security Agency, remarked: "I don't think anyone wants to see Osama bin Laden brought before a court here to be defended by Johnnie Cochran."[9]

Ruth Wedgwood, former federal prosecutor and professor of international law, spoke in favor of tribunals by picturing U.S. Marines having "to burrow down an Afghan cave to smoke out the leadership of al Qaeda." It would be "ludicrous," she said, "to ask that they pause in the dark to pull an Afghan-language Miranda card from their bag. This is war, not a criminal case."[10] Dispensing with Miranda warnings makes sense when apprehending suspects abroad, but it does not settle the merits of choosing between military tribunals and civilian courts. She regarded military courts as "the traditional venue for enforcing violations of the law of war" and described the logistics of trying combatants in a civilian court, with "carloads of federal marshals, rotated every two weeks, to protect each juror for the rest of his life." However, military tribunals also function with publicly known prosecutors and tribunal members. Would they need lifetime protection? Civilian trials, she warned, posed "severe limitations on what evidence can be heard by a jury." Hearsay statements, admissible in military tribunals, "cannot be considered in a trial by jury."[11] That point high-

8. Douglas W. Kmiec, "Military Tribunals Are Necessary in Times of War," Wall Street Journal, November 15, 2001, at 26.

9. Steven Lee Myers and Neil A. Lewis, "Assurances Offered About Military Courts," New York Times, November 16, 2001, at B10.

10. Ruth Wedgwood, "The Case for Military Tribunals," Wall Street Journal, December 3, 2001, at A18.

11. Id.

lights a distinguishing quality of tribunals: they allow the introduction of evidence that would be excluded in civilian court. That difference creates a permanent shadow over the fairness of the proceeding and the justice of a conviction.

The Critics

Opposition to the Bush military order centered on its scope, the absence of procedural safeguards, and the concentration of power within the executive branch. Kevin Ernst, a Detroit lawyer representing an individual arrested for fraudulent immigration documents and jailed for 25 days before being released, said he had "no idea they were going to try to use it for domestically detained people. It scares the hell out of me, I'll tell you that."[12]

Senator Patrick Leahy (D-Vt.), chairman of the Judiciary Committee, said that he and other lawmakers had learned about the tribunal by reading the newspapers: "We're really not being consulted at all, and it's hard to understand why."[13] Leahy is generally regarded as a liberal Democrat, but the same comment came from a conservative Republican, Rep. Bob Barr of Georgia. A member of the House Judiciary Committee, he remarked that he was "not aware that they're consulting at all."[14] Plans to detain and try suspects by military tribunal, Barr said, represented "fundamental changes to federal law and procedure."[15] Senator Ted Kennedy, a member of the Armed Services Committee, said he had received "absolutely no indication" of tribunals being authorized.[16]

Leahy expressed concern that other nations would use military tribunals against American citizens, sending "a message to the world that it is acceptable to hold secret trials and summary executions without the possibility of judicial review, at least when the defendant is a foreign national."[17] An editorial in the *Washington Post* cautioned that when Americans are accused

12. Bumiller and Myers, "Senior Administration Officials Defend Military Tribunals for Terrorist Suspects," New York Times, November 15, 2001, at B6.

13. Toner and Lewis, "White House Push on Security Steps Bypasses Congress," New York Times, November 15, 2001, at A1.

14. Id. at B7.

15. "Use of Military Tribunals Draws Objections on Hill," Washington Post, November 17, 2001, at A5.

16. "Department of Justice Oversight: Preserving Our Freedoms While Defending Against Terrorism," hearings before the Senate Committee on the Judiciary, 107th Cong., 1st Sess. 21 (2001).

17. Toner and Lewis, "White House Push on Security Steps Bypasses Congress," New York Times, November 15, 2001, at B7.

of terrorism in "secret courts by hooded judges in Peru or other nations, the U.S. government rightly objects."[18]

The U.S. State Department regularly protests to the use of military tribunals abroad to try civilians. Its annual Country Reports on Human Rights Practices evaluates foreign countries on their record of guaranteeing the right to a "fair public trial." The State Department criticizes the use of secret military trials in such countries as Burma, China, Columbia, Egypt, Kyrgyzstan, Malaysia, Nigeria, Peru, Russia, Sudan, and Turkey. For example, the State Department objects to military tribunals in Egypt because the judges are military officers appointed by the Ministry of Defense, verdicts may not be appealed, and they are subject to review only by a panel of other military judges and then confirmed by the President.[19] That comes close to the procedures adopted by U.S. military tribunals.

A conservative Republican, William Safire of the *New York Times,* wrote a series of op-ed pieces excoriating the military tribunal. He charged that Bush, "misadvised by a frustrated and panic-stricken attorney general," had seized "what amounts to dictatorial power to jail or execute aliens." A tribunal could operate by citing national security arguments to conceal evidence, "make up its own rules, find a defendant guilty even if a third of the officers disagree, and execute the alien with no review by a civilian court." Neither an independent jury nor a federal court would stand between the government and the accused.[20]

Career attorneys in the Judge Advocate General offices were offended when they first learned of the Bush military order by reading news reports.[21] A number of military lawyers objected to White House arguments that treated military tribunals as a wartime version of courts-martial. White House Counsel Alberto Gonzales championed tribunals by calling the American military justice system "the finest in the world, with longstanding traditions of forbidding command influence on proceedings."[22] To Gonzales, military tribunals and courts-martial seemed one and the same, but the history of tribunals is *not* one of forbidding command influence. Ronald W. Meister,

18. "End-Running the Bill of Rights," Washington Post, November 16, 2001, at A46.

19. Human Rights Watch Briefing Paper on U.S. Military Commissions, June 2003; http://www.hrw.org/press/2001/11/tribunals1128.htm.

20. William Safire, "Seizing Dictatorial Power," New York Times, November 15, 2001, at A31. See also his "Kangaroo Courts," New York Times, November 26, 2001, at A19.

21. Jeanne Cummings, "Gonzales Rewrites Laws of War," Wall Street Journal, November 26, 2002, at A4.

22. Alberto R. Gonzales, "Martial Justice, Full and Fair," New York Times, November 30, 2001, at A25.

a former Navy lawyer and judge, underscored the profound differences between military tribunals and courts-martial.[23] John S. Cooke, a retired Army judge, objected that military courts were tainted by being associated with tribunals.[24]

Congressional Hearings

Senator Arlen Specter (R-Pa.) called for hearings to explore why the White House bypassed Congress and unilaterally expanded executive power.[25] He believed that the matter should be considered by lawmakers because the Constitution grants to Congress "the authority to establish military courts and tribunals dealing with international law." Under the Constitution, "it is Congress that has the authority to establish the parameters and the proceedings under such courts."[26]

For three days, the Senate Judiciary Committee held hearings on the actions taken by the administration against terrorism. Leahy's opening statement said that the administration, rather than "respect the checks and balances that make up our constitutional framework," chose to "cut out Congress in determining the appropriate tribunal and procedures to try terrorists." He warned that the military tribunal authorized by Bush could become "a template for use by foreign governments against Americans overseas."[27] Several expert witnesses appeared to testify both for and against the military tribunal.[28] The committee also heard from Attorney General Ashcroft. His prepared statement made it clear that those who voiced their opposition to the administration gave aid and comfort to the terrorists:

> We need honest, reasoned debate, and not fear-mongering. To those who pit Americans against immigrants and citizens against non-citi-

---

23. William Glaberson, "Tribunal v. Court-Martial: Matter of Perception," New York Times, December 2, 2001, at B6.

24. Id.

25. Myers and Lewis, "Assurances Offered About Military Courts," New York Times, November 16, 2001, at B10.

26. 147 Cong. Rec. S11888 (daily ed. November 15, 2001).

27. "Department of Justice Oversight," hearings before the Senate Judiciary Committee, at 2.

28. Id. at 74–119, 135–97. See also Neil A. Lewis, "Justice Dept. and Senate Clash over Bush Actions," New York Times, November 29, 2001, at B7, and George Lardner Jr., "Democrats Blast Order on Tribunals," Washington Post, November 29, 2001, at A22.

zens, to those who scare peace-loving people with phantoms of lost liberty, my message is this: Your tactics only aid terrorists, for they erode our national unity and diminish our resolve. They give ammunition to America's enemies, and pause to America's friends. They encourage people of good will to remain silent in the face of evil.[29]

This broadside raised many questions. Who decides what is "honest" and "reasoned"? The administration? How much does the quest for "national unity" discourage individual dissent and subordinate Congress as a coequal branch? The executive branch can claim no monopoly on understanding, wisdom, or judgment. A day after the hearing, a spokesman for the Justice Department explained that Ashcroft did not intend to discourage public debate. What he found unhelpful to the country were "misstatements and the spread of misinformation about the actions of the Justice Department."[30] Yet the administration itself—as with any administration—contributed its share of "misstatements."

At the hearings, Ashcroft claimed that the President's authority to establish military tribunals "arises out of his power as Commander-in-Chief. For centuries, Congress has recognized this authority, and the Supreme Court has never held that any Congress may limit it."[31] Ashcroft appeared to claim that tribunals are created under the exclusive authority of the President and that, according to judicial precedents, Congress may not limit that authority. The legal and historical record of military tribunals presents quite a different picture. Congress has not recognized a unilateral presidential authority to create these tribunals, and the Supreme Court has repeatedly held that Congress has the constitutional authority to create tribunals, decide their authorities and jurisdiction, and limit the President if he acts unilaterally by military order or proclamation to establish these tribunals.[32] In the

29. "Department of Justice Oversight," hearings before the Senate Judiciary Committee, at 313.

30. Dan Eggen, "Ashcroft Aide Says Criticism Wasn't Aimed at Policy Foes," Washington Post, December 8, 2001, at A11.

31. "Department of Justice Oversight," hearings before the Senate Judiciary Committee, at 314.

32. For example, 1 Ops. Att'y Gen. 233 (1818); 11 Ops. Att'y Gen. 297 (1865); William Winthrop, Military Law and Precedents 831 (2000 ed.); Ex parte Milligan, 71 U.S. 2, 121–22 (1866); Coleman v. Tennessee, 97 U.S. 509, 514 (1878); Ex parte Quirin, 317 U.S. 1, 28–29 (1942); In re Yamashita, 327 U.S. 1, 10–11, 16, 23 (1946); Duncan v. Kahanamoku, 327 U.S. 304 (1946); Madsen v. Kinsella, 343 U.S. 341, 348–49 (1952). In the latter case, the Court noted that in the "absence of attempts by Congress to limit the President's power, it appears that, as Commander-in-Chief of the Army and Navy of the

face of this record, would it make any sense to say that Ashcroft's "misstatements and the spread of misinformation" give aid to terrorists?

Constitutional scholars urged Congress to step in and pass legislation to give military tribunals statutory support.[33] Several hundred law professors and lawyers wrote to Senator Leahy, stating that the Bush military order "undermines the tradition of the Separation of Powers" and that Article I provides that "the Congress, not the President, has the power to 'define and punish . . . Offenses against the Law of Nations.'"[34] Ruth Wedgwood, while strongly supporting the Bush order, agreed that congressional input "will be useful to the administration in crafting rules of procedure and evidence."[35] After the hearing by Senate Judiciary, several lawmakers considered the need for legislation to codify into law the procedures for tribunals.[36] Law professors proposed specific ideas to be incorporated in a statute.[37] Newspaper editorials encouraged the administration to work jointly with Congress in fashioning rules for the tribunals.[38]

Lawmakers introduced bills to authorize the President to convene military tribunals for trying suspects (other than U.S. citizens and lawful resident aliens) outside the United States. These bills would have preserved the right to petition for habeas corpus.[39] Senator Leahy introduced legislation to authorize military tribunals for al Qaeda members and for those who aided or abetted al Qaeda terrorist activities against the United States. The bill exempted U.S. citizens from the jurisdiction of the tribunals.[40] Senator Specter offered a bill to set forth certain requirements for trials and

---

United States, he may, in time of war, establish and prescribe the jurisdiction and procedure of military commissions, and of tribunals in the nature of such commissions, in territory occupied by Armed Forces of the United States." The Court added: "The policy of Congress to refrain from legislating in this uncharted area does not imply its lack of power to legislate." 343 U.S. at 348–49.

33. George Lardner Jr., "Legal Scholars Criticize Wording of Bush Order," Washington Post, December 3, 2001, at A10.

34. 147 Cong. Rec. S3277 (daily ed. December 14, 2001).

35. Ruth Wedgwood, "The Case for Military Tribunals," Wall Street Journal, December 3, 2001, at A18.

36. Elisabeth Bumiller and Katherine Q. Seelye, "Bush Defends Wartime Call for Tribunals," New York Times, December 5, 2001, at A1, B7.

37. Walter Dellinger and Christopher H. Schroeder, "The Case for Judicial Review," Washington Post, December 6, 2001, at A39.

38. "John Ashcroft Misses the Point," New York Times, December 7, 2001, at A28.

39. H.R. 3468, 107th Cong., 1st Sess. (December 12, 2001).

40. S. 1941, 107th Cong., 2d Sess. (2002); 148 Cong. Rec. S741 (daily ed. February 13, 2002).

sentencing by military tribunals.[41] Rep. Dennis Kucinich introduced a companion bill to the one introduced by Senator Leahy.[42] However, Congress never acted on these bills or any other form of legislation to give the administration firm legal backing for military tribunals.[43]

International Resistance

Several countries, including allies, reacted negatively to the Bush military order. Spain said it would not extradite eight men it had charged with complicity in the 9/11 attacks unless the United States agreed to try them by civilian court.[44] Other countries in the 15-nation European Union were expected to resist handing prisoners over to the United States unless they received similar assurances. In addition to objections to military tribunals, the countries belonging to the European Union had all renounced the death penalty. Geoffrey Robertson, a British human rights lawyer, said that military officers paid by the U.S. government "are not regarded as independent or impartial," and that European treaties required public, not secret, trials.[45] The European human rights convention, agreed to by 34 nations, prohibits the death penalty and requires public trials, the right to a jury, the right to confront witnesses, and the right to an attorney.[46] All of those safeguards would be violated either by the Bush military tribunal or the administration's handling of "enemy combatants" such as Hamdi and Padilla.

ABA Task Force

A Task Force on Terrorism and the Law, organized by the American Bar Association (ABA), issued a January 4, 2002, report on military commis-

---

41. S. 1937, 107th Cong., 2d Sess. (2002); 148 Cong. Rec. S733 (daily ed. February 13, 2002).

42. H.R. 4035, 107th Cong., 2d Sess. (2002); 148 Cong. Rec. E421 (daily ed. March 21, 2002). See also legislation by Rep. Adam Schiff, 148 Cong. Rec. H4402 (daily ed. July 9, 2002) and H.R. 1290, 108th Cong., 1st Sess. (2003).

43. Adriel Bettelheim, "Lawmakers Still Feeling Their Way on Whether to Intervene in Plan for Military Tribunals," CQ Weekly Report, December 15, 2001, at 2984.

44. Sam Dillon and Donald G. McNeil Jr., "Spain Sets Hurdle for Extraditions," New York Times, November 24, 2001, at A1.

45. Id. at B4.

46. T. R. Reid, "Europeans Reluctant to Send Terror Suspects to U.S.," Washington Post, November 29, 2001, at A23.

sions. It concluded that the Bush military order raised many important issues of constitutional and international policy, creating a "potential reach quite broad" for which there is "no clear, controlling precedent."[47] The Task Force stated that the scope of presidential power "to act alone with respect to military commissions has not been developed in case law." The President's constitutional authority to use military tribunals "is least open to question when the President consults with and has the support of Congress."[48]

Of particular concern to the task force was the order's broad sweep covering all noncitizens. Aliens in the United States consist of two groups: those present lawfully and those without authorization. The first group includes "lawful permanent residents; nonimmigrants (such as diplomats, and temporary visitors for work, study, or pleasure); and certain persons in humanitarian categories." The second category includes "undocumented aliens, that is, persons who entered the United States without authorization or inspection and who have not acquired lawful status; and, status violators, that is, persons who entered the United States with authorization but who overstayed a visa or otherwise violated the terms of admission."[49]

The task force pointed out that aliens not within the United States have "few, if any, constitutional protections," whereas aliens present within the United States "are entitled to due process protections."[50] For that reason, subjecting non–U.S. citizens outside the United States to the jurisdiction of military tribunals "raises the least likelihood of constitutional impediments, and also appears less objectionable on policy grounds. With respect to aliens already in the United States, such jurisdiction raises much more serious questions."[51]

As to the section of the Bush order that appears to deny defendants access to civilian courts, the task force noted that the broad language "does not expressly suspend the writ of habeas corpus, and it is most unlikely that it could."[52] The task force pointed to such cases as *Quirin* and *Yamashita,* in which defendants brought their applications for writ of habeas corpus to the Supreme Court. If the Bush order led to a trial before a military commission, "it can be assumed that the validity of the order and the jurisdic-

47. American Bar Association, Task Force on Terrorism and the Law, Report and Recommendations on Military Commissions, January 4, 2002, at 1.
48. Id. at 15 (Point 6).
49. Id. at 9, n. 21.
50. Id. at 9–10.
51. Id. at 10.
52. Id. at 11.

tion of such commissions will be reviewed in federal courts—at least with respect to any persons or trials within the United States, if the defendant has legal counsel who seeks review notwithstanding the prohibitory language of the President's order."[53]

The task force recommended that military tribunals "should be limited to narrow circumstances in which compelling security interests justify their use." Unless specifically authorized by Congress, the task force concluded that the following persons should not be tried by military tribunals: "persons lawfully present in the United States; persons in the United States suspected or accused of offenses unconnected with the September 11 attacks; and persons not suspected or accused of violations of the law of war."[54] Further, the task force recommended that the procedures adopted for military tribunals should be guided by the appropriate principles of law and rules of procedures and evidence prescribed for courts-martial, and should conform to Article 14 of the International Covenant on Civil and Political Rights. Included within Article 14 are provisions for an independent and impartial tribunal, access to the press and public (except for specific and compelling reasons), and various rights for the defendant, including presumption of innocence, prompt notice of charges, adequate time and facilities to prepare a defense, trial without undue delay, and other procedural safeguards. Moreover, anyone tried by a military tribunal in the United States "should be permitted to seek habeas corpus relief in United States courts."[55]

DOD Regulations

The Defense Department took the ABA study and other recommendations into account in preparing detailed procedures for military tribunals. Those procedures were released on March 21, 2002, as Military Commission Order No. 1. At a news briefing that day, DOD General Counsel William J. Haynes II cited the 1942 decision in *Quirin* for legal support. The Supreme Court, he said, "found that the president's order in that case was constitutional and properly applied."[56] However, the order released by Haynes

53. Id.
54. Id. at 16.
55. Id. at 17.
56. DOD News Briefing on Military Commissions, March 21, 2002, at 14; http://www.defenselink.mil/news/Mar2002/t03212002_t0321sd.html.

looks less like the 1942 tribunal than it does the 1945 tribunal, because it relies much more on legal expertise within the offices of Judge Advocate General.

The March 21 order changed some of the procedures included in the Bush order of November 13, 2001. The responsibility for appointing military tribunals now fell to the Secretary of Defense "or a designee." The tribunals established under this authority "shall have jurisdiction over violations of the laws of war and all other offenses triable by military commission." A tribunal shall consist of at least three but no more than seven members, each of them a commissioned officer of the U.S. armed forces. The presiding officer of the tribunal, who must be a judge advocate of any U.S. armed force, is responsible for admitting or excluding evidence.

The chief prosecutor shall be a judge advocate of any U.S. armed force. The defense counsel shall also be a judge advocate of any U.S. armed force, but the accused may retain the services of a civilian attorney, at no expense to the U.S. government, provided that the attorney is a U.S. citizen and meets certain other criteria detailed in the order. The accused shall be "presumed innocent until proven guilty." In finding a vote of guilty, a tribunal member must be convinced "beyond a reasonable doubt." The accused is not required to testify during the trial, and the tribunal may not draw "adverse inference" from the accused's decision not to testify. If the accused elects to testify, the accused shall be subject to cross-examination.

The accused may obtain witnesses and documents for the accused's defense, "to the extent necessary and reasonably available" as determined by the presiding officer. The accused may be present at every stage of the trial, unless the accused engages in disruptive conduct that justifies exclusion by the presiding officer, or unless a hearing is closed for security purposes. The defense counsel may not be excluded from any portion of the trial proceeding. The accused is entitled to a trial open to the public, although the presiding officer has authority to close proceedings, or portions of proceedings, in accordance with the procedures set forth in the order.

Instead of the two-thirds majority to convict and sentence in the Bush military order, the two-thirds is retained for conviction, but a sentence of death requires "a unanimous, affirmative vote of all of the members." For death penalty cases, seven officers are required. Whereas under the Bush order the trial record would go directly from the tribunal to him or to the Secretary of Defense, the March 21 regulations require a three-member review panel appointed by the Secretary of Defense. At least one member shall have experience as a judge, and civilians may also be commissioned to serve on the review panel. Within 30 days the review panel shall either

(a) forward the case to the Secretary of Defense with a recommendation as to its disposition, or (b) return the case to the appointing authority for further proceedings, provided that a majority of the review panel "has formed a definite and firm conviction that a material error of law occurred."

The Secretary of Defense shall review the trial record and the recommendation of the review panel, either returning the case for further proceedings or forwarding it to the President with a recommendation as to its disposition. The case then goes to the President for review and final decision unless the President designates the Secretary to perform that function. At a March 21 news briefing at the Pentagon, General Counsel Haynes acknowledged that "somebody could be tried and acquitted of that charge, but may not necessarily automatically be released." When questioned about the exclusion of the Supreme Court from the review process, Under Secretary of Defense for Policy Douglas Feith responded: "I don't think you'll find anything that excludes the Supreme—it's not within our power to exclude the Supreme Court from the process. . . . as far as whether the Supreme Court gets involved in the process, that's beyond our authority to say." Haynes added: "Far be it from me to tell the Supreme Court not to do something."[57]

List of Crimes

On February 28, 2003, the Defense Department released draft instructions on "Crimes and Elements for Trials by Military Commission." The draft listed 24 categories of crimes, including attacks on civilians, property, pillaging, taking hostages, employing poison or "analogous weapons," mutilation or maiming, degrading treatment of a dead body, and hijacking or hazarding a vessel or aircraft. Some of the listed crimes were parallel to the Articles of War, such as aiding the enemy and spying. Although the tribunals were created to deal with Taliban and al Qaeda members, Defense Secretary Rumsfeld said that the rules could apply to Iraqi suspects held in custody by the U.S. military if the United States went to war against Iraq.[58] The language "poison or analogous weapons" may have been intended as a warning signal to Iraqi military and civilian leaders.[59]

---

57. Id. at 18.

58. "The Pentagon Releases a Proposed List of War Crimes to Be Judged by Tribunals," New York Times, March 1, 2003, at A11.

59. Susan Schmidt, "U.S. Lists Crimes Subject to Tribunals," Washington Post, March 1, 2003, at A12.

Some crimes, associated with past international tribunals, were omitted, such as genocide and crimes against humanity. Another potential crime that was excluded: mere membership in an organization (such as al Qaeda). Membership in the Nazi Party was a category used at the Nuremberg tribunals.[60] Pentagon briefers explained that the omission of genocide and crimes against humanity did not mean that those offenses were not triable in another type of tribunal or court. Those categories were excluded because they did not seem "appropriately within the jurisdiction of a military commission."[61]

Several organizations responded to the draft instructions. One critique, prepared by the National Association of Criminal Defense Lawyers (NACDL), focused on the fundamental right of Congress, not the President, to decide what constitutes a crime: "The bottom line is that the President does not have the authority to unilaterally 'legislate' crimes and their elements."[62] The authority to define crimes and its elements "is a quintessential *legislative* function."[63] The NACDL cited this language from the Supreme Court's decision in *Talbot v. Seeman* (1801):

> The whole powers of war being, by the constitution of the United States, vested in congress, the acts of that body can alone be resorted to as our guides in this enquiry. It is not denied, nor in the course of the argument has it been denied, that congress may authorize general hostilities, in which case the general laws of war apply to our situation; or partial hostilities, in which case the laws of war, so far as they actually apply to our situation, must be noticed.[64]

The NACDL pointed out that the draft instruction made no mention of the Uniform Code of Military Justice (UCMJ), which Congress enacted in 1950 when it incorporated earlier Articles of War. The reason for the omission, the association suggested, was the limitation that Article 36 of the UCMJ placed on the President's authority to prescribe rules:

> (a) Pretrial, trial, and post-trial procedures, including modes of proof, for cases arising under this chapter triable in courts-martial, military

60. U.S. Department of Defense News Transcript, "Release of the Military Commission Draft Crimes and Elements Instruction," February 28, 2003, at 3.
61. Id. at 7.
62. National Institute of Military Justice, Military Commission Instructions: Sourcebook 30 (2003).
63. Id. at 32 (emphasis in original).
64. Id. at 33.

commissions and other military tribunals, and procedures for courts of inquiry, may be prescribed by the President by regulations which shall, so far as he considers practicable, apply the principles of law and the rules of evidence generally recognized in the trial of criminal cases in the United States district courts, but which may not be contrary to or inconsistent with this chapter.

(b) All rules and regulations made under this article shall be uniform insofar as practicable.[65]

From Justice Jackson's concurrence in the Steel Seizure Case of 1952, the association borrowed his warning that "emergency powers are consistent with free government only when their control is lodged elsewhere than in the Executive who exercises them."[66] To demonstrate that Congress had already spoken on what constitutes a war crime, the association pointed to a number of congressional statutes that defined various crimes, including acts of terrorism and war crimes.[67]

Turning to another problem, the NACDL cited language in the draft instruction: "This document does not preclude trial for crimes that occurred prior to its effective date." To the association, this language "clearly raises the *specter* of *ex post facto* proceedings." Especially was that so because of other language in the draft instruction: "The absence of a particular offense from the corpus of those enumerated therein does not preclude trial for that offense."[68] Not only would defense counsel have to prepare for the 24 listed crimes, but also for those unlisted. The association quoted this language from the Supreme Court's ruling in the Yamashita case: "We do not make the laws of war but we respect them so far as they do not conflict with the commands of Congress or the Constitution."[69]

The Defense Department responded to comments from a variety of organizations and released final instructions on "Crimes and Elements for Trials by Military Commissions" on April 30, 2003. With regard to the concern about ex post facto proceedings, the department added this sentence: "No offense is cognizable in a trial by military commission if that offense did not exist prior to the conduct in question."[70] It also stated: "Because

---

65. Id.
66. Id. (citing Youngstown Co. v. Sawyer, 343 U.S. 579, 652 (1952)).
67. Id. at 35.
68. Id. at 36.
69. Id. (citing In re Yamashita, 327 U.S. 1, 16 (1946)).
70. Id. at 73 (Department of Defense, Military Commission Instruction No. 2, April 30, 2003, § 3(A)).

this document is declarative of existing law, it does not preclude trial for crimes that occurred prior to its effective date."[71] The department continued to assert its right to define crimes and their elements.

Also on April 30, 2003, the department released a series of other Military Commission Instructions: No. 3, "Responsibilities of the Chief Prosecutor, Prosecutors, and Assistant Prosecutors"; No. 4, "Responsibilities of the Chief Defense Counsel, Detailed Defense Counsel, and Civilian Defense Counsel"; No. 5, "Qualifications of Civilian Defense Counsel"; No. 6, "Reporting Relationships for Military Commission Personnel"; No. 7, "Sentencing"; and No. 8, "Administrative Procedures."[72] On December 30, 2003, the department released Instruction No. 9 to establish procedures for military tribunal review panels. The panels serve as the court of appeals for the tribunal process.

The Appeals Process

At the end of 2003, the Pentagon announced the appointment of four civilian lawyers to serve on a review panel to hear appeals of decisions made by military tribunals. The individuals included Griffin B. Bell, Attorney General during the Carter administration; former Transportation Secretary William T. Coleman Jr.; Frank J. Williams, Chief Justice of the Rhode Island Supreme Court; and Edward G. Biester Jr., a former Pennsylvania attorney general, former member of Congress, and currently a judge in the Court of Common Pleas in Bucks County, Pennsylvania. Several other individuals were expected to be named to the panel. Three members drawn from the panel would hear appeals of tribunal cases. The members of the review panel would be commissioned as major generals in the Army for the duration of their two-year terms.[73]

The purpose of commissioning the members of the review panel was to underscore that the tribunal process would remain solely within the military. Eugene R. Fidell, a Washington lawyer specializing in military law, regarded it as "odd" to give the rank of general to prominent civilian lawyers: "The fact that they're drafting civilians and camouflaging them as military casts a shadow of doubt over the proposition." David Sheldon, a military lawyer in Washington, regarded the appeals court as "window

---

71. Id.

72. Id. at 107–64.

73. Thomas E. Ricks, "Tribunals' Review Panel Picked," Washington Post, December 31, 2003, at A2.

dressing" over a fundamentally flawed process. He asked: "If the trial itself isn't conducted in accordance with the rules that govern courts-martial, how can the process be fair?"[74]

Pentagon officials explained that if the review panel sent a case back down for further proceedings or decided to dismiss charges, those actions would be binding. However, if the panel concluded that the trial was conducted appropriately and forwarded a recommendation to the Secretary of Defense, its action would be "just a recommendation" and "not necessarily binding on the secretary." At that point, either the secretary or the President "will make a final decision on the case."[75]

Five military lawyers, assigned to defend detainees at Guantánamo Bay, filed an amicus brief to the Supreme Court to assert that prisoners convicted by military tribunal should have the right to appeal to civilian courts, not to the appeals panel established by the Pentagon. Although it was highly unusual for military lawyers to publicly challenge the procedures adopted for military trials, they decided that it was necessary to meet their obligations as defense attorney. They acted in the spirit of Col. Royall in the Nazi saboteur case. The brief argued that the denial of appeals to civilian courts gives the President "monarchical" powers.[76]

One of these military attorneys, Maj. Michael Mori, charged that the commission process "has been created and controlled by those with a vested interest only in convictions." He feared that the model created by the United States would be used by other nations against American civilians: "What's to stop the North Koreans from arresting a [U.S.] contractor as a spy and trying him under the very rules we set up? We wouldn't tolerate it."[77] At a London news conference, Mori said that the "system is not set up to provide even the appearance of a fair trial."[78]

Lt. Cmdr. Charles Swift, one of the five military lawyers who signed the amicus brief, filed a petition in federal court saying that the tribunals are

---

74. Id.

75. U.S. Department of Defense News Transcript, "Announcements of Key Personnel for Military Commissions; Issuance of Military Commission Instruction No. 9 on Military Commissions Review Panel," December 30, 2003, at 3.

76. John Mintz, "Military Lawyers Question Tribunal Rules," Washington Post, January 13, 2004, at A7. See also Vanessa Blum, "Military Lawyers Urge Role for High Court," Legal Times, January 19, 2004, at 1, and Neil A. Lewis, "Lawyer Says Detainees Face Unfair System," New York Times, January 22, 2004, at A21.

77. John Mintz, "Lawyer Criticizes Rules for Tribunals," Washington Post, January 22, 2004, at A3.

78. Neil A. Lewis, "Military Defenders For Detainees Put Tribunals on Trial," May 4, 2004, at A19.

illegal under U.S. and international law. He argued that the tribunals unconstitutionally target only aliens and not U.S. citizens, and that President Bush lacked statutory authority.[79] Swift's suit asserted that the Constitution guarantees civilian court review over any proceeding in the military court system.[80]

Recruiting Defense Counsel

Although the Pentagon's response to studies by the ABA and other organizations produced more detailed regulations and greater protections to suspects, the regulations continued to draw criticism. In an op-ed written late in 2003, Philip Allen Lacovara said he had raised his voice "in strong support of military commissions" after the Bush order of November 13, 2001. As he watched the Pentagon spell out the procedures for tribunals, he now "reluctantly conclude[d] that the administration's approach to military commissions confirms many of the critics' worst fears." He said that the procedures departed substantially from standards of fair procedure. They "undermine the basic right to effective counsel by imposing significant legal constraints on civilian defense attorneys." Customary attorney-client confidentiality was negated by authorizing the withholding of evidence from defendants and their counsel. Moreover, the rules allowed the Defense Department to restrict the ability of defense counsel to speak publicly about a case, "while Pentagon officials face no such constraint." The government reserved the right to listen to attorney-client communications, while defendants and their counsel "may be denied access to relevant and even exculpatory information if the military concludes that concealment is 'necessary to protect the interests of the United States.'"[81]

In response to a number of objections, the Pentagon on February 5, 2004, announced changes in the rules for tribunals. Defense attorneys would now be notified if the government decided to electronically monitor their conversations with clients. The modification responded to the refusal of a number of defense attorneys to participate in tribunal proceedings. The new regulation provided that only military officials responsible for security, but not government prosecutors, could order the eaves-

---

79. John Mintz, "Yemeni's Attorney Tries to Halt Tribunals," Washington Post, April 8, 2004, at A15.

80. Neil A. Lewis, "Suit Contests Military Trials of Detainees at Cuba Base," New York Times, April 8, 2004, at A19.

81. Philip Allen Lacovara, "Trials and Errors," Washington Post, December 12, 2003, at A23.

dropping. The information obtained would not, according to the procedure, be shared with prosecutors. The new rules also allowed defense attorneys to ask for trial delays for personal or professional reasons, a right denied under the former rules.[82]

The Pentagon had difficulty attracting defense counsels to serve the terrorist suspects. Don Rehkopf, a Rochester lawyer who serves as cochairman of the NACDL's military law committee, said that the military rules were so stacked against the defense that few lawyers would be interested: "It would be unethical for any attorney to agree to the conditions they've set. You have to agree to waive the attorney-client privilege so that the government can monitor your conversations."[83] The Pentagon addressed that problem, at least in part, but defense attorneys used to operating under the procedures of civilian trials would find the tribunal rules objectionable. Neal R. Sonnett, the chairman of the ABA's task force on the treatment of enemy combatants, said that it would be "almost impossible to render effective assistance of counsel" under the rules established for military tribunals.[84]

Lawrence S. Goldman, NACDL president, explained why it was difficult to solicit experienced defense attorneys to assist tribunal defendants. Pentagon rules placed restrictions on information gathering and the privacy of lawyer-client conversations. In view of those restrictions, he said, "with considerable regret, we cannot advise any of our members to act as civilian counsel at Guantánamo. The rules regulating counsel's behavior are just too restrictive to give us any confidence that counsel will be able to act zealously and professionally."[85]

The National Institute of Military Justice discouraged any effort by civilian lawyers to boycott the tribunal proceedings. It would be "unfortunate," it said, if competent civilian defense counsel did not make themselves available to the tribunals. Grant Lattin, a civilian lawyer and retired lieutenant colonel in the Marine Corps, thought that many lawyers with experience in military law would want to participate. Some of the factors making that an uphill struggle were regulations that required defense lawyers

---

82. John Mintz, "Pentagon to Alter Military Tribunal Rules," Washington Post, February 6, 2004, at A11.

83. Katharine Q. Seelye, "Staffing Defense at Guantánamo," New York Times, May 23, 2003, at A16.

84. Adam Liptak, "Tribunals Move from Theory to Reality," New York Times, July 4, 2003, at A11.

85. Neil A. Lewis, "Rules Set Up for Terror Tribunals May Deter Some Defense Lawyers," New York Times, July 13, 2003, at 1.

to pay for their own transportation to and from Guantánamo and for the cost of a security clearance, which can be as much as $2,800.[86] Even with those hurdles, Lattin thought that civilian lawyers had a duty to be involved: "Let's face it—if nobody participates, these people are going to be prosecuted without any input from the civilian defense bar."[87] To remove some of the disincentives, the Pentagon eliminated a requirement that civilian lawyers perform their case work at Guantánamo.[88]

Selecting the Defendants

By April 2003, the Pentagon had reached agreement on the rules and proceedings for military tribunals. It was expected that the trials would take place at the U.S. naval base at Guantánamo Bay. President Bush's fiscal 2003 supplemental budget included funds for the construction of facilities to house military tribunals at the base.[89] The administration placed the highest priority on gathering intelligence from detainees. Only after that objective had been satisfied would some of the detainees be brought before a military tribunal. Since the Bush military order focused on members of al Qaeda or those who engaged in, aided, abetted, or conspired with al Qaeda to injure the United States, people captured in Iraq were not expected to be tried by tribunal.[90]

During the following month, U.S. military officials began drawing up a list of detainees they thought should be tried by tribunal.[91] The Pentagon reviewed the cases of at least ten prisoners held at Guantánamo.[92] The Defense Department selected Air Force Col. Will A. Gunn as the chief defense attorney and Army Col. Frederic L. Borch III as the lead prosecutor. Borch emphasized that tribunal rules had been written to make the proceedings similar to those in regular military courtrooms, but significant differences remained. Gunn conceded: "This is certainly a foreign envi-

---

86. Id. at 14.

87. Vanessa Blum, "Tribunals Put Defense Bar in a Bind," Legal Times, July 14, 2003, at 1, 14.

88. Id. at 14.

89. Vanessa Blum, "DOD Readies Teams For Terror Trials," Legal Times, April 14, 2003, at 1.

90. Neil A. Lewis, "Tribunals Nearly Ready for Afghanistan Prisoners," New York Times, April 8, 2003, at B1.

91. John Mintz, "List Created of Captives to Be Tried by Military Tribunals," Washington Post, May 3, 2003, at A17.

92. John Mintz, "Prosecutor Says Tribunals Will Be Fair Trials," Washington Post, May 23, 2003, at A3.

ronment . . . quite a bit different than the environment that I am accustomed to practicing in."[93]

On June 23, 2003, President Bush designated Ali al-Marri an enemy combatant. He had been held by civilian courts in a federal jail in Illinois, but after his designation he was transferred to a naval brig in South Carolina. Al-Marri had arrived in the United States the day before 9/11, having been trained in computer hacking and the use of poisons, according to information the U.S. government obtained from several al Qaeda operatives. Officials in the Bush administration said he could eventually be brought before a military tribunal.[94] An attorney for al-Marri went to federal court, asking the government to justify its reasons for holding him and designating him an enemy combatant.[95] A district court in Illinois, holding that the proper venue was South Carolina, dismissed the habeas petition.[96] That ruling was affirmed by the Seventh Circuit.[97]

Following al-Marri's designation, Bush named six detainees on July 3, 2003, as eligible for military tribunals.[98] To go from eligibility to actual trial required an additional step. Deputy Defense Secretary Paul Wolfowitz would have to determine that a detainee should be brought before a tribunal.[99] The effect of a designation by President Bush was to establish a grant of jurisdiction over the individual. Whether that person was actually tried would depend on evidence put before Wolfowitz and considered by him.[100] John D. Altenburg Jr., who served in the Army as a major general and as Assistant Judge Advocate General, later replaced Wolfowitz as the appointing authority.

Newspaper stories reported that of the six people considered eligible for military tribunals, two were Britons. The British government reacted by expressing "serious concerns about the military commission process." The

---

93. Id.

94. Susan Schmidt, "Qatari Man Designated An Enemy Combatant," Washington Post, June 24, 2003, at A1; Eric Lichtblau, "Bush Declares Student an Enemy Combatant," New York Times, June 24, 2003, at A15.

95. "Enemy Combatant Designation Challenged in Court," Washington Post, July 10, 2003, at A11.

96. Al-Marri v. Bush, 274 F.Supp.2d 1003 (C.D. Ill. 2003).

97. Al-Marri v. Rumsfeld, 360 F.3d 707 (7th Cir. 2004).

98. Neil A. Lewis, "Six Detainees Soon May Face Military Trials," New York Times, July 4, 2003, at A1.

99. John Mintz, "6 Could Be Facing Military Tribunals," Washington Post, July 4, 2003, at A1.

100. U.S. Department of Defense News Transcript, "Background Briefing on Military Commissions," July 3, 2003, at 1.

two men were identified as Moazzam Begg, 35, from Birmingham, and Feroz Abbasi, 23, from south London. In a separate action, the Australian government announced that one of its nationals, David Hicks, was among the six.[101]

President Bush and Prime Minister Tony Blair met with reporters on July 17 to discuss a number of issues, including the detainees (Britons among them) at Guantánamo. Bush said: "The only thing I know for certain is that these are bad people."[102] His comment provoked this response from a British reporter: "Mr. President, do you realize that many people hearing you say that we know these are 'bad people' in Guantanamo Bay will merely fuel their doubts that the United States regards them as innocent until proven guilty and due a fair, free, and open trial?"[103] Bush and Blair told the reporters that they were about to discuss the dispute over the British detainees and would put out a statement the following day.[104]

On July 18, President Bush announced that he had temporarily halted military proceedings against the two Britons and the Australian. Administration officials explained that the decision was a political favor to British Prime Minister Tony Blair, whose support had plummeted at home. The reversal seemed to show favoritism toward two allies in the wars in Afghanistan and Iraq.[105] British legal officials pressed for other changes for Britons held at Guantánamo, such as allowing British lawyers to be part of the defense team and assigning a British officer to serve on a tribunal created to judge a Briton.[106] Later, U.S. officials agreed to allow British defendants to use British lawyers as consultants.[107]

The Pentagon made other adjustments. U.S. and Australian officials announced that the two Australians held at Guantánamo would not face the death penalty if convicted, and the Pentagon agreed that if the two British suspects held at Guantánamo were convicted, they would not be

---

101. Glenn Frankel and John Mintz, "2 Britons, Australian Among Six Facing Trial," Washington Post, July 5, 2003, at A13. See also Sarah Lyall, "Families of 2 British Terrorism Suspects Oppose Military Trials by the U.S.," New York Times, July 5, 2003, at A7.

102. 39 Weekly Compilation of Presidential Documents 929 (2003).

103. Id. at 930.

104. Id.

105. Mike Allen and Glenn Frankel, "Bush Halts Military Proceedings Against 3," Washington Post, July 19, 2003, at A15. See also Neil A. Lewis, "Bowing to Ally, Bush to Rethink Tribunals for British Subjects," New York Times, July 19, 2003, at A3.

106. "U.S. Pressed on Military Trials," Washington Post, July 22, 2003, at A3.

107. Bradley Graham and Tania Branigan, "Two Britons at Guantanamo Will Not Face the Death Penalty," Washington Post, July 23, 2003, at A18.

subject to the death penalty either.[108] If any were sentenced to be confined, it would be served within his own country and not at Guantánamo. The agreements invited the charge that if suspected al Qaeda operators belonged to a country considered by the United States as a close ally, they would receive concessions not available to other detainees.

Political leverage loomed large again in a story reported on July 4, 2004, in the *New York Times*. According to senior American and British officials, three countries agreed to swap detainees held at Guantánamo and in Saudi Arabia. Five Saudi prisoners were transferred from the naval base to Riyadh, Saudi Arabia, in May 2003. Three months later, the Saudis agreed to release five Britons and two others convicted of terrorist attacks in Saudi Arabia. Some U.S. officials objected to the trade because they wondered whether the returned Saudis would remain imprisoned or subjected to prosecution.[109]

Charging Detainees

The date for the first tribunal slipped from month to month. An article in the *Washington Post* on May 3, 2003, reported that U.S. officials expected that some prosecutions "could move forward in the next few months."[110] On July 4, 2003, a *New York Times* story said that some administration officials expected military tribunals to begin "before the end of the summer."[111] The *Washington Post* on October 31, 2003, included this prediction from Col. Borch: "Our start is imminent, soon."[112] Time passed by without any tribunals.

The first charges against al Qaeda defendants did not come until February 2004. Pentagon officials announced that they were bringing charges against two detainees at Guantánamo: Ali Hamza Ahmed Sulayman al-

108. John Mintz, "Pentagon to Review Rules for Tribunals," Washington Post, November 26, 2003, at A17; Bradley Graham and Tania Branigan, "Two Britons at Guantanamo Will Not Face the Death Penalty," Washington Post, July 23, 2003, at A18.

109. Don Van Natta Jr. and Tim Golden, "Officials Detail a Detainee Deal by 3 Countries," New York Times, July 4, 2004, at 1.

110. John Mintz, "List Created of Captives to Be Tried by Military Tribunals," Washington Post, May 3, 2003, at A17.

111. Neil A. Lewis, "Six Detainees Soon May Face Military Trials," New York Times, July 4, 2003, at A1.

112. John Mintz, "First Trial by Tribunal 'Imminent' Official Says," Washington Post, October 31, 2003, at A10.

Bahlul of Yemen, and Ibrahim Ahmed Mahmoud al-Qosi of Sudan. They were charged with acting in conspiracy with bin Laden to commit both terrorism and war crimes against civilians. The administration described Bahlul as an al Qaeda propagandist who prepared a video that celebrated the bombing of the American destroyer *Cole* in 2000 in the Yemeni port of Aden, and al-Qosi as a senior accountant who served as the deputy to al Qaeda's chief financial officer. For these two men, Col. Borch regarded the death penalty as inappropriate.[113] To give defense attorneys time to prepare, the trial was expected to begin in late spring or early summer.[114] Bahlul and al-Qosi were among the six detainees earlier named as eligible for military tribunals, but their names had been kept secret.

The trial did not begin as expected because of delays in naming the members of the tribunal. Finally, on June 29, 2004, the Pentagon selected the officers to make up the tribunal that would evaluate the charges against Bahlul, al-Qosi, and David Hicks.[115] Earlier in the month, on June 10, the Pentagon announced three criminal charges against the Australian: conspiracy to commit war crimes, attempted murder, and aiding the enemy. His defense counsel, Maj. Michael Mori, said that Hicks had not committed any crime: "There is no statement that David Hicks shot any service member or planted any bombs."[116] Australia understood that if Hicks were convicted and sentenced to a prison term, he would serve that time in an Australian jail.[117] No date was set for the trials of Bahlul, al-Qosi, and Hicks, but a Pentagon spokesman thought the cases could be tried by the end of the year.[118] The trials began in August 2004. By that time, the number of detainees selected to be tried as enemy combatants had increased to fifteen.

113. Neil A. Lewis, "U.S. Charges Two at Guantánamo with Conspiracy," New York Times, February 25, 2004, at A1.

114. John Mintz, "U.S. Charges 2 as Bin Laden Aides," Washington Post, February 25, 2004, at A1, A18.

115. "Pentagon Appoints Officers For First Tribunal; No Date Set," Washington Post, June 30, 2004, at A6.

116. Bradley Graham, "3 Charges Placed Against Detainee," Washington Post, June 11, 2004, at A3.

117. Eric Schmitt and Kate Zernike, "U.S. Charges an Australian with Fighting for Taliban," New York Times, June 11, 2004, at A12.

118. "Pentagon Appoints Officers for First Tribunal; No Date Set," Washington Post, June 30, 2004, at A6.

Treatment of Prisoners

During the military operations in Afghanistan in late 2001, U.S. forces captured several thousand fighters thought to be associated with the Taliban and al Qaeda. Many were eventually transferred to Guantánamo, leading to debates within the administration on what standards of treatment to apply. Were the detainees entitled to protection under the Geneva Conventions? Could interrogation be more harsh to pry out needed intelligence? Executive officials divided on such questions. When the Justice Department participated in oral argument before the Supreme Court in April 2004 on the Hamdi, Padilla, and Guantánamo cases, the Justices sought assurance that the administration had a reliable screening process to separate the guilty from the innocent. Justice lawyers told the Court that torture would never be used. Yet on the evening of the final oral argument, the entire world began to see photos of U.S. soldiers abusing detainees at the Abu Ghraib prison in Iraq. Scrambling for higher ground, the administration released a number of documents to explain the legal analysis that guided the treatment of prisoners. Newspapers released other agency documents that had been leaked to them but withheld from Congress.

Departmental Infighting

In the early months of 2002, disputes broke out within the administration on whether detainees at Guantánamo should be treated humanely and in accordance with treaties and statutes. The Defense Department and probably the CIA wanted substantial latitude when interrogating prisoners, whereas the State Department insisted that the United States was obliged to comply with the four Geneva Conventions, completed in 1949 and agreed to by the United States in 1955. The first Geneva Convention covers armed forces in the field, the second armed forces at sea, the third prisoners of war, and the fourth civilian persons.[119]

On January 25, 2002, White House Counsel Alberto Gonzales summed up departmental conflicts in a memo to President Bush. He advised Bush that the OLC in the Department of Justice had issued a formal legal opinion, concluding that the Third Geneva Convention on the treatment of prisoners of war (GPW) did not apply to the conflict with al Qaeda. In addition, Justice found "reasonable grounds" why the Geneva Convention did

---

119. 6 UST 3114, 3217, 3316, 3516 (1955).

not apply to the Taliban. It was Gonzales's understanding that Bush decided that Geneva did not apply "and, accordingly, that al Qaeda and Taliban detainees are not prisoners of war under the GPW." Gonzales called the OLC interpretation "definitive."[120]

Gonzales advised Bush that Secretary of State Colin Powell asked that the decision on prisoner treatment be reconsidered. Powell thought that GPW did apply to both al Qaeda and the Taliban. His arguments for reconsideration included these factors: (1) the United States had never denied the applicability of the Geneva Conventions to either U.S. or opposing forces engaged in armed conflict; (2) if the administration now decided against compliance with Geneva, the United States could not invoke the GPW if enemy forces threatened to mistreat U.S. or coalition forces captured during operations in Afghanistan; (3) noncompliance with Geneva would invite condemnation from allies; and (4) other countries would be less inclined to turn over terrorists if the United States did not recognize a legal obligation to comply with GPW.[121]

For Gonzales, as spelled out in his memo to Bush, the arguments for reconsideration and reversal were, on balance, "unpersuasive."[122] Terrorist actions in recent years represented a "new type of warfare—one not contemplated in 1949 when the GPW was framed—and requires a new approach in our actions towards captured terrorists."[123] Although the administration would not feel bound by GPW, in the treatment of detainees "the U.S. will continue to be constrained by (i) its commitment to treat the detainees humanely and, to the extent appropriate and consistent with military necessity, in a manner consistent with the principles of GPW, (ii) its applicable treaty obligations, (iii) minimum standards of treatment universally recognized by the nations of the world, and (iv) applicable military regulations regarding the treatment of detainees."[124]

The Gonzales memo seems to support the need for humane treatment of detainees, but several factors weakened this commitment. First, Gonzales said that the United States would continue to be "constrained" by treaty obligations and military regulations. Being constrained is not the same as being legally bound. Second, Gonzales spoke about President Bush's "pol-

---

120. Memorandum from Gonzales to Bush, "Decision re Application of the Geneva Convention on Prisoners of War to the Conflict with Al Qaeda and the Taliban," January 25, 2002, at 1.
121. Id. at 3.
122. Id.
123. Id.
124. Id. at 4.

icy of providing humane treatment to enemy detainees."[125] Policy does not carry the same weight and import as binding legal obligations.

This preference for policy over law appears in a President Bush memo of February 7, 2002. He accepted the legal conclusion of the Justice Department that none of the Geneva provisions should apply to al Qaeda. He also accepted the legal conclusion of the Attorney General and the Justice Department that he had authority under the Constitution "to suspend Geneva as between the United States and Afghanistan, but I decline to exercise that authority at this time. Accordingly, I determine that the provisions of Geneva will apply to our present conflict with the Taliban."[126] The conditional "at this time" indicated that Bush could suspend Geneva protections to the Taliban if he so decided. Moreover, he determined that the Taliban detainees "are unlawful combatants and, therefore, do not qualify as prisoners of war under Article 4 of Geneva."[127] Instead of being legally bound by Geneva, Bush treated U.S. obligations as discretionary and purely of a policy nature:

> Of course, our values as a Nation, values that we share with many nations in the world, call for us to treat detainees humanely, including those who are not legally entitled to such treatment. Our Nation has been and will continue to be a strong supporter of Geneva and its principles. As a matter of policy, the United States Armed Forces shall continue to treat detainees humanely and, to the extent appropriate and consistent with military necessity, in a manner consistent with the principles of Geneva.[128]

Had this presidential policy been posted at prison sites in Guantánamo, Afghanistan, and Iraq, it might have sent a healthy and salutary signal to U.S. soldiers to treat detainees humanely, even with the caveats of "military necessity" and the decision to act "consistent" with the principles of the

125. Id. at 3.

126. "Humane Treatment of al Qaeda and Taliban Detainees," memorandum of February 7, 2002, from President Bush to the Vice President, the Secretary of State, the Secretary of Defense, the Attorney General, Chief of Staff to the President, Director of Central Intelligence, Assistant to the President for National Security Affairs, and Chairman of the Joint Chiefs of Staff, at 1–2.

127. Id. at 2.

128. Id.; Katharine Q. Seelye, "In Shift, Bush Says Geneva Rules Fit Taliban Captives," New York Times, February 8, 2002, at A1; John Mintz and Mike Allen, "Bush Shifts Position on Detainees," Washington Post, February 8, 2002, at A1.

Geneva Convention. However, the Bush memo remained classified until June 17, 2004. The manner of its implementation would therefore depend on how those who received it, and shared it with others, decided to fulfill administration policy. During a press briefing on June 22, 2004, Gonzales told reporters that the language on "military necessity" was intended "to reflect the fact that as a legal matter, Geneva doesn't apply."[129]

A number of legal analyses at the time of the Gonzales and Bush memos suggested that U.S. interrogators could act with considerable freedom. On December 28, 2001, two high-ranking attorneys in the Justice Department sent a memo to William J. Haynes II, General Counsel of the Defense Department. They concluded that the "great weight" of legal authority indicated that a federal district court "could not probably exercise habeas jurisdiction" over an alien detained at Guantánamo.[130] In short, there was little reason to worry about federal court scrutiny if U.S. interrogators failed to treat detainees humanely.

Another Justice Department memo, by two OLC attorneys, offered 42 pages of legal analysis to reach the conclusion that international treaties and federal laws did not apply to al Qaeda and Taliban detainees.[131] It was this OLC analysis that Gonzales, in his memo to Bush, regarded as "definitive." And it was on the basis of this OLC opinion that Attorney General John Ashcroft wrote to Bush on February 1, 2002, outlining various legal options.[132] Ashcroft advised Bush about a variety of techniques that would shield U.S. interrogators from possible criminal prosecution. If Bush determined that Afghanistan was a "failed state" and therefore unable to be a party to the Geneva Conventions, the treaty's protections would not apply and "various legal risks of liability, litigation, and criminal prosecutions are minimized."[133]

129. Press Briefing by White House Counsel Judge Alberto Gonzales, DOD General Counsel William Haynes, DOD Deputy General Counsel Daniel Dell'Orto and Army Deputy Chief of Staff for Intelligence Gen. Keith Alexander, June 22, 2004, at 16; http://www/prnewswire,com/cgi-bin/shores.pl?ACCT=109&STORY=/www/story/06-22-2.

130. Memorandum for William J. Haynes II, General Counsel, Department of Defense, from Patrick F. Philbin, Deputy Assistant Attorney General, and John C. Yoo, Deputy Assistant Attorney General, December 29, 2001, at 1.

131. Memorandum for William J. Haynes II, General Counsel, Department of Defense, from John Yoo, Deputy Assistant Attorney General, and Robert J. Delahunty, Special Counsel, January 9, 2002.

132. For example, Yoo and Delahunty cite the Supreme Court's decision in Clark v. Allen, 331 U.S. 503 (1947), for the proposition that when the President makes a determination about a treaty, it becomes a political question that a court will not decide. Id. at 16, 24. Ashcroft refers to this case in his letter to Bush on February 1, 2002.

133. Letter from Ashcroft to Bush, February 1, 2002, at 1.

Ashcroft pointed to a Supreme Court opinion that when a President *determines* that a treaty does not apply, his determination is "fully discretionary and will not be reviewed by the federal courts." Thus, a Bush determination against treaty applicability "would provide the highest assurance that no court would subsequently entertain charges that American military officers, intelligence officials, or law enforcement officials violated Geneva Convention rules relating to field conduct, detention conduct or interrogation of detainees." Ashcroft advised Bush that the War Crimes Act of 1996 "makes violation of parts of the Geneva Convention a crime in the United States."[134]

If the Bush administration intended to treat prisoners humanely, why the concerted and exhaustive efforts of top administration officials to demonstrate that federal courts would have no jurisdiction to review detention practices? Why the concern of the Attorney General that interrogation officials might face criminal prosecution and his suggestions on how that could be averted? What techniques of interrogation were executive officials considering?

The principal opposition to the White House policy came from Secretary of State Powell and his legal advisers. Powell wrote directly to Gonzales, expressing his concern that the draft memorandum being prepared for Bush "does not squarely present to the President the options that are available to him. Nor does it identify the significant pros and cons of each option."[135] Powell called the draft memo "inaccurate or incomplete in several respects."[136] On February 2, 2002, William H. Taft IV, the legal adviser at the State Department, also wrote to Gonzales, urging that Bush be told that a decision that Geneva does apply "is consistent with the plain language of the Conventions and the unvaried practice of the United States in introducing its forces into conflicts over fifty years."[137]

These departmental battles hit the press almost immediately. The Gonzales memo to Bush on January 25, 2002, wound up in the hands of the *Washington Times* the very same day, in time to make a story the next day.[138] An

---

134. Id. at 1.

135. Memorandum from Powell to Gonzales, "Draft Decision Memorandum for the President on the Applicability of the Geneva Convention to the Conflict in Afghanistan," undated but probably in mid-January 2002, at 1.

136. Id. at 4.

137. Memorandum from Taft to Gonzales, "Comments on Your Paper on the Geneva Conventions," February 2, 2002, at 1.

138. Rowan Scarborough, "Powell wants detainees to be declared POWs," Washington Times, January 1, 2002, at A1.

article in the *New York Times* remarked that the Gonzales memo "leaked with astonishing speed."[139] Much of the coverage in the newspapers focused on the question of whether the detainees at Guantánamo should be classified as POWs. Under Article 17 of the Third Geneva Convention, every POW, when questioned, "is bound to give only his surname, first names and rank, date of birth, and army, regimental, personal or serial number, or failing this, equivalent information."[140] The administration wanted interrogators to go beyond those elementary facts in order to uncover intelligence about past and planned terrorist actions.[141]

Abu Ghraib

In April 2004, three national security cases reached the Supreme Court for oral argument. On April 20, the Court heard the Guantánamo case. Eight days later the Justices heard both the Hamdi and the Padilla cases. During the Hamdi oral argument, Justice Stevens asked Deputy Solicitor General Paul Clement whether he thought there was "anything in the law that curtails the method of interrogation that may be employed." Clement assured him that safeguards existed: "I think that the United States is signatory to conventions that prohibit torture and that sort of thing. And the United States is going to honor its treaty obligations."[142] To Clement, drawing on the judgment of those involved in interrogations, "the last thing you want to do is torture somebody or try to do something along those lines."[143] He explained that using coercion to get information leaves one wondering "about the reliability of the information you were getting," and that the experience of interrogators is that the way to "get the best information from individuals is that you interrogate them, you try to develop a relationship of trust."[144]

---

139. David E. Sanger, "Prisoners Straddle an Ideological Chasm," New York Times, January 27, 2002, at 14. See also Katharine Q. Seelye, "Powell Asks Bush to Review Stand on War Captives," New York Times, January 27, 2002, at 1.

140. 6 UST 3330.

141. John Mintz, "On Detainees, U.S. Faces Legal Quandary," Washington Post, January 27, 2002, at A22; John Mintz, "Debate Continues on Legal Status of Detainees," Washington Post, January 28, 2002, at A15; Katharine Q. Seelye, "Detainees Are Not P.O.W.'s, Cheney and Rumsfeld Declare," New York Times, January 28, 2002, at A6; Katherine Q. Seelye and David E. Sanger, "Bush Reconsiders Stand on Treating Captives of War," New York Times, January 29, 2002, at A1; Katherine Q. Seelye, "A P.O.W. Tangle: What the Law Says," New York Times, January 29, 2002, at A14.

142. U.S. Supreme Court, Yaser Esam Hamdi v. Rumsfeld, oral argument, April 28, 2004, at 48–49.

143. Id. at 50.

144. Id.

The issue of torture also came up in the Padilla oral argument. Clement argued that the President should be free to use "traditional authority to make discretionary judgments" in deciding what is the necessary appropriate force for military actions, as in Afghanistan. He counseled against "judicial management of the executive's war-making power."[145] One of the Justices said that "if the law is what the executive says it is, whatever is necessary and appropriate in the executive's judgment," the result would be an "executive, unchecked by the judiciary." In that case, "what is it that would be a check against torture?" Clement replied: "Well, first of all, there are treaty obligations." Moreover, if a U.S. military person committed a war crime "by creating some atrocity on a harmless, you know, detained enemy combatant or a prisoner of war," the government would put the soldier or officer on trial in a court-martial.[146]

Here is Clement at oral argument describing treaty obligations as binding, whereas his colleagues in the Justice Department had been arguing (quite likely without his knowledge) that it would be appropriate to comply with Geneva Conventions on a voluntary basis, for policy reasons, but not feel legally compelled. Also, he anticipated that soldiers who committed torture on detainees would face disciplinary procedures. The Justice Department attorneys, including the Attorney General, appeared confident that punishment was unlikely.

The Justices expressed other concerns to Clement. One asked what would happen if the President or executive officials said that mild torture would be helpful in extracting information. What would constrain such conduct? "Is it just up to the good will of the executive? Is there a judicial check?" Clement held his ground. The fact that executive discretion during war "can be abused is not a good and sufficient reason for judicial micromanagement and overseeing of that authority." In time of war "you have to trust the executive to make the kind of quintessential military judgments that are involved in things like that."[147]

The Hamdi and Padilla oral arguments began at 10:19 AM on April 28 and ended at 12:20 PM. Later that day, the public began to see photos of U.S. abuse toward prisoners at the Abu Ghraib detention center in Iraq. Some of the photos were broadcast that evening by the CBS News program 60 Minutes. Viewers from around the world saw prisoners forced to conduct simulated sex acts and assume positions of sexual humiliation. In one

145. U.S. Supreme Court, Rumsfeld v. Padilla, oral argument, April 28, 2004, at 17.
146. Id. at 22.
147. Id. at 23.

photo, a prisoner was shown standing on a box, his head covered, with wires attached to his fingers, toes, and penis. He was told if he fell off the box he would be electrocuted. Female U.S. soldiers, grinning and with cigarettes in their mouth, stood next to naked Iraqi prisoners, pointing at their genitals.[148]

The U.S. military had already ordered an inquiry into these abuses on January 19, 2004, resulting in the appointment of Maj. Gen. Antonio M. Taguba to conduct the investigation. His report, which began circulating on Web sites in early May, described "numerous incidents of sadistic, blatant, and wanton criminal abuses" inflicted on detainees. The abuse was "systemic and illegal."[149] Taguba concluded that several U.S. soldiers had committed "egregious acts and grave breaches of international law."[150] His report described such actions as keeping detainees naked for several days at a time, a male military police guard having sex with a female detainee, using unmuzzled dogs to intimidate and frighten detainees, and sodomizing a detainee with a chemical light and perhaps a broomstick.[151]

Taguba's report, although thorough and highly detailed, was limited to the 800th Military Police Brigade and the Abu Ghraib prison. Abuses in other prisons in Afghanistan and Iraq were not covered, nor was there an effort to examine criminal conduct outside the MP brigade, particularly commanders at a high level and officials in the executive branch who might have known about the incidents and condoned them. Gen. Taguba recommended that certain officers and sergeants be reprimanded and relieved from their duties,[152] and recommended reprimands for two civilian contractors.[153] But criminal charges were initially filed only against seven enlisted men and women from a reserve unit.[154] Although evidence suggested that military intelligence officers played a key role in encouraging the abuses, the initial round of criminal charges did not include them.[155]

---

148. "Photos Show U.S. Troops Abusing Iraqi Prisoners," Los Angeles Times, April 29, 2004, at A4; James Risen, "G.I.'s Are Accused of Abusing Iraqi Captives," New York Times, April 29, 2004, at A13; "Photographs Reveal Atrocities by U.S. Soldiers," Washington Times, April 29, 2004, at A5.

149. Article 15-6 Investigation of the 800th Military Police Brigade, at 16.

150. Id. at 50.

151. Id. at 16–17.

152. Id. at 44–47.

153. Id. at 48.

154. Sewell Chan and Jackie Spinner, "Allegations of Abuse Lead to Shakeup at Iraqi Prison," Washington Post, April 30, 2004, at A24.

155. Sewell Chan and Michael Amon, "Prisoner Abuse Probe Widened: Military Intelligence at Center of Investigation," Washington Post, May 2, 2004, at A1; Eric Schmitt

So discredited was the conduct at Abu Ghraib that American commanders began to release detainees and send them home. A group of 454 were released on May 21, 2004. Twenty more were let go on May 24, another 624 on May 28, and 320 on June 6. About 400 prisoners were released on June 14, bringing the total to almost two thousand.[156] The release of such large numbers in a brief period gave the impression that U.S. soldiers had indiscriminately rounded up Iraqis in the streets and had detained and abused many of them for no reason. It undermined the administration's claim that it was arresting only those who were either terrorists or extremely dangerous. The shadow of Abu Ghraib would play over the considerations of Supreme Court Justices when they began to write the opinions in the Hamdi, Padilla, and Guantánamo cases, discussed in the next chapter.

Although President Bush in February 2002 determined that the Geneva Conventions applied to the Taliban but not to al Qaeda, White House Counsel Gonzales in a May 15, 2004, op-ed piece stated that Iraq was a party to the Geneva Conventions and that the United States "recognizes that these treaties are binding in the war for the liberation of Iraq." He said there "has never been any suggestion by our government that the conventions do not apply in that conflict." Responding to news reports that questioned the U.S. commitment to the treaties, he wrote: "make no mistake that the United States is bound to observe the rules of war in the Geneva Conventions."[157] Even with this understanding that Geneva represented a binding commitment towards detainees in Iraq, prison abuses were rampant.

---

and Douglas Jehl, "M.P.'s Received Orders to Strip Iraqi Detainees: Colonel Recalls Role of Intelligence Officers," New York Times, May 18, 2004, at A1; Josh White and Scott Higham, "Sergeant Says Intelligence Directed Abuse," Washington Post, May 20, 2004, at A1; R. Jeffrey Smith, "Memo Gave Intelligence Bigger Role," Washington Post, May 21, 2004, at A17; Douglas Jehl and Eric Schmitt, "Dogs and Other Harsh Tactics Linked to Military Intelligence," New York Times, May 22, 2004, at A1.

156. Jackie Spinner, "Hundreds Freed at Abu Ghraib," Washington Post, May 22, 2004, at A19; Jackie Spinner, "Abu Ghraib Prisoners Freed During Sit-In," Washington Post, May 25, 2005, at A14; Christine Hauser, "To Frenzied Scenes, Abu Ghraib Frees 624 Prisoners," New York Times, May 29, 2004, at A8; Jackie Spinner and Bassam Sebti, "U.S. Frees Hundreds from Abu Ghraib," Washington Post, May 29, 2004, at A18; James Glanz, "U.S. Releases More Prisoners; Bombings Kill at Least 21 Iraqis," New York Times, June 7, 2004, at A11; Jackie Spinner, "For Freed Iraqis, Mixed Emotions," Washington Post, June 15, 2004, at A1.

157. Alberto R. Gonzales, "The Rule of Law and the Rules of War," New York Times, May 15, 2004, at A27.

Agency Legal Analysis

What accounts for the U.S. atrocities in Iraqi and Afghanistan prisons? The classified nature of President Bush's February 7, 2002, memo, promising humane treatment of detainees, placed a heavy burden on careful guidance and instruction by the administration, communicating clearly from the top to the field. Much of that potential care and professionalism was lost when the administration decided to exclude military lawyers from the policy-making and implementation processes. Military lawyers had been actively involved in supervising interrogations in the Iraq war in 1991. John Norton Moore, a law professor and former American diplomat, stated: "We had JAG officers at all of the detention facilities where interrogations took place."[158] The presence of military officers helped sensitize commanders that certain conduct could make them guilty of violating the Geneva Conventions. From the drafting of the Bush military order, issued November 13, 2001, to the interrogation of detainees, military lawyers were largely excluded.

Also contributing to lax standards during the interrogation process were a series of agency legal memos that were either leaked to the press or voluntarily surrendered by the administration after the Abu Ghraib scandal. The most disturbing analysis appears in a 50-page memo written by the OLC head, Jay S. Bybee, to White House Counsel Gonzales. Bybee first addressed the meaning of the U.S. statute that implements the Convention Against Torture and Other Cruel, Inhuman and Degrading Treatment or Punishment. The statute defines torture as an act committed by a person "acting under the color of law specifically intended to inflict severe physical and mental pain or suffering (other than pain or suffering incidental to lawful sanctions) upon another person within his custody or physical control." The phrase "severe mental pain or suffering" means the prolonged mental harm caused by or resulting from "(A) the intentional infliction or threatened infliction of severe physical pain or suffering, (B) the administration or application, or threatened administration or application, of mind-altering substances or other procedures calculated to disrupt profoundly the senses or the personality, (C) the threat of imminent death, and (D) the threat that another person will imminently be subject to death, severe physical pain or suffering, or the administration or application of mind-altering substances or other procedures calculated to disrupt profoundly

---

158. Adam Liptak, "Legal Review Could Have Halted Abuse, Lawyer Says," New York Times, May 19, 2004, at A14.

the sense or personality."[159] The statute applies to actions by U.S. individuals "outside the United States" and includes fines and imprisonment not more than 20 years, unless death results from conduct prohibited by the statute, in which case punishment can be death or imprisonment for any term of years or for life.[160]

Bybee advised Gonzales that for an act to constitute torture as defined by the statute "it must inflict pain that is difficult to endure." And then came this understanding of physical pain: "Physical pain amounting to torture must be equivalent in intensity to the pain accompanying serious physical injury, such as organ failure, impairment of bodily function, or even death."[161] These extreme pains do not come from the torture statute. Bybee finds them by looking to other statutes that have nothing to do with torture or interrogation (such as statutes that define an emergency medical condition for the purpose of providing health benefits).[162] By combining elements of different statutes, he concluded that American interrogators can inflict physical pain so long as it does not result in organ failure, impairment of bodily function, or death.

Next, Bybee looked at the statutory meaning of "specifically intended." He concluded that in order for a defendant to have acted with specific intent, "he must expressly intend to achieve the forbidden act." The infliction of pain "must be the defendant's precise objective." If the defendant acted knowing that severe pain or suffering was "reasonably likely to result from his actions, but no more, he would have acted only with general intent" and not specific intent.[163] Thus, even if the defendant knows that severe pain will result from his actions, "if causing such harm is not his objective, he lacks the requisite specific intent even though the defendant did not act in good faith. Instead, a defendant is guilty of torture only if he acts with the express purpose of inflicting severe pain or suffering on a person within his custody or physical control."[164] Under this reading, if the objective of an American is to pry loose important intelligence from a detainee, and his interrogation inflicts severe pain or suffering, the American has not violated the statute. The severe pain or suffering was incidental, not the intended purpose.

---

159. 18 U.S.C. § 2340 (2000).

160. Id. at § 2340A.

161. Memorandum from Bybee to Gonzales, "Re: Standards of Conduct for Interrogation under 18 U.S.C. §§ 2340–2340A," August 1, 2002, at 1.

162. Id. at 5–6.

163. Id. at 3–4.

164. Id. at 4.

Bybee took the same approach to mental pain or suffering. To commit torture, an interrogator "must specifically intend to cause prolonged mental harm." The interrogator "could negate a showing of specific intent to cause severe mental pain or suffering by showing that he had acted in good faith that his conduct would not amount to the acts prohibited by the statute." If the interrogator "has a good faith belief that his actions will not result in prolonged mental harm, he lacks the mental state necessary for his actions to constitute torture," even if the detainee suffers from prolonged mental harm.[165]

Looking to the ratification history of the Convention Against Torture (CAT), Bybee said that the Reagan administration took the position that CAT "reached only the most heinous act." The Reagan administration included the following understanding: "The United States understands that, in order to constitute torture, an act must be a deliberate and calculated act of an extremely cruel and inhuman nature, specifically intended to inflict excruciating and agonizing physical or mental pain or suffering."[166] Read in this light, many of the actions cited in the Taguba report might not constitute "torture," and it could be argued that the Bush administration was complying with treaty obligations and committed to following the law.

Similarly, the Reagan administration distinguished torture from "lesser forms of cruel, inhuman, or degrading treatment or punishment, which are to be deplored and prevented, but are not so universally and categorically condemned as to warrant the severe legal consequences that the Convention provides in cases of torture."[167] Relying on this distinction, an administration could permit cruel, inhuman, or degrading treatment of detainees and claim, at the same time, that it has complied fully with the Convention Against Torture and the torture statute. Bybee summed up the text of CAT to conclude that the torture statute "was intended to proscribe only the most egregious conduct," and that CAT's text, ratification history, and negotiating history "all confirm that Section 2340A reaches only the most heinous acts."[168]

Possibly the most remarkable section of Bybee's memo is his interpretation of the President's powers as Commander in Chief. He said that even if an interrogation method arguably violated the torture statute, the statute would be unconstitutional "if it impermissibly encroached on the Presi-

165. Id. at 8.
166. Id. at 16.
167. Id. at 17.
168. Id. at 22.

dent's constitutional power to conduct a military campaign." As Commander in Chief, the President "has the constitutional authority to order interrogations of enemy combatants to gain intelligence information concerning the military plans of the enemy."[169] Because this power, as read by Bybee, comes from the Constitution, no statute or treaty can limit it.

In light of the President's "complete authority" over the conduct of war, Bybee was loath to read a criminal statute (like the torture statute) "as infringing on the President's ultimate authority in these areas." The torture statute "must be construed as not applying to interrogations undertaken pursuant to his Commander-in-Chief authority."[170] Because of this interpretation, even if a U.S. interrogator flatly violated the torture statute, the Justice Department would not prosecute if it concluded that the interrogation was conducted to further the President's authority as Commander in Chief. Referring to an earlier OLC opinion in 1984, involving executive privilege, Bybee said that if executive officials were subject to prosecution for interrogations conducted to carry out the President's Commander in Chief powers, "it would significantly burden and immeasurably impair the President's ability to fulfill his constitutional duties."[171]

Just as OLC had earlier opposed prosecutions related to the President's assertion of executive privilege, Bybee had "even greater concerns with respect to prosecutions arising out of the exercise of the President's express authority as Commander-in-Chief."[172] If a U.S. interrogator violated the torture statute, even by committing egregious and heinous acts, prosecution would not be considered if the Justice Department decided that the interrogation was a legitimate means of furthering the President's constitutional duties as Commander in Chief.

Bybee concluded his memo by considering defenses that could be advanced by U.S. interrogators who faced possible prosecution and punishment. This is a fascinating section of the memo. Even if an interrogator violated the torture statute, and somehow the Justice Department decided that the interrogation could not be justified under the Commander in Chief power, Bybee still offered a number of reasons why the prosecution would not be successful. Certain "justification defenses might be available that would potentially eliminate criminal liability." Standard criminal law defenses, ranging from necessity to self-defense, "could justify interrogation methods

169. Id. at 31.
170. Id. at 34.
171. Id. at 35.
172. Id. at 36.

needed to elicit information to prevent a direct and imminent threat to the United States and its citizens."[173]

These pages provide a handy road map to guide the interrogator and his defense counsel. How often does the Justice Department and the OLC offer helpful hints and litigation strategy to those who violate the law? Anthony Lewis thought this kind of memo "read like the advice of a mob lawyer to a mafia don on how to skirt the law and stay out of prison."[174] Clearly Bybee understood that the administration was preparing to use more aggressive methods of interrogation in order to secure needed intelligence, and it was his purpose to assure U.S. forces that prosecution by the Justice Department was a remote and unlikely prospect.

A Defense Department memo, dated October 11, 2002, discusses "more aggressive interrogation techniques than the ones presently used" at Guantánamo. These techniques "may be required in order to obtain information from detainees that are resisting interrogation efforts and are suspected of having significant information essential to national security." Interestingly, the memo states that the detainees at Guantánamo "are not protected by the Geneva Conventions (GC)."[175] The Bush memo of February 7, 2002, stated that the Taliban would be covered by Geneva. Bush indicated that his decision on that issue stood "at this time" and reserved the right to change his decision "in this or future conflicts." Had Bush changed his determination on the Taliban, or did the Defense Department have an incorrect impression of presidential policy?

On January 15, 2003, Defense Secretary Rumsfeld directed his general counsel to establish a Working Group within the department "to assess the legal, policy, and operational issues relating to the interrogation of detainees held by the U.S. Armed Forces in the war on terrorism."[176] This memo was issued before U.S. troops began military operations against Iraq, but the scope of the Rumsfeld memo was broad enough to cover all detainees, whether in Guantánamo, Afghanistan, or Iraq.

When the report of the Working Group was released, first as a draft on

---

173. Id. at 39.

174. Anthony Lewis, "Making Torture Legal," New York Review of Books, July 15, 2004, at 4.

175. Department of Defense, "Legal Brief on Proposed Counter-Resistance Strategies," Memorandum for Commander, Joint Task Force 170, JTF 170-SJA, October 11, 2002, at 1 (Paragraphs 1 and 2), declassified June 21, 2004.

176. Office of the Secretary of Defense, "Detainees Interrogations," Memorandum for the General Counsel of the Department of Defense, January 15, 2003, declassified June 21, 2004.

March 6, 2003, and later as a final report on April 4, 2003, they showed the heavy influence of Bybee's legal analysis. By the time of the final report, U.S. troops were fighting in Iraq. As with the Bybee memo, the reports are structured to cover the Geneva Conventions, the Convention Against Torture, the torture statute, interpretations of "specifically intended," the Commander in Chief authority, and an interrogator's access to the doctrines of necessity and self-defense.[177] Both reports state that the torture statute "does not apply to the conduct of U.S. personnel" at Guantánamo.[178] Both interpret the torture statute as not applying "to the President's detention and interrogation of enemy combatants pursuant to his Commander-in-Chief authority."[179]

As accessed on various Web sites, the March 6 draft stops in midsentence on page 56. The April 4 report, because it was declassified on June 21, 2004, is available in full and has some extremely interesting material. It states that under the Third Geneva Convention, U.S. forces are required to treat captured personnel as POWs until an official determination is made of their status. Once it is determined that captured personnel are unlawful combatants, "as is currently the case with captured Taliban and Al Qaida operatives, they do not have a right to the protections of the Third Geneva Convention."[180] The February 7, 2002, memo signed by President Bush applied Geneva to the Taliban.

The April 4 report explains that defenses related to the Commander in Chief authority, the doctrines of necessity and self-defense, and others, may be available to individuals whose actions during interrogation would violate the torture statute. "Where the Commander-in-Chief authority is being relied upon, a Presidential written directive would serve to memorialize this authority."[181] One of the recommendations at the end of the report elaborates on this: "As the Commander-in-Chief authority is vested in the President, we recommend that any exercise of that authority by DOD personnel be confirmed in writing through Presidential directive or other doc-

177. "Working Group Report on Detainee Interrogations in the Global War on Terrorism: Assessment of Legal, Historical, Policy, and Operational Considerations," March 6, 2003 (Draft); "Working Group Report on Detainee Interrogations in the Global War on Terrorism: Assessment of Legal, Historical, Policy, and Operational Considerations," April 4, 2003 (Final Report). I obtained the first from a Web site before the administration declassified these documents. The second was declassified June 21, 2004.

178. Page 7 of March 6 draft; page 8 of April 4 report.

179. Page 21 of each document.

180. Page 67 of April 4 report.

181. Id. at 68.

ument."[182] The vast outpouring of classified material released by the administration in June 2004 did not include this type of presidential document.

The April 4 report describes a number of authorized interrogation techniques that appear in the photos from Abu Ghraib. Hooding was permitted when "questioning the detainee with a blindfold in place." Clothing could be removed, "to be done by military policy if not agreed to by the subject." Nudity creates "a feeling of helplessness and dependence." Anxiety could be increased in various ways, including the "simple presence of dog without directly threatening action."[183]

Part of the April 4 report has a prescient quality. It anticipates the negative reaction if some of the interrogation methods became public. "Should information regarding the use of more aggressive interrogation techniques than have been used traditionally by U.S. forces become public, it is likely to be exaggerated or distorted in the U.S. and international media accounts, and may produce an adverse effect on support for the war on terrorism."[184] As it turned out, even the military and the administration condemned the actions at Abu Ghraib. More accurate was this observation: "Participation by U.S. military personnel in interrogations which use techniques that are more aggressive than those appropriate for POWs would constitute a significant departure from traditional U.S. military norms and could have an adverse impact on the cultural self-image of U.S. military forces."[185]

The shoddy quality of the agency legal memos, combined with their shock effect on the American public and other nations, forced the administration into a retreat. At a press briefing on June 22, 2004, White House Counsel Gonzales and three other executive officials met with reporters to clarify and modify what agency lawyers had been arguing. Gonzales said that to the extent that some of the documents, "in the context of interrogations, explored broad legal theories, including legal theories about the scope of the President's power as Commander-in-Chief, some of their discussion, quite frankly, is irrelevant and unnecessary to support any action taken by the President."[186] Clearly that was aimed at the Bybee memo and its inclusion in the Working Group reports. Gonzales continued: "Unnec-

---

182. Id. at 70.
183. Id. at 64–65.
184. Id. at 69.
185. Id.
186. Press Briefing by White House Counsel Judge Alberto Gonzales, DOD General Counsel William Haynes, DOD Deputy General Counsel Daniel Dell'Orto and Army Deputy Chief of Staff for Intelligence Gen. Keith Alexander, June 22, 2002, at 2; http://www/prnewswire.com/cgi-bin/stories.pl?ACCT=109&STORY=/www/story/06-22-2.

essary, over-broad discussions in some of these memos that address abstract legal theories, or discussions subject to misinterpretation, but not relied upon by decision-makers are under review, and may be replaced, if appropriate, with more concrete guidance addressing only those issues necessary for the legal analysis of actual practices."[187]

Gonzales set the record straight on a number of issues. He referred to the Bush memo of February 7, 2002, as "the only formal, written directive from the President regarding treatment of detainees."[188] However, he also said that the briefing "does not include CIA activities."[189] When one of the reporters asked, "Are we wrong to assume then, that the CIA is not subject to these categories of interrogation technique?" Gonzales replied that he was not going "to get into questions related to the CIA."[190] His response raised the question of whether the White House applied one rule to interrogations conducted by the Defense Department, and left open another rule for the CIA.

The November 13, 2001 military order, authorizing the creation of military tribunals, was fashioned largely on the basis of the military order and proclamation issued in 1942 by President Roosevelt. As a result, it failed to benefit from the instructive lessons learned by the Roosevelt administration early in 1945 when it decided to use tribunals a second time against saboteurs who came from Germany by submarine. On the other hand, whereas the Roosevelt administration instituted a tribunal in 1942 without first issuing rules and regulations, the Bush administration spent several years fashioning the procedures that would guide tribunals. It benefitted from recommendations by private organizations to the draft instructions. In August 2004, with the start of tribunal proceedings at Guantánamo, the rules were still in flux, making it difficult for defense attorneys to prepare their case.[191] How to apply those instructions to specific individuals was less clear. As the next chapter explains, the administration initially decided to rely on civilian courts in prosecuting alleged terrorists and in many cases simply detained suspects without charging them and bringing them to trial, either civilian or military.

187. Id.
188. Id. at 4.
189. Id.
190. Id. at 21. See also Mike Allen and Susan Schmidt, "Memo on Interrogation Tactics Is Disavowed," Washington Post, June 23, 2004, at A1, and Richard W. Stevenson, "White House Says Prisoner Policy Set Humane Tone," New York Times, June 23, 2004, at A1.
191. Vanessa Blum, "Combatants To Go Before Military Panel," Legal Times, August 23, 2004, at 1.

8

JUDICIAL PROCESS AGAINST TERRORISTS

The Bush administration adopted a variety of procedures for handling terrorist suspects. For the most part, it depended on regular civil proceedings to indict individuals and prosecute them in court. It also detained hundreds of individuals at Guantánamo Bay and designated them and others "enemy combatants." By placing people in this category, the government claimed the right to deny the person the right to counsel and to hold him incommunicado for as long as necessary in an effort to obtain information about past and future terrorist operations. Detention could last years without charging the individual or bringing him to trial. All of these issues, initially explored by district and appellate courts, reached the Supreme Court in 2004.

Relying on Civilian Courts

Notwithstanding the administration's emphasis on military tribunals, the Justice Department regularly went to civilian courts to prosecute terrorists charged with assisting the Taliban and al Qaeda. John Walker Lindh, born in California but captured in Afghanistan among Taliban forces, was tried in civil court. He pled guilty to assisting the Taliban government in Afghanistan.[1] Richard E. Reid, the British "shoe bomber," was tried and convicted in civil court.[2] The Justice Department prosecuted six Yemenis from Lackawanna, New York. The men admitted to attending an al Qaeda training camp in Afghanistan during the spring of 2001.[3] Indictments were brought against an Algerian and three Moroccans in Detroit for being members of a terror cell.[4] Two were convicted and two acquitted.[5] The outcome was

1. United States v. Lindh, 227 F.Supp.2d 565 (E.D. Va. 2002).
2. Pamela Ferdinand, "Would-Be Shoe Bomber Gets Life Term," Washington Post, January 31, 2003, at A1.
3. Michael Powell, "No Choice but Guilty: Lackawanna Case Highlights Legal Tilt," Washington Post, July 29, 2003, at A1; Matthew Purdy and Lowell Bergman, "Unclear Danger: Inside the Lackawanna Terror Case," New York Times, October 12, 2003, at 1.
4. Danny Hakim, "Trial Set to Begin for Four Men Accused of Being in Terror Cell," New York Times, March 17, 2003, at A14.
5. Danny Hakim, "2 Arabs Convicted and 2 Cleared Of Terrorist Plot Against the U.S.," New York Times, June 4, 2003, at A1.

later thrown in doubt when it appeared that prosecutors might have withheld key exonerating evidence.[6] In September 2004, a federal judge threw out the two convictions because of prosecutorial abuse.[7] Maher Hawash, a software engineer in Portland, Oregon, pled guilty in civil court to assisting the Taliban.[8] Many other terrorist suspects faced charges in civil court.

Moussaoui in Civil Court

Zacarias Moussaoui, a 33-year-old French citizen of Moroccan descent, was arrested on immigration charges in Minneapolis on August 16, 2001, after he had enrolled in a flight school to learn how to fly a Boeing 747 commercial jet. He was first held in federal prison in New York as a material witness. Later he was suspected of being part of the Osama bin Laden conspiracy on 9/11. Several lawmakers thought he was precisely the type of person the administration had in mind when it authorized the tribunals. Senator Joseph I. Lieberman (D-Conn.) asked: "If we will not try Zacarias Moussaoui before a military tribunal, who will we try by a military tribunal?"[9] Senator Carl Levin (D-Mich.) expressed surprise that Moussaoui was not brought before a tribunal: "The glove fits so perfectly here."[10]

The administration had debated whether it was best to prosecute Moussaoui in civil court by the Justice Department or in a tribunal by the Defense Department. This dispute was aired in front of the Senate Armed Services Committee. Deputy Secretary of Defense Paul Wolfowitz told Senators that "just the existence of a military tribunal is a deterrence" because it put foreign terrorists who are considering an attack on U.S. targets "on notice that you'll be under a different [legal] process."[11] His explanation seemed to concede that despite the promise of a "full and fair" trial before a tribunal, it would be easier to intimidate, convict, and execute terrorists by avoiding civilian courts.

6. Robert E. Pierre, "Terrorism Case Thrown Into Turmoil," Washington Post, December 31, 2003, at A5.

7. Danny Hakim, "Judge Reverses Convictions in Detroit Terrorism Case," New York Times, September 3, 2004, at A10.

8. Blaine Harden, "Ore. Man Pleads Guilty to Helping Taliban," Washington Post, August 7, 2003, at A8.

9. Walter Pincus, "Senators Ask: Why No Tribunal for Suspect?," Washington Post, December 13, 2001, at A14.

10. Katharine Q. Seelye, "Justice Department Decision to Forgo Tribunal Bypasses Pentagon," New York Times, December 13, 2001, at B6.

11. Walter Pincus, "Senators Ask: Why No Tribunal for Suspect?," Washington Post, December 13, 2001, at A14.

On December 11, 2001, a federal grand jury indicted Moussaoui for being part of the al Qaeda conspiracy to kill and maim persons and destroy structures in the United States. The indictment included six counts: conspiracy to commit acts of terrorism transcending national boundaries, conspiracy to commit aircraft piracy, conspiracy to destroy aircraft, conspiracy to use weapons of mass destruction, conspiracy to murder U.S. employees, and conspiracy to destroy property. The indictment listed two supporting conspirators: Ramzi bin al-Shibh and Mustafa Ahmed al-Hawsawi, and stated that bin al-Shibh had wired approximately $14,000 to Moussaoui from Germany.[12] These allegations would complicate the trial after bin al-Shibh was apprehended in Pakistan and Moussaoui insisted he had a right to confront him in court.

The government chose to bring Moussaoui before a civil court in Alexandria, Virginia, which has a strong history of imposing the death penalty.[13] The decision to seek the death penalty marked the first of many complications with the Moussaoui case. Capital punishment has been abolished in all 15 countries of the European Union. For that reason, such countries as France and Germany were unwilling to release key evidence to the United States.[14] That problem was overcome when French and German authorities agreed to hand over documents on the condition that the Justice Department would not use the material to seek or impose the death penalty.[15]

The Charges

Exactly what criminal conduct the government suspected Moussaoui of shifted with time. Initially, high-ranking officials in the Bush government, including Vice President Cheney, regarded Moussaoui as the "20th hijacker." The three planes that hit the World Trade Center and the Pentagon had five terrorists each. The plane that crashed in a field in Stony Township, Pennsylvania, had only four terrorists. Federal investigators soon suspect-

---

12. United States of America v. Zacarias Moussaoui, Criminal No. 01-455-A, U.S. District Court for the Eastern District of Virginia, Alexandria Division, July 2002 Term, Superseding Indictment, at 6, 17 (hereafter "Moussaoui Indictment").

13. Don Van Natta Jr. with Benjamin Weiser, "Compromise Settles Debate over Tribunal," New York Times, December 12, 2001, at B1.

14. Peter Finn, "Germany Reluctant to Aid Prosecution of Moussaoui," Washington Post, June 11, 2002, at A1.

15. Dan Eggen, "U.S. to Get Moussaoui Data from Europe," Washington Post, November 28, 2002, at A19.

ed that a Yemeni citizen might have been meant to be the hijacker aboard that plane.[16]

The Justice Department never fully embraced the theory of Moussaoui being the 20th hijacker, a notion that became increasingly difficult to defend. Later, Moussaoui learned through court documents that the Justice Department believed he was involved in a "fifth plane" to be crashed into the White House.[17] His attorneys sought access to those statements, made in a secret court hearing, and Judge Leonie M. Brinkema agreed that access was appropriate.[18] The Justice Department told Brinkema it had evidence that Moussaoui was plotting to fly a hijacked plane into the White House in 2001, an attack separate from the 9/11 attacks.[19] Newspaper reports said that the Justice Department, by August 2003, had backed away from the "fifth plane" theory, which appeared to be based on information from some al Qaeda prisoners but contradicted by other prisoners.[20] With complications mounting in civil court, the administration debated again the merits of shifting Moussaoui to a military tribunal.[21]

Moussaoui Represents Himself

The trial stretched from month to month, in part because of Judge Brinkema's decision to let Moussaoui serve as his own lawyer. He used that opportunity to promote al Qaeda goals and create a circus atmosphere. Representing oneself in court is almost always ill-advised, even for seasoned attorneys. For Moussaoui, it was especially harmful. Court-appointed attorneys with security clearances could have been given access to evidence and witnesses. Moussaoui would never have such rights. Even so, prosecutors

---

16. Don Van Natta Jr., "Debate Centers on Which Court Will Decide Fate of Arab Man," New York Times, November 22, 2001, at B6.

17. Philip Shenon, "Prosecution Says Qaeda Member Was to Pilot 5th Sept. 11 Jet," New York Times, April 16, 2003, at B10.

18. United States v. Moussaoui, April 28, 2003, Order by Judge Brinkema, 2003 WL 21266341 (E.D. Va. 2003); Philip Shenon, "Moussaoui Should Get Details in '5th Plane' Theory, Judge Says," New York Times, April 29, 2003, at A13.

19. Philip Shenon, "White House Called Target of Plane Plot," New York Times, August 9, 2003, at A7.

20. Josh White, "FBI Intercepts Moussaoui's Mail," Washington Post, August 9, 2003, at B2.

21. Philip Shenon and Eric Schmitt, "White House Weighs Letting Military Tribunal Try Moussaoui, Officials Say," New York Times, October 20, 2002, at 15; Bradley Graham and dan Eggen, "Moussaoui Case May Be Moved to Military Tribunal," Washington Post, November 11, 2002, at B7.

managed to inadvertently place some classified materials in his hands.[22]
Moreover, Judge Brinkema authorized a limited disclosure of classified
information to Moussaoui.[23]

After almost two years of the trial, Judge Brinkema decided on November 14, 2003, to remove Moussaoui's right to represent himself. She had put
him on notice that he could no longer act as his own lawyer if he continued to file frivolous, repetitive, and disrespectful motions. His handwritten
motions had called Judge Brinkema the "death judge" and a would-be Nazi
SS officer. He responded, she said, with two more pleadings that "include
contemptuous language that would never be tolerated from an attorney,
and which will no longer be tolerated from this defendant."[24] She appointed his standby attorneys to officially represent him. The Fourth Circuit prohibited Moussaoui from filing pleadings unless they were routed through
his attorneys.[25]

Right of Confrontation

The trial took on new complexity in September 2002 with the capture of
Ramzi bin al-Shibh, a young Yemeni apprehended in Pakistan. He was
accused of being a key planner of the 9/11 attacks and had been identified in Moussaoui's indictment. Now that the Justice Department had
decided to try Moussaoui in civil court, he was entitled under the Sixth
Amendment to seek witnesses to prove his innocence and to confront witnesses against him. The rights in the Sixth Amendment apply to any
"accused" in a criminal proceeding, not just to a U.S. citizen. Again the government wondered whether it was now time to turn Moussaoui over to the
Defense Department to be tried by tribunal.[26]

Khalid Sheik Mohammed, an al Qaeda operations chief captured in
Pakistan, told U.S. interrogators that Moussaoui was not part of the 9/11
attacks, but was in the United States to take part in a second-wave attack.
According to press reports, both Mohammed and bin al-Shibh came to dis-

---

22. United States v. Moussaoui, March 19, 2003, Order by Judge Brinkema, 2003 WL
18777698 (E.D. Va. 2003).

23. United States v. Moussaoui, May 7, 2003, Order by Judge Brinkema, 2003 WL
21266319 (E.D. Va. 2003).

24. Jerry Markon, "Lawyers Restored for Moussaoui," Washington Post, November 15,
2003, at A2.

25. Jerry Markon, "Court Reins in Terror Suspect," Washington Post, December 30,
2003, at B3.

26. Susan Schmidt, "Prosecution of Moussaoui Nears a Crossroad," Washington Post,
January 21, 2003, at A8.

trust Moussaoui and found him unreliable.[27] It was reported that Moussaoui offered a third explanation, saying he was to take part in another al Qaeda operation outside the United States after the 9/11 attacks.[28]

On January 30, 2003, Judge Brinkema ordered the government to allow Moussaoui's lawyers to take a video deposition of bin al-Shibh. The government balked at her order, arguing that any questioning by his attorneys would disrupt ongoing interrogations and jeopardize access to crucial evidence needed by the government in the war against terrorism. Yet the government's indictment charged that bin al-Shibh had wired Moussaoui at least $14,000, making both men part of the conspiracy.[29] A defendant in civil court has a right to challenge a government's witness. After Khalid Sheik Mohammed was captured in Pakistan, Moussaoui's attorneys sought access to him and others. In one memo, Judge Brinkema advised the government that when it chose to bring Moussaoui to trial in a civilian court, "it assumed the responsibility of abiding by well-established principles of due process."[30]

When the government appealed Brinkema's order, the Fourth Circuit sent the case back to district court, urging the two sides to find a middle ground that would allow Moussaoui some access to bin al-Shibh.[31] On May 15, Brinkema rejected the government's proposal that would give the defense access to some of bin al-Shibh's statements, but deny it the right to depose bin al-Shibh and other potential witnesses.[32]

Although a civil trial is open for public viewing, much of the Moussaoui trial was conducted in secret. Judge Brinkema's order to give Moussaoui's attorneys access to bin al-Shibh was made in secret, as was the government brief to the Fourth Circuit appealing her ruling, and also a key hearing before the Fourth Circuit on May 6, 2003.[33] Several news organizations

27. Susan Schmidt and Ellen Nakashima, "Moussaoui Said Not to Be Part of 9/11 Plot," Washington Post, March 28, 2003, at A4.

28. Jerry Markon, "Moussaoui Says He Was to Aid Later Attack," Washington Post, May 14, 2003, at A2.

29. Moussaoui Indictment, at 17; Susan Schmidt and Dana Priest, "Judge Orders Access to Detainee for Moussaoui's Lawyers," Washington Post, February 1, 2003, at A9.

30. Josh White, "Memos Reveal Doubt on Proper Court for Moussaoui," Washington Post, June 3, 2003, at A8.

31. Jerry Markon, "Court Seeks Deal on Terror Witness Access," Washington Post, April 16, 2003, at A12.

32. Jerry Markon, "Judge Rejects Bid to Block Access to Sept. 11 Planner," Washington Post, May 16, 2003, at A3.

33. Jerry Markon, "U.S. Files Terror Briefs in Secrecy," Washington Post, March 15, 2003, at A6; Jerry Markon, "Moussaoui's Hearing Closed to Public," Washington Post, March 25, 2003, at A2.

went to court to demand access to these secret court documents.[34] Judge Brinkema criticized the "shroud of secrecy" surrounding the Moussaoui case, expressing doubt that the government could prosecute the case in open court.[35] In response to the action by the news organizations and Brinkema's statement, the government agreed to unseal some of the secret documents.[36] Also, the Fourth Circuit ruled that part of a hearing scheduled for June 3 be open to the public.[37]

At a hearing before the Fourth Circuit, Assistant Attorney General Michael Chertoff told the court that Moussaoui's rights were trumped by national security interests. Chief Judge William W. Wilkins Jr. responded: "National security interests cannot override a defendant's right to a fair trial."[38] Chertoff insisted that "this is not a Sixth Amendment case," and that what Moussaoui "wants is to expand the Sixth Amendment."[39] Chertoff denied that the Sixth Amendment could be extended overseas to potential witnesses who are enemy combatants, and that any effort to interrogate bin al-Shibh would "change the course of a military operation."[40]

Waiting for a "Final Decision"

On June 26, 2003, the three-judge panel ducked these constitutional issues by holding that Brinkema's order was not yet subject to appeal because it was not technically a "final decision."[41] The order would not become final, in a legal sense, "unless and until the Government refuses to comply and the district court imposes a sanction."[42] The Justice Department had asked the Fourth Circuit to issue a mandamus, reversing the district court's order, but the Fourth Circuit declined to provide that relief.[43]

34. Philip Shenon, "News Groups Want Terror Case Files," New York Times, April 4, 2003, at B13.

35. United States v. Moussaoui, April 4, 2003, Order by Judge Brinkema, 2003 WL 21266379 (E.D. Va. 2003). See also Patricia Davis and Jerry Markon, "U.S. Secrecy Criticized by Moussaoui Judge," Washington Post, April 5, 2003, at A9.

36. Philip Shenon, "Government Agrees Some Secret Documents in Terror Case Can Be Unsealed," New York Times, April 22, 2003, at A12.

37. Philip Shenon, "In Shift, Appeals Court Opens Hearing on a 9/11 Suspect," New York Times, May 14, 2003, at A15.

38. Jerry Markon, "Appeals Panel Hears Arguments on Deposition Sought by Moussaoui," Washington Post, June 4, 2003, at A10.

39. Philip Shenon, "Justice Dept. Warns of Risk to Prosecution and Security," New York Times, June 4, 2003, at A21.

40. Id.

41. United States v. Moussaoui, 333 F.3d 509, 513–14 (4th Cir. 2003).

42. Id. at 515.

43. Id. at 516–17.

The government asked the Fourth Circuit to reconsider its ruling, but on July 3 the court refused.[44] Rebuffed, the government asked the entire Fourth Circuit to rehear the case. Divided 7 to 5, the appellate court voted against an en banc rehearing.[45] The next step was now quite predictable: the government defied Brinkema's order to give Moussaoui access to bin al-Shibh. Instead of taking the case immediately to a military tribunal, the Justice Department hoped to return to the Fourth Circuit and this time secure a favorable ruling.[46] In late August, Brinkema granted Moussaoui access to two al Qaeda operatives: Khalid Sheik Mohammed and Mustafa Ahmed al-Hawsawi, a Saudi man who reportedly served as paymaster to the 9/11 hijackers and is named in the indictment against Moussaoui.[47] The Justice Department told Judge Brinkema that it would refuse to produce either man for deposition.[48]

The government's threat to take Moussaoui out of civil court and try him before a military tribunal was fraught with risks. Had he been apprehended abroad, the government could have relied on *Eisentrager* that federal courts would have no jurisdiction over him. But Moussaoui was arrested in Minnesota. To eliminate the possibility of any legal review by the courts, the administration might have designated Moussaoui as an "enemy combatant," but the multiyear delay in making such a determination would have met with skepticism and incredulity.

By late September, it appeared that the Justice Department would not object if Brinkema accepted a defense motion to dismiss the indictment. That step would allow the government to have a final order it could appeal to the more friendly Fourth Circuit.[49] However, Brinkema had other options. She could strike portions of the indictment dealing with al Qaeda prisoners, presenting an issue the government would find more difficult to win

44. Jerry Markon, "Moussaoui Prosecution Is Dealt Setback," Washington Post, July 4, 2003, at A8.

45. United States v. Moussaoui, 336 F.3d 279 (4th Cir. 2003).

46. Jerry Markon, "Moussaoui Prosecutors Defy Judge," Washington Post, July 15, 2003, at A1; Philip Shenon, "U.S. Will Defy Court's Order in Terror Case," New York Times, July 15, 2003, at A1.

47. Jerry Markon, "Moussaoui Granted Access to Witnesses," Washington Post, August 30, 2003, at A12; Moussaoui Indictment, at 6.

48. Jerry Markon, "U.S. Refuses to Produce Al Qaeda Officials as Witnesses," Washington Post, September 11, 2003, at A7.

49. Jerry Markon, "Defense Calls for Dismissal of Sept. 11 Case," Washington Post, September 25, 2003, at A15; Philip Shenon, "In Maneuver, U.S. Will Let Terror Charges Drop," New York Times, September 26, 2003, at A1.

on appeal.[50] Another option, which she selected on October 2, was to prevent prosecutors from seeking the death penalty for Moussaoui because there was insufficient evidence linking him to 9/11, and he was "a remote or minor participant" in al Qaeda's actions against the United States.[51] Judge Brinkema also ruled that it would be fundamentally unfair to require Moussaoui to defend himself against accusations without the opportunity to seek testimony from witnesses held by the government.[52] Under her ruling, Moussaoui could still be prosecuted for participating in a broad al Qaeda conspiracy against the United States, leading perhaps to life in prison.[53]

Searching for a Compromise

Judge Brinkema's ruling put pressure on the government to either allow Moussaoui to depose bin al-Shibh and other government witnesses, or take the case out of civil court and assign it to a military tribunal. The judges on the Fourth Circuit suggested a compromise that would allow Moussaoui access to statements made by three key al Qaeda detainees without letting him or his attorneys interview them in person. These witness statements were called "substitutions." The government thought that the substitutions "may be a way of securing the defendant's rights," but Moussaoui's attorneys indicated that the compromise was not comparable to the witnesses' live testimony.[54] One of his attorneys remarked: "It's hard for us to consider substitutions for witnesses that we can't see or talk to."[55]

After a lengthy delay, the Fourth Circuit issued a decision on April 22, 2004, that gave a little to each side. It rejected the government's claim that Judge Brinkema exceeded her authority by granting Moussaoui access to the witnesses, and it affirmed her conclusion that the witnesses could provide material, favorable testimony on Moussaoui's behalf. It further agreed with Brinkema that the government's proposed substitutions for deposition

50. Philip Shenon and Neil A. Lewis, "Appeals Strategy Lies Behind Prosecutors' Decision in Terror Case," New York Times, September 30, 2003, at A21.

51. Moussaoui v. United States, 282 F.Supp.2d 481, 486 (E.D. Va. 2003).

52. Id. at 482.

53. Jerry Markon, "Ruling Shakes Up Moussaoui Terror Case," Washington Post, October 3, 2003, at A1; Philip Shenon, "Judge Rules Out a Death Penalty for 9/11 Suspect," New York Times, October 3, 2003, at A1.

54. Jerry Markon, "Compromise Hinted in Moussaoui Case," December 4, 2003, at A10.

55. Jerry Markon, "U.S. Might Compromise in Moussaoui Dispute," December 17, 2003, at A14.

testimony were inadequate. It reversed Brinkema's conclusion that it was not possible to craft adequate substitutions, and remanded the case to her with instructions to craft substitutions that would be acceptable to each side.[56]

As to the government's argument that the Sixth Amendment's right of confrontation did not extend to witnesses outside the country, the Fourth Circuit accepted the *Eisentrager* principle that the writ of habeas corpus did not extend to enemy aliens held abroad, but rejected the assumption that territorial limitations apply to lesser writs. It was clear to the Fourth Circuit that Judge Brinkema could reach beyond the boundaries of her district in order to issue a testimonial writ. It ruled that a testimonial writ issued by her would not implicate the separation of powers. Moussaoui's Sixth Amendment right to the testimony of witnesses held by the government would have to be balanced against the government's interest in preventing disruption of its detention of the witnesses.[57]

The Fourth Circuit concluded that several statements by the witnesses tended to exculpate Moussaoui by undermining the theory that he was to pilot a fifth plane into the White House. The statements also supported the position that he was relatively unimportant in the conspiracy, and that he was not involved in the 9/11 attacks. On those grounds, Moussaoui had made a sufficient showing that evidence from the witnesses "would be more helpful than hurtful, or at least that we cannot have confidence in the outcome of the trial" without evidence from the witnesses.[58]

Judge Karen Williams concurred in part and dissented in part. She thought that separation of powers principles prohibited the district court from giving Moussaoui access to the witnesses' testimony. She was concerned that the approach offered by the Fourth Circuit "impermissibly jeopardizes the security of our Nation and its allies by intruding on the Executive's ability to perform its war-making, military, and foreign relations duties."[59] Although she concluded that separation of powers principles place the witnesses beyond the reach of the district court, and that Moussaoui had no Sixth Amendment right to their compulsion, she believed that he had a right grounded in due process under the Fifth Amendment to introduce "material, favorable information from these people that is already in the Government's possession."[60] She agreed that Moussaoui had made "a sufficient

56. United States v. Moussaoui, 365 F.3d 292 (4th Cir. 2004).
57. Id. at 304.
58. Id. at 310.
59. Id. at 317.
60. Id. at 318 (emphasis in original).

showing that the information provided by the witnesses is material and favorable."[61]

Judge Roger Gregory also wrote a separate opinion, concurring in part and dissenting in part. He concurred that the witnesses would provide material, favorable testimony on Moussaoui's behalf, but he disagreed with the majority's decision to vacate Judge Brinkema's order striking the government's intention to seek the death penalty. Moussaoui's inability to depose the witnesses and to have them present to enable the jury to judge their credibility prevented him from producing mitigating factors that would weigh against a sentence of death. For Judge Gregory, a penalty of death "cannot be imposed unless the defendant has been accorded the opportunity to defend himself fully."[62] On that ground, he would have upheld Judge Brinkema.

Moussaoui's trial encountered another complication in June 2004 when the 9/11 commission released information to the public, describing how al Qaeda figures differed on Moussaoui's role in the 9/11 attacks. The coordinator of the 9/11 plot (bin al-Shibh) told interrogators that it was his understanding that Moussaoui would be a participant, but another top al Qaeda detainee (Khalid Sheik Mohammed) expected Moussaoui to be part of a second wave of attacks. An attorney for Moussaoui criticized the 9/11 commission for disclosing the information and the government for declassifying it. He called the disclosure "selective" and damaging to Moussaoui's ability to get a fair trial.[63] Judge Brinkema had agreed to provide classified statements from the two al Qaeda figures to the 9/11 commission, but with the condition that they would not be made public. She told investigators: "As long as the classified summaries remain out of the public's view, I have no objection."[64]

"Enemy Combatants"

A number of suspected terrorists were not charged in civil court or taken before a military tribunal. Instead, they were designated "enemy combat-

---

61. Id. at 326.

62. Id. at 332.

63. Jerry Markon, "Al Qaeda Figures Split on Moussaoui's Role in 9/11," Washington Post, June 17, 2004, at A15. See also Eric Lichtbau, "Report Says Arrest Thwarted Use of Substitute 9/11 Pilot," New York Times, June 17, 2004, at A18.

64. Jerry Markon, "Moussaoui Judge Expected Statements to Stay Classified," Washington Post, June 18, 2004, at A7.

ant" and held incommunicado without access to an attorney. The Justice Department argued that whenever the government decides to place someone in that category, federal judges have no right to interfere with the executive judgment. A government brief in the Fourth Circuit argued that courts "may not second-guess the military's determination that an individual is an enemy combatant and should be detained as such. . . . Going beyond that determination would require the courts to enter an area in which they have no competence, much less institutional expertise, intrude upon the constitutional prerogative of the Commander in Chief (and military authorities acting at his control), and possibly create 'a conflict between judicial and military opinion highly comforting to enemies of the United States.'"[65]

In other briefs, the Justice Department conceded that federal judges may have a review function in determining whether the President has properly designated an individual as an enemy combatant, but the review function "is limited to confirming based on some evidence the existence of a factual basis supporting the determination."[66] The government wanted the judiciary to accept as "some evidence" whatever executive officials submitted without any opportunity for an accused enemy combatant, supported by counsel, to challenge the executive assertion. The courts cannot determine that something is legitimate on its face if they hear only one side.

"Enemy combatant" is another term for "unlawful combatant," which the Court used in *Quirin*. Lawful combatants are held as prisoners of war and may not be prosecuted for criminal violations for belligerent acts that do not constitute war crimes. Lawful combatants wear uniforms or display a fixed distinctive emblem, to distinguish them from unlawful combatants, and conduct their operations in accordance with the laws and customs of war.[67] On November 26, 2002, the General Counsel of the Defense Department defined "enemy combatant" as "an individual who, under the laws and customs of war, may be detained for the duration of an armed conflict. In the current conflict with Al Qaida and the Taliban, for example, the term includes a member, agent, or associate of Al Qaida or the Taliban. In applying this definition, we note our consistency with the observation of the Supreme Court of the United States in *Ex parte Quirin,* 317 U.S. 1(1942):

---

65. "Brief for Respondents-Appellants," Hamdi v. Rumsfeld, No. 02-6895 (4th Cir.), at 29–30, 31. See Tom Jackman and Dan Eggen, "'Combatants' Lack Rights, U.S. Argues," Washington Post, June 20, 2002, at A10.

66. "Repondents' Response to, and Motion to Dismiss, the Amended Petition for a Writ of Habeas Corpus," Padilla v. Bush, at 15.

67. Hague Convention of October 18, 1907, 36 Stat. 2296.

'Citizens who associate themselves with the military arm of the enemy government, and with its aid, guidance and direction enter this country bent on hostile acts are enemy belligerents within the meaning of the Hague Convention and the law of war.'"[68]

Enemy combatants who are American citizens can appeal to this provision in the U.S. Code: "No citizen shall be imprisoned or otherwise detained by the United States except pursuant to an Act of Congress."[69] In 1981, the Supreme Court interpreted the "plain language" of this provision as "proscribing detention *of any kind* by the United States, absent a congressional grant of authority to detain."[70] The Bush administration, however, argued that it was not limited by this statute because "Article II alone gives the President the power to detain enemies during wartime, regardless of congressional action,"[71] or, alternatively, that the Use of Force Act of 2001, authorizing military operations against Afghanistan, represented an act of Congress that satisfied the statutory requirement.

Yaser Esam Hamdi

Yaser Esam Hamdi, born in Louisiana and captured in the same Afghan prison rebellion as John Walker Lindh, was first held at Guantánamo Bay but moved to a brig at the Norfolk Naval Station and still later to Charleston, South Carolina. Designated an enemy combatant, he was not charged but held incommunicado without access to an attorney. A federal district judge several times rejected the broad arguments put forth by the Justice Department, which relied on an administration affidavit (the "Mobbs Declaration") as sufficient evidence that Hamdi was legitimately classified as an enemy combatant. The district judge, insisting that Hamdi had a right of access to the public defender and without the presence of military personnel, was repeatedly reversed by the Fourth Circuit.[72] In a ruling of January 8, 2003, again overturning the district court, the Fourth Circuit juggled two values—the judiciary's duty to protect constitutional rights versus

---

68. Letter of November 26, 2002, from William J. Haynes II, General Counsel, Department of Defense, to Senator Carl Levin, at 1–2.

69. 18 U.S.C. § 4001(a) (2000).

70. Howe v. Smith, 452 U.S. 473, 479 n. 3 (1981) (emphasis in original).

71. Letter of September 23, 2002, from William J. Haynes II, General Counsel, Department of Defense, to Alfred P. Carlton Jr., President, American Bar Association, at 2.

72. Hamdi v. Rumsfeld, 294 F.3d 598 (4th Cir. 2002); Hamdi v. Rumsfeld, 296 F.3d 278 (4th Cir. 2002).

the judiciary's decision to defer to military decisions by the President—and came down squarely in favor of presidential power.

Judicial Deference

The Fourth Circuit arrived at its position through a strange reading of separation of powers. It cited an opinion by the Supreme Court in 1991 that the "ultimate purpose of this separation of powers is to protect the liberty and security of the governed."[73] Instead of reading this language as an affirmation of the checks and balances that prevent an accumulation of power in a single branch, the Fourth Circuit interpreted the Court's sentence as a warning to the federal judiciary not to interfere with powers vested in another branch: "For the judicial branch to trespass upon the exercise of the warmaking powers would be an infringement of the right to self-determination and self-governance at a time when the care of the common defense is most critical." What kind of "self-determination" and "self-governance" exists when power is concentrated in the executive branch? The reading is bizarre because whereas the Fourth Circuit acquiesced wholly to the judgment of the President, the Supreme Court in 1991 expressly intervened to strike down a statutory procedure adopted by Congress. No philosophy of deference appears in the 1991 decision.

Although the Fourth Circuit payed lip-service to independent judicial scrutiny ("The detention of United States citizens must be subject to judicial review"[74]), the review scarcely existed. The Fourth Circuit left little doubt about its willingness to defer to the President. "The judiciary is not at liberty to eviscerate detention interests directly derived from the war powers of Articles I and II."[75] With such a frame of reference, judicial review is emptied of meaning. Judicial deference or abdication is reflected in the statement by the Fourth Circuit that "it is undisputed" that Hamdi was captured "in a zone of active combat in a foreign theater of conflict."[76] *Undisputed?* The court heard only the government's side. Hamdi, through his attorney, was given no opportunity to challenge assertions by executive officials or their informers.

On July 9, 2003, the full bench of the Fourth Circuit voted 8 to 4 to deny

73. Hamdi v. Rumsfeld, 316 F.3d 450, 463 (4th Cir. 2003), citing Metro. Wash. Airports Auth. v. Citizens for the Abatement of Aircraft Noise, Inc., 501 U.S. 252, 272 (1991).
74. Id. at 464.
75. Id. at 466.
76. Id. at 459.

a petition requesting a rehearing of its January panel ruling.[77] Judges
Wilkinson and Traxler filed opinions supporting the denial, while Judges
Luttig and Motz wrote separate dissenting opinions. The Luttig opinion
faulted the panel for calling Hamdi's seizure "undisputed." Hamdi, he said,
"has not been permitted to speak for himself or even through counsel as
to those circumstances." However, Luttig tilted toward presidential power
by criticizing the panel's refusal "to rest decision on the proffer made by
the President of the United States . . . all but eviscerat[ing] the President's
Article II power to determine who are and who are not enemies of the
United States during times of war."[78] Luttig wanted the full panel to rehear
the case and resolve those issues. Unless the judiciary clarified the range
of executive power, an "embedded journalist or even the unwitting tourist
could be seized and detained in a foreign combat zone," without meaningful judicial review.[79] However, what kind of judicial review is possible
if the Court should defer—as Luttig urged—to the President?

Judge Motz regarded the Mobbs Declaration as a pure hearsay statement
by "an unelected, otherwise unknown, government 'advisor.'"[80] Mobbs did
not claim "*any* personal knowledge of the facts surrounding Hamdi's capture and incarceration."[81] Instead, Mobbs merely reviewed "undisclosed
and unenumerated 'relevant records and reports.'"[82] She also noted: "The
panel's decision marks the first time in our history that a federal court has
approved the elimination of protections afforded a citizen by the Constitution solely on the basis of the Executive's designation of that citizen as an
enemy combatant, without testing the accuracy of the designation. Neither
the Constitution nor controlling precedent sanction this holding."[83]

Newspaper stories explain that, according to Pakistani intelligence sto-
ries, Northern Alliance commanders were slated to receive $5,000 for each
Taliban prisoner and $20,000 for al Qaeda fighters.[84] Obviously, Northern
Alliance commanders had a clear financial incentive to assert that a cap-
tured prisoner, no matter how ambiguous his standing, belonged to al
Qaeda.

With the Hamdi case headed for the Supreme Court, the Bush adminis-

---

77. Hamdi v. Rumsfeld, 337 F.3d 335 (4th Cir. 2003).
78. Id. at 357.
79. Id. at 358.
80. Id. at 368.
81. Id. at 373 (emphasis in original).
82. Id.
83. Id. at 369
84. "Petition for Writ of Certiorari," Hamdi v. Rumsfeld, at 9 n. 8.

tration on December 2, 2003, decided to strengthen its case by giving Hamdi access to a lawyer. The Defense Department announced that he would be allowed to see a lawyer "as a matter of discretion and military policy" rather than a constitutional right. The government's statement emphasized that there was no obligation to make a lawyer available and that its decision "should not be treated as a precedent."[85] Pentagon officials stated that the Defense Department had "completed its intelligence collection" with Hamdi and that access to an attorney would not now harm national security.[86] That decision happened to occur at the same time that the case was before the Supreme Court.

When Hamdi's attorney was allowed to see him several months later, the government insisted that a military observer remain in the room in order to record the session. The attorney, Frank W. Dunham Jr., said he considered canceling the meeting because it would violate the tradition of attorney-client privilege. He finally agreed to go, knowing that he would be prohibited from discussing the conditions of Hamdi's confinement or talking to him "about anything that's substantive to the case."[87]

Not so Fast, Mr. Bush

On June 28, 2004, eight Justices rejected the government's central argument that Hamdi's detention was quintessentially a presidential decision, not to be reevaluated and second-guessed by the courts. Only Justice Thomas parted company from the position of the eight Justices that courts have the competence to check and override presidential decisions in the field of national security. However, instead of offering a clean 8–1 ruling, the case offered various combinations from a plurality of four (O'Connor, Rehnquist, Kennedy, and Breyer), joined at times by a concurrence/dissent from Souter and Ginsburg, and at other times by a dissent from Scalia and Stevens. Several of the plurality's judgments and prescriptions were shallow and contradictory.

Writing for the plurality, Justice O'Connor supplied language that found ready use in newspaper and media coverage: "we necessarily reject the Government's assertion that separation of powers principles mandate a heavily circumscribed role for the courts in such circumstances. . . . We

85. Jerry Markon and Dan Eggen, "U.S. Allows Lawyer for Citizen Held as 'Enemy Combatant,'" Washington Post, December 3, 2003, at A1.

86. Id. at A7.

87. Jerry Markon, "Military to Watch Prisoner Interview," Washington Post, January 31, 2004, at B3.

have long since made clear that a state of war is not a blank check for the President when it comes to the rights of the Nation's citizens. . . . Whatever power the United States Constitution envisions for the Executive in its exchanges with other nations or with enemy organizations in times of conflict, it most assuredly envisions a role for all three branches when individual liberties are at stake."[88] On such general principles the plurality was joined by Souter, Ginsburg, Scalia, and Stevens.

The plurality held that an enemy combatant "must receive notice of the factual basis for his classification, and a fair opportunity to rebut the Government's factual assertions before a neutral decisionmaker."[89] That position attracted the support of Souter and Ginsburg, but they did so with quite different reasoning. They found Hamdi's detention forbidden by §4001(a) (the Non-Detention Act) and unauthorized by the Use of Force Act, which Congress enacted to authorize military operations against Afghanistan. Without reaching any questions of the process that would be appropriate for Hamdi in litigating his release, they said that the government had "failed to justify holding him in the absence of a further Act of Congress, criminal charges, a showing that the detention conforms to the laws of war, or a demonstration that §4001(a) is unconstitutional." Unable to command a majority of the Court for their view, Souter and Ginsburg reluctantly joined with the plurality in ordering remand on terms "closest to those I would impose." The terms of the plurality's remand "will allow Hamdi to offer evidence that he is not an enemy combatant, and he should at the least have the benefit of that opportunity." It was on that ground that Souter and Ginsburg agreed that someone in Hamdi's position "is entitled at a minimum to notice of the Government's claimed factual basis for holding him, and to a fair chance to rebut it before a neutral decision maker."[90]

Scalia and Stevens, in their dissent, did not express views about the need for notice to Hamdi and an opportunity to present his case before a neutral decision maker. They went to more fundamental grounds, concluding that Hamdi was entitled to a habeas decree requiring his release "unless (1) criminal proceedings are promptly brought, or (2) Congress has suspended the writ of habeas corpus."[91]

The plurality held that Hamdi "unquestionably has the right to access to counsel in connection with the proceedings on remand."[92] Souter and

88. Hamdi v. Rumsfeld, 124 S.Ct. 2633, 2650 (2004).
89. Id. at 2648.
90. Id. at 2660.
91. Id. at 2671.
92. Id. at 2652.

Ginsburg said they did not disagree with this affirmation of Hamdi's right to counsel.[93] Scalia and Stevens offered no views on the right to counsel because they objected vehemently to the plurality's effort to prescribe a host of procedural rules to guide a future trial, such as putting the burden of proof on the citizen rather than on the government, and allowing testimony by hearsay rather than live witnesses.[94] To Scalia and Stevens, the Court had no competence to offer such procedures. Those questions should be left to Congress: "If civil rights are to be curtailed during wartime, it must be done openly and democratically, as the Constitution requires, rather than by silent erosion through an opinion of this Court."[95]

On other issues the eight Justices, after combining to reject much of the government's case, differed sharply. The plurality described *Quirin* as "a unanimous opinion. It both postdates and clarifies *Milligan*, providing us with the most apposite precedent that we have on the question of whether citizens may be detained in such circumstances."[96] To Scalia and Stevens, the Nazi saboteur case "was not this Court's finest hour."[97] They pointed to a number of problems, such as the fundamental difference between the fate of eight saboteurs who were "admitted enemy invaders" (citing *Quirin*) and Hamdi, who "insists that he is *not* a belligerent."[98]

The plurality agreed with the government's assertion that the Use of Force Act constituted "explicit congressional authorization for the detention of individuals," thus satisfying §4001(a).[99] The plurality cited nothing in the text or legislative history of the Use of Force Act that "explicitly" indicated a willingness by Congress to authorize the detention of U.S. citizens. In fact, a few paragraphs later the plurality said "it is of no moment" that the Use of Force Act "does not use specific language of detention."[100] Somewhere, in the language of the Use of Force Act, the plurality found implicit support for the detention of U.S. citizens, although no member of Congress referred to detention in debating the statute.

Souter and Ginsburg disagreed sharply with the plurality on this point, stating that the government had "failed to demonstrate that the Force Resolution authorizes the detention complained of here even on the facts the

---

93. Id. at 2660.
94. Id. at 2672.
95. Id. at 2674.
96. Id. at 2643.
97. Id. at 2669.
98. Id. at 2670 (emphasis in original).
99. Id. at 2639–40.
100. Id. at 2641.

Government claims. If the Government raises nothing further than the record now shows, the Non-Detention Act entitles Hamdi to be released."[101] They pointed out that the Use of Force Act "never so much as uses the word detention."[102] They noted also that 38 days after completing action on the Use of Force Act, Congress passed the USA Patriot Act, which authorized the detention of alien terrorists for no more than seven days unless the government pressed criminal charges or instituted deportation proceedings.[103]

Scalia and Stevens also strongly objected to the plurality's position that Hamdi's imprisonment could be justified on the basis of the Use of Force Act. They said the statute did not authorize the detention of a U.S. citizen "with the clarity necessary to satisfy the interpretive canon that statutes should be construed so as to avoid grave constitutional concerns."[104] Thomas's dissent agreed with the plurality that Congress had authorized the President to detain U.S. citizens by passing the Use of Force Act.[105]

In deciding how to balance the interests of the government with the liberty interests of an individual, the plurality curiously relied on *Mathews v. Eldridge* (1976), a case that involved the right of the government to withdraw disability benefits.[106] By using this decision to weigh the government's interest over the rights of a detainee, the plurality arrived at its judgment that a detainee required notice and an opportunity to challenge the government's assertion before a neutral decision maker. Scalia and Stevens took special offense at deciding a national security case on the basis of a ruling that concerned "newly recognized property rights."[107] In his dissent, Thomas did not agree with the plurality that "the balancing approach" of *Mathews* "is the appropriate analytical tool with which to analyze this case."[108]

Finally, the plurality endorsed Hamdi's right to "a fair opportunity to rebut the Government's factual assertions before a neutral decisionmaker," drawing attention to earlier rulings that due process requires a "neutral and detached judge."[109] The plurality later insisted that "an independent tribu-

101. Id. at 2653.
102. Id. at 2657.
103. Id. at 2659.
104. Id. at 2671.
105. Id. at 2679.
106. Id. at 2646.
107. Id. at 2672.
108. Id. at 2683.
109. Id. at 2648.

nal," an "independent review," and an "impartial adjudicator" would not overtax the executive branch or interfere with military operations.[110] However, the plurality appeared to be satisfied by some kind of review panel within the executive branch, perhaps even "an appropriately authorized and properly constituted military tribunal."[111]

The plurality seemed to lose sight of how Hamdi became an "enemy combatant." The person who made that designation was President Bush. No review panel within the executive branch, much less within the military, could possibly possess the sought-for qualities of neutrality, detachment, independence, and impartiality in passing judgment on a presidential decision. Instead of a military panel reviewing Hamdi's status, the Court's decision prompted the government to release Hamdi rather than try him. Conditions of release included that he renounce his U.S. citizenship, move to Saudi Arabia, and agree not to sue the federal government on the ground that his civil rights were violated.[112]

Jose Padilla

Jose Padilla, born in New York, was held by the military as a suspect in a plot to detonate a radiological dispersal device—or "dirty bomb"—in the United States. Although the administration designated both Hamdi and Padilla as enemy combatants, their cases are quite different. As explained by Judge Wilkinson of the Fourth Circuit, to compare the battlefield capture of Hamdi "to the domestic arrest in *Padilla v. Rumsfeld* is to compare apples and oranges."[113] The FBI arrested Padilla in Chicago on May 8, 2002, on a material witness warrant to secure his testimony before a grand jury in New York City. After President Bush designated him an enemy combatant, the material witness warrant was withdrawn and the government moved Padilla to a Navy brig in Charleston, South Carolina. He had access to an attorney, Donna Newman, in New York City, but not after his removal to Charleston, with the exception of brief, monitored visits after the Supreme Court agreed to hear the case.

110. Id. at 2649–50.

111. Id. at 2651.

112. Jerry Markon, "U.S. to Free Hamdi, Send Him Home," Washington Post, September 23, 2004, at A1; "Hamdi set to Be Flown Home," Washington Post, September 28, 2004, at A28.

113. Hamdi v. Rumsfeld, 337 F.3d at 344.

If the government's facts on Hamdi are correct, there would be a basis for designating him an "enemy combatant." It is much more a stretch to make that case for Padilla, because the government did not claim that he participated in hostilities in Afghanistan or engaged in any way as a "combatant" on a battlefield. But according to the government, one can be an enemy combatant without ever fighting on a battlefield: "In a time of war, an enemy combatant is subject to capture and detention wherever found, whether on a battlefield or elsewhere abroad or within the United States."[114] A definition of that breadth goes far beyond the traditional meaning of "enemy combatant" and brings within it a multitude of activities that have, in the past, been litigated in civil court.

Access to Counsel

On December 4, 2002, a district judge in New York City ruled that Padilla had a right to consult with counsel under conditions that would minimize the likelihood that he could use his lawyers as "unwilling intermediaries for the transmission of information to others."[115] Judge Michael B. Mukasey held that Padilla had a right to present facts and the most convenient way to do that was to present them through counsel.[116] Moreover, on the issue of Padilla's status, Mukasey insisted on evidence from the government to support Bush's finding that Padilla is an enemy combatant.

Mukasey did not grant to Padilla the right of counsel because of the Sixth Amendment, which applies only to "all criminal prosecutions." With no charges filed against him, there was no criminal proceeding. Instead, Mukasey looked to congressional policy on habeas corpus petitions, entitling an applicant to "deny any of the facts set in the return or allege any other material facts" (28 U.S.C. § 2243). As to the government's concern that Padilla might somehow use his attorney to communicate to the enemy, Mukasey noted that such an argument would even prohibit an indicted member of al Qaeda from consulting with counsel in an Article III proceeding.[117]

After Judge Mukasey granted the government's request to reconsider his ruling, he again held that Padilla was entitled to consult with counsel to

---

114. "Respondents' Response to, and Motion to Dismiss, the Amended Petition for a Writ of Habeas Corpus," Padilla v. Bush, U.S. District Court for the Southern District of New York, at 23.

115. Padilla ex rel. Newman v. Bush, 233 F.Supp.2d 564, 569 (S.D.N.Y. 2002).

116. Id. at 599.

117. Id. at 603–4.

aid his habeas petition. Mukasey described the government's new arguments as "permeated with the pinched legalism one usually encounters from non-lawyers."[118] The government thought the "some evidence" standard supported the lawfulness of Padilla's detention, but Mukasey replied that no court of which he was aware had applied that standard "to a record that consists solely of the government's evidence, to which the government's adversary has not been permitted to respond."[119]

Mukasey also underscored the difference between the Hamdi and Padilla cases: "Unlike Hamdi, Padilla was detained in this country, and initially by law enforcement officers pursuant to a material witness warrant. He was not captured on a foreign battlefield by soldiers in combat. The prospect of courts second-guessing battlefield decisions, which they have resolutely refused to do, . . . does not loom in this case."[120] The government decided to appeal to the Second Circuit.

Like Hamdi, Padilla was designated an enemy combatant on the basis of a Mobbs Declaration. Padilla's attorneys, Donna Newman and Andrew Patel, said that Mobbs's own footnotes "conceded that the government's 'confidential sources' probably were not 'completely candid,' and that one source subsequently recanted and another was being treated with drugs." Patel remarked: "Someone who's a confirmed liar and someone else who's on drugs and one of the two has recanted. You really think someone should be locked up for a year in solitary confinement based on *that?*"[121]

The Second Circuit

On December 18, 2003, the Second Circuit held that the President lacked inherent constitutional authority as Commander in Chief to detain American citizens on American soil outside a zone of combat. To justify such detentions, he needed specific congressional authorization. As the court noted, the Non-Detention Act (§ 4001(a)) specifically prohibited the President from detaining an American citizen on American soil. Passed in 1971, the statute reads: "No citizen shall be imprisoned or otherwise detained by the United States except pursuant to an Act of Congress." The court ruled that the Use of Force Act, passed shortly after 9/11 to authorize military

118. Padilla ex rel. Newman v. Rumsfeld, 243 F.Supp.2d 42, 47 (S.D.N.Y. 2003).
119. Id. at 54.
120. Id. at 56.
121. Paula Span, "Enemy Combatant Vanishes into a 'Legal Black Hole,'" Washington Post, July 30, 2003, at A8 (emphasis in original).

action against Afghanistan, did not represent an authorization for detentions.[122]

Before reaching those substantive points, the court addressed some preliminary issues. It ruled that Padilla's attorney, Donna Newman, had a sufficiently close relationship to him to have standing as "next friend" to bring a habeas petition on his behalf. The court said there was no dispute that Padilla "is unable to file a petition on his own behalf—he is being held incommunicado," and there was no issue "as to Newman's professional relationship with Padilla."[123] She was assigned to represent him when he was first brought to the Southern District and before he was transferred to military custody.

The government argued that the petition for a writ of habeas corpus directed to Secretary Donald Rumsfeld should be dismissed or transferred to the district court in South Carolina, where Padilla was being held. The proper custodian, said the government, was Commander Melanie A. Marr, the commander of the brig in South Carolina. However, the court rejected this analysis as too formalistic. Rumsfeld was charged by President Bush with detaining Padilla, and Rumsfeld or his designees determined that Padilla would be sent to the brig in South Carolina. The "legal reality of control" was vested with Rumsfeld, "since only he—not Commander Marr—could inform the President that further restraint of Padilla as an enemy combatant is no longer necessary."[124] All of the initial actions regarding Padilla's status as enemy combatant were completed by Rumsfeld or his agents in the Southern District of New York, not in South Carolina.[125]

With regard to the constitutional issues, the Second Court relied largely on the Steel Seizure Case of 1952, where Justice Black wrote for the Court that presidential power "must stem either from an act of Congress or from the Constitution itself."[126] Justice Black held that President Truman's seizure of steel mills could not be justified as a function of the President's powers as Commander in Chief. A concurrence by Justice Jackson developed three categories for evaluating the exercise of emergency power by the President. First, when the President acts pursuant to an express or implied authorization from Congress, "his authority is at its maximum, for it includes all that he possesses in his own right plus all that Congress can

122. Padilla v. Rumsfeld, 352 F.3d 695 (2d Cir. 2003).
123. Id. at 703.
124. Id. at 707.
125. Id. at 710.
126. Id. at 711 (citing Youngstown Co. v. Sawyer, 343 U.S. 579, 585 (1952)).

delegate." Second, when the President acts in the absence of either a congressional grant or denial of authority, "he can only rely upon his own independent powers, but there is a zone of twilight in which he and Congress may have concurrent authority, or in which its distribution is uncertain." The third category included situations where the President takes measures that are incompatible with the express or implied policy of Congress. In such cases, the President's power "is at its lowest ebb, for then he can rely only upon his own constitutional powers minus any constitutional powers of Congress over the matter."[127]

The Second Circuit ruled that President Bush lacked inherent constitutional authority as Commander in Chief to detain American citizens on American soil outside a zone of combat, and concluded that the Non-Detention Act served as an explicit congressional denial of authority within the meaning of Steel Seizure Case, thus placing Bush's action in the third category. The Second Circuit also decided that the Constitution "entrusts the ability to define and punish offenses against the law of nations to the Congress, not the Executive."[128] Although Congress "may have the power to authorize the detention of United States citizens under the circumstances of Padilla's case, the President, acting alone, may not."[129]

The government argued that *Quirin* "conclusively establishes the President's authority to exercise military jurisdiction over American citizens."[130] The Second Circuit disagreed, stating that the Court's decision in 1942 "rested on express congressional authorization of the use of military tribunals to try combatants who violated the laws of war." Second, *Quirin* found it "unnecessary for present purposes to determine to what extent the President as Commander in Chief has constitutional power to create military commissions without the support of congressional legislation." Third, when the 1942 decision was issued, Section 4001(a) had not been enacted. Fourth, the German saboteurs "admitted that they were soldiers in the armed forces of a nation against whom the United States had formally declared war." Padilla made no such admission. He disputed his designation as an enemy combatant.[131]

Judge Wesley, concurring in part and dissenting in part, disagreed that the President lacked authority from Congress or the Constitution to order

127. Id. (Citing Youngstown Co. v. Sawyer, 343 U.S. at 637–38).
128. Id. at 714.
129. Id. at 715.
130. Id.
131. Id. at 716.

the detention and interrogation of Padilla. It was his view that the President, as Commander in Chief, "has the inherent authority to thwart acts of belligerency at home or abroad that would do harm to United States citizens."[132] He also believed that the Use of Force Act specifically authorized President Bush's decision to designate Padilla as an enemy combatant.[133] Even with these challenges to the majority's decision, Judge Wesley noted that Padilla's right to pursue a remedy through habeas corpus "would be meaningless if he had to do so alone. I therefore would extend to him the right to counsel as Chief Judge Mukasey did."[134]

Following the decision by the Second Circuit and the government's appeal to the Supreme Court, the Bush administration announced that it would permit Padilla to consult with Donna Newman. As with Hamdi, access to an attorney was "a matter of discretion and military authority," was not required by domestic or international law, and "should not be treated as a precedent."[135] On March 3, 2004, Newman and Padilla talked through a glass security window while two government officials listened to the conversation and videotaped the meeting. She said "this was not an attorney-client meeting." She was not allowed to ask "about the conditions of his confinement." She also wanted to be able to send Padilla documents without having them first reviewed by the government. As it was, she gave Padilla some newspaper articles about his case.[136] The government also consented to a longstanding request from the International Committee of the Red Cross to meet with Padilla.[137]

Comey's Statement

After the Court heard oral argument on Padilla's case and the Justices were busy drafting a decision, Deputy Attorney General James Comey made an extraordinary public statement on June 1, 2004. He explained that Senator Orrin Hatch had sent a letter to Attorney General Ashcroft, asking the Justice and Defense Departments to supply information about American

132. Id. at 726.
133. Id. at 728–31.
134. Id. at 732.
135. Thomas E. Ricks and Michael Powell, "2nd Suspect Can See Lawyer," Washington Post, February 12, 2004, at A16.
136. Michael Powell, "Lawyer Visits 'Dirty Bomb' Suspect," Washington Post, March 4, 2004, at A10.
137. Deborah Sontag, "Terror Suspect's Path from Streets to Brig," New York Times, April 25, 2004, at 1.

citizens being held as enemy combatants in the United States. Comey felt that much was known about Hamdi but "much less is known about Jose Padilla, in part because rules about classification have long restricted what we could say about him publicly." Even before receiving Hatch's letter, Comey said that the administration had been working to compile and declassify what was known about Padilla from his own statements, information obtained from al Qaeda detainees around the world, and from intelligence sources.[138]

As a result of those labors, Comey told reporters that the Justice Department was able "for the first time to tell the full story of Jose Padilla," permitting the American public "to understand the threat he posed and also [to] understand that the president's decision was and continues to be essential to the protection of the American people."[139] First, the claim of a "full story" was not credible if the source came from one side: the government's. Second, Comey's statement could easily be interpreted as an election year stunt to emphasize that President Bush was taking every necessary step to protect the American public. Third, the statement was released after about a month of the administration being steadily pounded by the disclosures of U.S. soldiers abusing prisoners in Abu Ghraib. Fourth, Comey's claim that the government was motivated by giving the public access to information jarred with the administration's established pattern of withholding information not only from the public but from Congress.

Finally, was Comey trying to influence the Justices, even in a ham-handed way? If he wanted to inform the public, why not wait a couple of weeks to let the decision come down? Court watchers could not recall a prosecutor releasing new information against an individual whose case was in the hands of Justices. Of course nothing is unusual if the Justice Department releases a one-sided indictment of an individual, and follows that with supplemental indictments. The difference with Padilla was that he was not being charged and thus had no opportunity to respond through an attorney. Padilla's attorney, Donna Newman, listened to Comey and thought: "Okay, that's his opening statement. Now when do I get to speak up? Everything my client says to me is classified. I can't offer any defense."[140]

138. U.S. Department of Justice, "Remarks of Deputy Attorney General James Comey Regarding Jose Padilla, June 1, 2004, at 1; http://www.justice.gov/dag/speech/2004/day6104.htm (hereafter "Remarks of Comey").

139. Id.

140. Michael Powell, "Padilla Case Puts Lawyers in Limbo, Too," Washington Post, June 5, 2004, at A3.

Legal experts referred to Comey's remarks as "the opening statement in a trial they have refused to allow."[141] An editorial in the *Washington Post* remarked that "the government has delivered a broadside smear against which no defense is possible."[142]

Much of what appeared in Comey's statement had appeared in print before. The fresh information was the claim that Padilla, supposedly involved in a dirty-bomb plot, also considered a plan to locate high-rise apartment buildings in the United States that had natural gas supplied to all floors. He and accomplices would rent two apartments in each building, "seal those apartments, turn on the gas, and set timers to detonate and destroy the buildings simultaneously at a later time."[143] How anyone, much less Padilla, could successfully carry out such an assignment was not explained by Comey.

No one questioned that Comey's statement had political appeal. He said that the administration decided to release the information "to help people understand why we are doing what we are doing in the war on terror."[144] The last line read: "We now know much of what Jose Padilla knows, and what we have learned confirms that the president of the United States made the right call, and that that call saved lives."[145] The not-so-hidden message: If the Justices disposed of the case in a way that put Padilla on the streets, the blood from any terrorist action would belong on their hands.

The press reacted to Comey's statement with considerable skepticism. Here is the lead sentence in the *New York Times:* "Just weeks before the Supreme Court is to decide whether the Bush administration improperly declared Jose Padilla an enemy combatant, the Justice Department on Tuesday released newly declassified documents that it said showed the grave terrorist threat he posed to the United States."[146] The Justice Department's move "appeared aimed at helping win over public opinion in a case in which even some conservatives have questioned the rationale for locking up Mr. Padilla indefinitely in military custody."[147] Subheads in a *Los Angeles Times* story offered these observations: "Allegations are released as

141. Dan Eggen, "U.S. Details Case Against Terror Suspect," June 2, 2004, at A8.
142. "No Defense Possible" (editorial), Washington Post, June 4, 2004, at A22.
143. Remarks of Comey, at 4.
144. Id. at 5.
145. Id.
146. Eric Lichtblau, "U.S. Spells Out Dangers Posed by Plot Suspect," New York Times, June 2, 2004, at A1.
147. Id.

the Supreme Court prepares to rule on his arrest and detention," and "Timing of Justice Department's Padilla's Allegations Questioned."[148]

The Court Ducks

On June 28, the Court divided 5–4 in deciding that Padilla's habeas petition had been filed with the wrong court. It should have been filed, said the majority, with a district court in South Carolina, where Padilla was housed in a naval brig, rather than with the southern district in New York. The southern district therefore lacked jurisdiction over the habeas petition and Padilla's attorney was advised to submit the petition to the "only proper respondent," which is "the person who has custody over [the petitioner]." That person, said the Court, was Commander Marr at the naval brig.[149]

The issue of the proper custodian was explored with some care during oral argument. Deputy Solicitor General Clement told the Court that the fact that Padilla was in New York "in the first place is a bit of happenstance." Justice Stevens corrected him: "No, but the Government is responsible for him being in New York," referring to the fact that it was the government who initially apprehended Padilla in Chicago and brought him to New York as a material witness.[150] Toward the end of the oral argument, Clement volunteered that on the question of jurisdiction, "it is true that the immediate custodian rule is not a hard and fast rule and it has been— exceptions have been made."[151] Justice O'Connor referred to considerable uncertainty: "Jurisdiction under the Habeas Statutes has been a bit of a confusion because, for instance, on behalf of aliens, I think we have allowed jurisdiction to be obtained in the manner it was here, have we not?" Clement disagreed.[152] Later, in a passage of some obscurity, he said that on questions of who is custodian "this Court has relaxed the rules. . . . but it has never deviated."[153]

Rehnquist, joined by O'Connor, Scalia, Kennedy, and Thomas, regarded

---

148. Richard B. Schmitt, "Government Says Padilla Plotted High-Rise Attacks," Los Angeles Times, June 2, 2004, at A1. For further criticism of Comey's statement, see Jonathan Turley, "You Have Rights—If Bush Says You Do," Los Angeles Times, June 3, 2004, at A15, and Scott Turow, "Trial by News Conference? No Justice in That," Washington Post, June 13, 2004, at B1.

149. Rumsfeld v. Padilla, 124 S.Ct. 2711 (2004).

150. U.S. Supreme Court, Rumsfeld v. Padilla, oral argument, April 28, 2004, at 18.

151. Id. at 56.

152. Id. at 5–6.

153. Id. at 16.

Commander Marr as the only proper respondent to the habeas petition because she, not Secretary Rumsfeld, was Padilla's custodian. He argued that limiting district courts to "their respective jurisdictions" helps prevent forum shopping by habeas petitioners.[154] Stevens, writing for the dissenters, agreed that habeas petitioners should not be allowed to engage in forum shopping. However, he pointed out that if the government had given Newman notice of its intent to ask the district court to vacate the material witness warrant and place Padilla in the custody of the Defense Department, with eventual transfer to South Carolina, she could have properly filed the petition in New York. Had she done so, Stevens said that the government could not then transfer Padilla to another district.[155] The dissenters objected that the government should not have had a tactical advantage in moving unilaterally and informing Newman several days later. She was entitled to fair notice to allow her to present in timely manner a habeas petition.[156] If anyone was doing forum shopping to gain an advantage it was the government, not the petitioner.

Guantánamo Detainees

During U.S. military operations in Afghanistan and Pakistan in late 2001 and 2002, the United States and its allies captured thousands of individuals thought to be connected with the Taliban regime and al Qaeda's terrorist network. The military determined that many of the individuals should be detained as enemy combatants, citing two reasons. Detention prevented them from continuing to aid the enemy and it offered an opportunity to gather intelligence to further military operations and the war against terrorism. The U.S. military transferred some of those combatants from Afghanistan to the American naval base at Guantánamo Bay, Cuba. In time, the number of detainees at the base reached about 700. The detainees were not charged with any crimes. None had access to attorneys.

In the D.C. Circuit

Aliens detained at the naval base petitioned for a writ of habeas corpus, and family members of 12 Kuwaiti nationals held at the base sought a pre-

154. Rumsfeld v. Padilla, 124 S.Ct. 2711, 2724–25 (2004).
155. Id. at 2731–32.
156. Id. at 2732.

liminary injunction on their behalf, alleging violations of due process, the Alien Tort Claims Act, and the Administrative Procedure Act. On July 30, 2002, District Judge Colleen Kollar-Kotelly held that the two cases would be considered only as petitions for writs of habeas corpus. On the merits, she ruled that aliens held by the United States outside the sovereign territory of the United States could not use federal courts to pursue petitions for habeas relief.[157]

At trial, the Justice Department conceded that "there's a body of international law that governs the rights of people who are seized during the course of combative activities." Yet the government argued that "the scope of those rights are for the military and political branches to determine—and certainly that reflects the idea that other countries would play a role in that process."[158] In short, allies would have an opportunity to participate in the decision on how to treat the detainees, but not the federal courts.

Judge Kollar-Kotelly relied on *Johnson v. Eisentrager* (1950) for the proposition that no court had authority to extend the writ of habeas corpus to aliens held outside the sovereign territory of the United States. The Court in 1950 noted that aliens within the country have a number of rights, including access to federal courts, and those rights expand as they declare an intent to become a U.S. citizen. She remarked that it was "undisputed that the individuals held at Guantanamo Bay do not seek to become citizens."[159] The detainees did not "fall into any of the categories of cases where the courts have entertained the claims of individuals seeking access to the country."[160]

Relying on the 1950 precedent, she noted that enemy aliens captured during war do not have even a qualified access to federal courts, compared to aliens living within the United States. The essential point, she said, was not that the detainees are enemy aliens, but that they are aliens held outside the territory over which the United States was sovereign. That conclusion required her to decide whether Guantánamo Bay was part of the sovereign territory of the United States. She said that both parties agreed that Guantánamo Bay "is not part of the sovereign territory of the United States."[161] Those who represented the detainees argued that the United

---

157. Rasul v. Bush, 215 F.Supp.2d 55 (D.D.C. 2002).
158. Id. at 56.
159. Id. at 66.
160. Id.
161. Id. at 69.

States "has de facto sovereignty over the military base at Guantanamo Bay" because the United States exercises control and jurisdiction over the base.

The United States occupies the base under a lease entered into with the Cuban government in 1903. The lease provides: "While on the one hand the United States recognizes the continuance of the ultimate sovereignty of the Republic of Cuba over [the military base at Guantánamo Bay], on the other hand the Republic of Cuba consents that during the period of occupation by the United States of said areas under the terms of this agreement the United States shall exercise complete jurisdiction and control over and within said areas with the right to acquire . . . for the public purposes of the United States any land or other property therein by purchase or by exercise of eminent domain with full compensation to the owners thereof."[162]

Judge Kollar-Kotelly concluded from this language that it "is clear from this agreement, the United States does not have sovereignty over the military base at Guantanamo Bay."[163] Unlike the relationship of the United States to Puerto Rico, Guam, or Micronesia, the military base at Guantánamo Bay "is nothing remotely akin to a territory of the United States, where the United States provides certain rights to the inhabitants." The United States "merely leases an area of land for use as a naval base."[164] Those observations only treat part of the case. Obviously the lease excludes U.S. sovereignty over the base and clearly the base is not analogous to other territories, but the question remained whether the United States had the type of "jurisdiction and control" to justify habeas review by federal courts.

Appealed to the D.C. Circuit, Judge Kollar-Kotelly's decision was affirmed on March 11, 2003. The appellate court agreed that *Eisentrager* was correctly cited for the principle that the aliens at Guantánamo could not seek habeas relief in federal court: "the Guantanamo detainees have much in common with the German prisoners in *Eisentrager*. They too are aliens, they too were captured during military operations, they were in a foreign country when captured, they are now abroad, they are in the custody of the American military, and they have never had any presence in the United States."[165] Left unexplored by the D.C. Circuit were critical differences between the German prisoners in *Eisentrager* and the detainees at Guantánamo. Those differences would be highlighted once the case reached the Supreme Court.

---

162. Id. at 69 n. 14.
163. Id.
164. Id. at 71.
165. Al Odah v. United States, 321 F.3d 1134 (D.C. Cir. 2003).

The Ninth Circuit

With the Bush administration winning handily in the D.C. Circuit, a different pattern developed in the Ninth Circuit. On February 21, 2002, District Judge A. Howard Matz held that a coalition of journalists, lawyers, and clergy, having filed for a writ of habeas corpus on behalf of the detainees at Guantánamo Bay, lacked standing as "next friend." Federal law provides that an application for a writ of habeas corpus must be signed and verified by the person seeking relief "or by someone acting in his behalf."[166] Courts use the term "next friend" to indicate the person who acts on behalf of the individual seeking relief. Next-friend status is typically allowed when the real party cannot appear because of mental incompetence, inaccessibility, or some other disability.[167] In the case before the district court, there was nothing in the record to indicate that the detainees supported the coalition's petition, or that it had even attempted to communicate with the detainees.[168] The district court concluded that it had no jurisdiction to issue the writ (citing *Eisentrager*), and that detainees had no right to a writ of habeas corpus.

The Ninth Circuit agreed that the coalition was not entitled to next-friend standing, but ruled that the district court did not have jurisdiction to decide that neither it nor any other federal court may properly entertain the habeas claims presented in the case. Having concluded that the coalition lacked standing, the Ninth Circuit declined to reach the remaining questions dealt with by the district court. Reaching those issues, particularly the application of *Eisentrager,* was "inappropriate" because federal courts "should not adjudicate rights unnecessarily."[169]

A second case emerged in the Ninth Circuit. On May 13, 2003, Judge Matz held that he had no jurisdiction over a habeas claim from the brother of Falen Gherebi, who was captured by the United States in Afghanistan and detained at Guantánamo. Judge Matz concluded that the privilege of litigation did not extend to aliens in military custody outside the United States. He relied on *Eisentrager* and subsequent rulings that construed that case.[170] The Ninth Circuit reversed his decision on December 18, 2003,

166. 28 U.S.C. § 2242 (2000).
167. Whitmore v. Arkansas, 495 U.S. 149, 161–64 (1990).
168. Coalition of Clergy v. Bush, 189 F.Supp.2d 1036, 1043 (C.D. Cal. 2002).
169. Coalition of Clergy, Lawyers, & Professors v. Bush, 310 F.3d 1153, 1164 (9th Cir. 2002).
170. Gherebi v. Bush, 262 F.Supp.2d 1064, 1066 (C.D. Cal. 2003).

holding that habeas jurisdiction existed over the petition filed on behalf of "enemy combatants" detained at Guantánamo. It said that for habeas purposes, the naval base was a part of the sovereign territory of the United States. Moreover, the Ninth Circuit ruled that the district court for the Central District of California had personal jurisdiction over the Secretary of Defense.[171]

The Ninth Circuit first stated that it shared the desire of all Americans that the President be granted the necessary power and flexibility to prevent terrorist attacks. However, even in times of national emergency "it is the obligation of the Judicial Branch to ensure the preservation of our constitutional values and to prevent the Executive Branch from running roughshod over the rights of citizens and aliens alike." It could not accept the government's position that the executive branch "possesses the unchecked authority to imprison indefinitely any persons, foreign citizens included, on territory under the sole jurisdiction and control of the United States, without permitting such prisoners recourse of any kind to any judicial forum, or even access to counsel, regardless of the length or manner of their confinement."[172]

Contrary to the government's contention, *Eisentrager* "neither requires nor authorizes" such a result.[173] In *Eisentrager*, the Court spoke both of U.S. "territorial jurisdiction" and "sovereignty."[174] The Ninth Circuit refused to accept the government's reading of *Eisentrager* as holding "that the prerequisite for the exercise of jurisdiction is *sovereignty* rather than *territorial jurisdiction*."[175] It was evident to the Ninth Circuit that the United States "exercises sole territorial jurisdiction over Guantanamo."[176] Because of U.S. territorial jurisdiction over the base, "habeas jurisdiction lies in the present case."[177]

Releasing Detainees

While these cases were being prepared for appeal to the Supreme Court, the administration began to free some detainees and send them home.

---

171. Gherebi v. Bush, 352 F.3d 1278 (9th Cir. 2003).
172. Id. at 1283.
173. Id.
174. Id. at 1287.
175. Id. (emphasis in original).
176. Id. at 1288.
177. Id. at 1289–90.

Their accounts differed on the treatment they received at Guantánamo Bay. Eighteen Afghan men set free on March 25, 2003, said they were generally fed well and received medical care, but at times were shackled, hit, and humiliated. They complained that American soldiers insulted Islam by sitting on the Koran or throwing it in the toilet. Some detainees acknowledged fighting with the Taliban, but said it was not by choice. Others claimed they were apprehended while working on farms, driving taxis, or attending school.[178] In a series of interviews with Amnesty International, prisoners released from Guantánamo and Bagram air base in Afghanistan said they were forced to stand or kneel for hours in painful positions.[179]

Children between the ages of 13 and 15 were kept in a separate facility at Guantánamo. They received schooling, counseling, and visits from social workers.[180] The teenagers were released on January 29, 2004, and flown back to Afghanistan. That brought the number of released detainees to 87.[181] One of the teenagers said he was looking for work when arrested by Afghan soldiers, expressing anger "with the Afghans who handed me over to the Americans. The Americans did not know what was happening."[182]

On February 11, U.S. authorities released another detainee from Guantánamo, this time a Spaniard. The mothers of some of the eight Russian detainees said they preferred that their sons remain at the naval base because letters from their sons described it as a benign environment. Russian prisons, said one of the mothers, are "worse than hell."[183] Nevertheless, on March 1 the United States turned seven of the detainees over to Russia for prosecution. The transfer came three days after the State Department issued a report harshly critical of Russia's record with human rights, concluding that "law enforcement personnel frequently engaged in torture,

178. Marc Kaufman and April Witt, "Returning Afghans Talk of Guantanamo," Washington Post, March 26, 2003, at A12.

179. Tania Branigan, "Ex-Prisoners Allege Rights Abuses by U.S. Military," Washington Post, August 19, 2003, at A2.

180. Tania Branigan, "3 Likely to Be Freed from Guantanamo," Washington Post, August 23, 2003, at A18.

181. John Mintz, "U.S. Releases 3 Teens From Guantanamo," Washington Post, January 30, 2004, at A1.

182. Carlotta Gall, "Freed Afghan, 15, Recalls a Year at Guantánamo," New York Times, February 11, 2004, at A3. See also Carlotta Gall, "3 Afghan Youths Question U.S. Captivity," New York Times, March 12, 2004, at A12.

183. John Mintz and Robin Wright, "Spanish Detainee Sent Home," Washington Post, February 12, 2004, at A31.

violence and other brutal or humiliating treatment and often did so with impunity."[184] On March 9, five Britons were released from Guantánamo and sent back to England.[185] By March 21, 2004, the number of released detainees had reached 131.[186]

Prosecutorial Abuse

The need for some kind of judicial scrutiny over the Guantánamo detainees was heightened by reports of prosecutorial abuse toward Arab Americans and Muslims. Much of the harshness, arbitrariness, and abuse by law enforcement officials fell on that community. Although many of those actions do not directly implicate military tribunals, they illustrate the danger of trusting solely in executive and military authorities who have repeatedly demonstrated a disregard for fundamental fairness and procedural safeguards, especially in time of war and terrorism. Examples of governmental abuse underscore once again the need for congressional oversight, judicial checks, and public awareness.

Dr. Al Bader al-Hamzi, a 34-year-old radiologist from Saudi Arabia, was arrested at his townhouse in San Antonio the day after the September 11 terrorist attacks. Held for 12 days before being allowed to answer questions put to him by authorities, he was released on September 24 with no charges ever brought against him.[187] Ali al-Maqtari, born in Yemen, came to the United States with the hope of becoming a French teacher. Four days after the 9/11 attacks, he arrived at Fort Campbell, Kentucky, to drop off his American wife, who was reporting for active duty with the U.S. Army. He was ordered out of the car and later detained for two months by the Immigration and Naturalization Service (INS) in Mason, Tennessee. He appeared before a Senate subcommittee to testify about his experience.[188]

On September 12, 2001, Hady Hassen Omar was placed in jail because the FBI was convinced he had some connections to al Qaeda. Born in

184. Peter Baker, "U.S. Sends to Russia 7 Held at Guantanamo," Washington Post, March 2, 2004, at A14.

185. Alan Cowell, "Five Britons Released From Guantánamo Arrive Home," New York Times, March 10, 2004, at A12.

186. John Mintz, "U.S. Faces Quandary in Freeing Detainees," Washington Post, March 22, 2004, at A1, A16.

187. Elizabeth A. Palmer and Adriel Bettleheim, "War and Civil Liberties: Congress Gropes for a Role," CQ Weekly Report, December 1, 2001, at 2820.

188. "Department of Justice Oversight: Preserving Our Freedoms While Defending Against Terrorism," hearings before the Senate Committee on the Judiciary, 107th Cong., 1st Sess. 211–17 (2001).

Egypt, he lived in Fort Smith, Arkansas, with his American wife and baby daughter. A deputy from the local sheriff's office asked him to come to the station for a few questions. He was then held in captivity for 73 days, some of it in solitary confinement, until he became suicidal. He was released, but legal expenses left the couple broke and he was fired from his job. The government never presented charges against him.[189] These are only a few samples of prosecutorial abuse. They help explain why some procedure—independent from the executive branch—is necessary to check and verify governmental claims that someone is an enemy combatant and should be detained.

One of the most egregious cases was that of Capt. James Yee, a Muslim chaplain who ministered to military personnel and detainees at Guantánamo. Even though he faced relatively minor charges of mishandling classified documents,[190] he was confined for 76 days at a naval brig in South Carolina on suspicion of espionage. During that time, he was kept in solitary confinement and at times in chains and manacles. Upon release, the military announced that it was investigating new charges of possible violations of the Uniform Code of Military Justice, including contentions that he had kept pornography on his government computer and had an extramarital affair. His attorney, Eugene R. Fidell, said that the government had "destroyed this man's reputation for what turns out to be no good reason, and now it appears they are pursuing matters in a completely vindictive manner."[191] John L. Fugh, a retired major general and former judge advocate general, said the "whole thing makes the military prosecutors look ridiculous." Having failed on the espionage claims, to add "these Mickey Mouse charges just makes them look dumb, in my mind."[192]

The government eventually dropped the charges that Yee had mishandled classified information, possessed pornography, and committed adultery. That eliminated the prospect of a court-martial,[193] but the case then moved to a nonjudicial, administrative proceeding to consider the pornography and adultery charges. In this noncriminal action, a U.S. Army gener-

189. Matthew Brzesinski, "Hady Hassan Omar's Detention," New York Times Magazine, October 27, 2002, at 50–55.

190. John Mintz, "Ex-Muslim Cleric at Guantanamo Faces Minor Charges," Washington Post, October 11, 2003, at A6.

191. Neil A. Lewis, "Chaplain Held in Espionage Case Is Freed," New York Times, November 26, 2003, at A22.

192. Neil A. Lewis and Thom Shanker, "As Chaplain's Spy Case Nears, Some Ask Why It Went So Far," New York Times, January 4, 2004, at 1, 14.

193. Neil A. Lewis, "Charges Dropped Against Chaplain," New York Times, March 20, 2004, at A1.

al issued a reprimand to be added to Yee's permanent military record.[194] On appeal, Gen. James Hill threw out the reprimand, saying that while he believed that Yee's misconduct was wrong, "I do not believe, given the extreme notoriety of his case in the news media, that further stigmatizing Chaplain Yee would serve a just and fair purpose."[195]

Access to Federal Courts

The Supreme Court did not grant cert on the case out of the Ninth Circuit (*Gherebi*), but it did agree to hear the consolidated cases out of the D.C. Circuit (*Rasul* and *Al Odah*). When the case was argued on April 20, 2004, matters did not go well for the government. John J. Gibbons, for the detainees, told the Justices that officials from the executive branch "assert that their actions are absolutely immune from judicial examination whenever they elected to detain foreign nationals outside our borders."[196] Could the government detain U.S. citizens as well as foreign nationals? The habeas statute is not limited to U.S. citizens. With certain exceptions, the writ of habeas corpus extends to a "prisoner."[197]

The Justices asked Solicitor General Ted Olson whether citizens held at Guantánamo would be beyond the reach of a habeas petition. He assured the Court that there would be "more protection for citizens" than for aliens.[198] If a citizen were held at the naval base and sought a habeas petition, "we would not be contesting it."[199] That question, Olson cautioned, "is not before the Court."[200] Nevertheless, he admitted that "there is enhanced respect with respect to the power of the Court under the habeas corpus jurisdiction with respect to questions involving citizenship."[201]

Even with that issue put to the side, several Justices expressed discomfort with the scope of power sought by the government. Justice Breyer conceded that Olson's position "has a virtue of clarity." If the petitioner is not a citizen, and is outside the United States, "you don't get your foot in

---

194. "Yee Guilty on Adultery, Porn Charges," Washington Post, March 23, 2004, at A4.
195. "Reprimand of Muslim Chaplain Thrown Out," Washington Post, April 15, 2004, at A5.
196. U.S. Supreme Court, Rasul v. Bush, oral argument, April 20, 2004, at 3.
197. 28 U.S.C. § 2241(c) (2000).
198. U.S. Supreme Court, Rasul v. Bush, oral argument, at 37.
199. Id.
200. Id. at 39.
201. Id. at 28.

the door." But Breyer identified two problems. The first: "It seems rather contrary to an idea of a Constitution with three branches that the executive would be free to do whatever they want, whatever they want without a check." The second: "several hundred years of British history" interpreting habeas corpus ran contrary to the government's claim of power.[202]

Some of the Justices thought that relief to the detainees was barred by *Eisentrager*. Gibbons disagreed, pointing out several distinctions between the two cases. *Eisentrager* covered admitted enemy aliens who had received a hearing before a military tribunal. The detainees at Guantánamo did not admit to being enemy aliens and had never received a hearing. These differences would be discussed later in the Court's decision.[203] Throughout oral argument, several Justices regarded *Eisentrager* as "a hard opinion to fathom," a "very difficult decision to understand," and "ambiguous and not clearly determinative."[204]

Gibbons was later asked about the situation of a lawful combatant in a declared war, where an enemy of the United States is captured and detained. Would he have access to a habeas petition? Gibbons replied: "Absolutely not." He elaborated: "In the zone of active military operations or in an occupied area under martial law, habeas corpus jurisdiction has never extended."[205]

Toward the end of oral argument, Olson staked out a position he would eventually lose. On the issue of whether Guantánamo was outside the jurisdiction of federal courts to give habeas relief, he said that the "question of sovereignty is a political decision. It would be remarkable for the judiciary to start deciding where the United States is sovereign and where the United States has control."[206] He tried to liken the situation to military detainees "in a field of combat where there are prisons in Afghanistan where we have complete control with respect to the circumstances." Justices did not buy the analogy, pointing out that Afghanistan "is not a place where American law is, and for a century, has customarily been applied to all aspects of life," as at the naval base.[207]

On June 28, 2004, in a 6–3 decision, the Court refused to treat *Eisentrager* as an automatic bar on detainee access to a habeas petition. It ruled

202. Id. at 42.
203. Id. at 9.
204. Id. at 30–31, 44.
205. Id. at 15.
206. Id. at 51.
207. Id. at 52.

that federal courts have jurisdiction to consider challenges to the legality of the detention of foreign nationals captured abroad, in connection with hostilities, and held at Guantánamo. Writing for the majority, Justice Stevens pointed to six critical facts in the *Eisentrager* case: the prisoners were (1) enemy aliens, (2) had never been or resided in the United States, (3) were captured outside of U.S. territory and held there in military custody as a POW, (4) were tried and convicted by a military tribunal sitting outside the United States, (5) were convicted for offenses against laws of war committed outside the United States, and (6) were at all times imprisoned outside the United States. By contrast, the detainees at Guantánamo were not nationals of countries at war with the United States, had denied being engaged in or plotting acts of aggression against the United States, were never afforded access to any tribunal or even charged with or convicted of wrongdoing, and for two years had been detained in a territory over which the United States exercises exclusive jurisdiction and control.[208]

Drawing from a Court decision of 1973, Stevens noted that a prisoner's presence within the territorial jurisdiction of a district court is not "an invariable prerequisite" to the exercise of district court jurisdiction under the habeas statute, and that a district court acts within its respective jurisdiction as long as "the custodian can be reached by service of process."[209] Nothing in *Eisentrager* or any other case, Stevens said, "categorically excludes aliens detained in military custody outside the United States from the 'privilege of litigation' in U.S. courts." Federal courts, he maintained, "have traditionally been open to nonresident aliens."[210] Left hanging at the end of the majority's decision: to which federal courts could the detainees file a habeas petition?

Justice Kennedy concurred with the majority opinion, distinguishing *Eisentrager* by first describing Guantánamo as "in every practical respect a United States territory, . . . one far removed from any hostilities," and noting that what "matters is the unchallenged and indefinite control that the United States has long exercised over Guantanamo Bay." He also objected that the detainees at the naval base "are being held indefinitely, and without benefit of any legal proceedings to determine their status."[211]

Justice Scalia wrote a dissenting opinion, joined by Rehnquist and Thomas. He insisted that the majority opinion "overrules *Eisentrager*," even

---

208. Rasul v. Bush, 124 S.Ct. 2686, 2693 (2004).
209. Id. at 2695.
210. Id. at 2698.
211. Id. at 2700.

though the majority and Kennedy took pains to show how *Eisentrager* differed from the detainees at Guantánamo.[212] For Scalia, the fact that the detainees at the naval base "are not located within the territorial jurisdiction of any federal district court" should "end this case."[213] Having warned of the concentration of executive power in his Hamdi decision, in the Guantánamo case he worries that the extension of habeas petitions to the detainees will force federal courts "to oversee one aspect of the Executive's conduct of a foreign war,"[214] and warns that the majority's opinion "has a potentially harmful effect upon the Nation's conduct of a war." He believed that the "Commander in Chief and his subordinates had every reason to expect that the internment of combatants at Guantanamo Bay would not have the consequence of bringing the cumbersome machinery of our domestic courts into military affairs."[215] Under his prediction, the detainees at the naval base "can petition in any of the 94 federal judicial districts," opening the door to forum shopping.[216]

Two days after its opinion in the Guantánamo case, the Court issued an order to the Ninth Circuit to revive the Gherebi case. The Court granted cert and directed the appellate court to proceed in light of *Rumsfeld v. Padilla*.[217] The purpose appeared to require the Ninth Circuit either to explain why *Padilla* does not prevent a Guantánamo detainee from being heard in California or to suggest a more appropriate location, closer to the detainee.[218]

The Government's Response

On July 2, 2004, the administration granted approval to the lawyers for the 13 detainees at Guantánamo to travel to the naval base and meet with their clients.[219] Five days later, the Defense Department responded to *Rasul* by establishing a Combatant Status Review Tribunal, thus providing detainees

212. Id. at 2706.
213. Id. at 2701.
214. Id. at 2707.
215. Id. at 2710–11.
216. Id. at 2711.
217. Bush v. Gherebi, 124 S.Ct. 2932 (2004), granting motion of respondent for leave to proceed in forma pauperis, granting cert, vacating judgment, and remanding the case to the Ninth Circuit.
218. Charles Lane, "Justices Move to Define Detainees' Court Access," Washington Post, July 1, 2004, at A7.
219. Neil A. Lewis, "U.S. Allows Lawyers to Meet Detainees," New York Times, July 3, 2004, at A14.

at Guantánamo with notice to explain the grounds for their detention and an opportunity to contest their designation as enemy combatants. The panels consisted of three military officers who had nothing to do with the capture of a detainee or with interrogation procedures. Each detainee would have a "personal representative"—a military officer, not a lawyer—with access to information in DOD files on the detainee's background. The detainee could appear before the panel to present evidence and call witnesses if "reasonably available."[220]

Proceedings by the three-person panels were generally closed to the media and the public.[221] In seeking to challenge their detentions, prisoners were not entitled to access to their own lawyer. A brief by the Justice Department, filed in federal court, maintained: "As aliens detained by the military outside the sovereign territory of the United States and lacking a sufficient connection to the country, petitioners have no cognizable constitutional rights."[222] Jeff Fogel, legal director for the Center for Constitutional Rights, called the panel hearings "a sham." The detainees "are given no access to counsel, have no right to meaningfully contest any classified evidence against them and no meaningful way to call any witnesses in their favor."[223] On August 3, 2004, in response to a court challenge brought by lawyers for detainees at Guantánamo, a federal district judge refused to halt the panel hearings.[224]

Other details of these panels were made public. A military officer explained that a detainee "doesn't have to come to the proceeding."[225] The hearings, eventually open to a small number of reporters, lasted about two hours for each prisoner. The detainee's personal representative can pass along to the panel any evidence the detainee wants to offer, but the detainee is denied information "about how, where and from whom the information about the accusations supporting the enemy combatant charge originated if officials deem it classified."[226] The detainee thus had no

---

220. Department of Defense, News Transcript, "Defense Department Background Briefing on the Combatant Status Review Tribunal," July 7, 2004, at 1–2.

221. "Military Hearing for Guantanamo Detainee Is a First," Washington Post, July 31, 2004, at A24.

222. "New Fight on Guantánamo Rights," New York Times, July 31, 2004, at A28.

223. Mary Fitzgerald, "Detainees Seeking to End Hearings Without Counsel," Washington Post, August 3, 2004, at A13.

224. "Judge Refuses to Halt Military Hearings on Detainees," Washington Post, August 4, 2004, at A2.

225. Neil A. Lewis, "Scrutiny of Review Tribunals As War Crimes Trials Open," New York Times, August 24, 2004, at A12.

226. Id.

opportunity to judge whether the accusation was made by someone who acted out of malice, vengeance, or even ignorance.

After deciding 30 cases, the administration determined in early September 2004 that 29 detainees were legitimately held as enemy combatants but one was not. Held for almost three years at Guantánamo, this individual was released to be sent home to his native country. Anthony Romero, executive director of the American Civil Liberties Union, objected that it should not take years "for the U.S. military to determine that we were holding someone who is apparently not an enemy combatant."[227] Navy Secretary Gordon R. England, the top Pentagon official responsible for overseeing the panels, explained: "These are very complex issues. The information, many times it's ambiguous, it's conflicting. It's not always black and white."[228] He added: "it's very difficult to separate fact from fiction."[229] Yet the information was considered sufficiently "solid" to hold someone wrongly for nearly three years.

While these panel operations were underway, the administration began tribunal hearings for those who had already been designated as enemy combatant and eligible for the tribunals. Four trials were open to news media representatives, human rights organizations, and legal observers. Two of the tribunals involved Ali Hamza Ahmed Sulayman al-Bahlul and Salim Ahmed Hamdan, both of Yemen. The third concerned David Hicks of Australia, and the fourth Ibrahim Ahmed al-Qosi of Sudan. Rules adopted for the proceedings allowed witnesses to testify anonymously for the prosecution. It was uncertain how the tribunal would judge whether evidence or testimony had been obtained by coercion.[230] How would defense counsel know that incriminating statements had been obtained through coercion, or that the statements were false? What would happen if the government withheld exculpatory evidence? How would defense counsel even learn of such decisions?

Other questions concerned the qualifications of the five military officers who served on the tribunal. The defense counsel for Hamdan charged that the presiding officer of the tribunal, Col. Peter E. Brownback III, should be removed because of his close contacts with Pentagon officials who set up

227. Josh White, "Suspect Is Freed From Guantanamo," Washington Post, September 9, 2004, at A3.

228. Id.

229. Neil A. Lewis, "U.S. Will Send Detainee Home From Cuba," New York Times, September 9, 2004, at A18.

230. Neil A. Lewis, "U.S. Terrorism Tribunals Set to Begin Work," New York Times, August 22, 2004, at 17.

the tribunals, particularly with Maj. Gen. Altenburg, the appointing authority for the tribunals.[231] The credentials of other tribunal members were challenged as well. Brownback's colleagues included an officer who served in intelligence operations in the Middle East, one who sent detainees from Afghanistan to Guantánamo Bay, another who commanded a Marine who died in the 9/11 attack on the World Trade Center, and a fourth who, when asked if he knew what the Geneva Conventions were, answered: "Not specifically, no, sir."[232] Other defense counsel expressed concern that Brownback, the only lawyer on the tribunal, would exert excessive influence.[233] Although the Pentagon had spent considerable time in devising, in advance, the rules of procedure for military tribunals, observers at Guantánamo remarked that an entirely new set of rules were being "written on the run."[234]

The judicial process against al Qaeda and Taliban terrorists began with a combination of traditional indictments in federal district courts and the designation of "enemy combatant" to be applied to detainees at Guantánamo and such individuals as Hamdi and Padilla. After the three Supreme Court decisions on June 28, 2004, the administration established tribunals at the naval base to allow the detainees to challenge their designation as enemy combatant. The jurisdiction of district courts to hear habeas petitions was considerably broadened by distinguishing contemporary detainees from those at issue in *Eisentrager*. As a result, executive judgments and actions were now more open to scrutiny by another branch.

231. Neil A. Lewis, "First War-Crimes Case Opens at Guantánamo Base," New York Times, August 25, 2004, at A14; Scott Higham, "Hearings Open With Challenge to Tribunals," Washington Post, August 29, 2004, at A12, A13.

232. Scott Higham, "Bin Laden Aide Is Charged at First Tribunal," Washington Post, August 25, 2004, at A1.

233. Neil A. Lewis, "Australian Pleads Not Guilty to Terrorism Conspiracy," New York Times, August 26, 2004, at A13.

234. Neil A. Lewis, "Terror Tribunal Defendant Demands to Be Own Lawyer," New York Times, August 27, 2004, at A14.

9

CONCLUSIONS

Through the express grants of authority in Article I of the Constitution, Congress is empowered to be the dominant branch in creating and defining military courts, both courts-martial and military tribunals. William Winthrop, the premier nineteenth-century authority on military law, wrote: "in general, it is those provisions of the Constitution which empower Congress to 'declare war' and 'raise armies,' and which, in authorizing the initiation of war, authorize the employment of all necessary and proper agencies for its due prosecution, from which this tribunal [the military commission] derives its original sanction."[1]

Over the years, statutory actions that adopted and modified the Articles of War demonstrated the preeminent legislative role. Executive initiatives were taken at times, including the tribunals established by Gen. Scott in Mexico, but at every step he acknowledged Congress as the superior power and conceded that whatever policies he announced could be countermanded by Congress through the legislative process. This congressional presence has been absent in recent periods. Presidents have assumed the major role in creating tribunals and lawmakers have done little but watch.

The result is a stunning transformation from a republican form of government, characterized by legislative control and a vigorous system of checks and balances, to a system of military tribunals that concentrates power in the executive branch and particularly in the presidency. Tribunals are created by Presidents, staffed by Presidents, and guided by rules and procedures developed by the executive branch, all with little or minimal involvement of the other two branches. It is a form of government that the framers would find repugnant. The three national security decisions issued by the Supreme Court on June 28, 2004, restored a semblance of judicial supervision, but they represent only a first and halting step in checking presidential power.

The military tribunals authorized after 9/11 leaned heavily on the Supreme Court's opinion in the Nazi saboteur case, *Ex parte Quirin* (1942). The Court received great credit for meeting in special session to consider

---

1. William Winthrop, Military Law and Precedents 831 (1920) (emphasis in original).

the legal rights of the eight defendants. The haste with which it moved, however, left doubts in the minds of some whether justice had been served. Were nine hours of oral argument an impressive display of judicial independence and the rule of law, or largely show? A repeat German sabotage effort late in 1944, with the submarine this time discharging its passengers off the coast of Maine, led to heated debate within the administration on the proper organization and procedures for military tribunals. As a result, significant changes were instituted to minimize presidential involvement and maximize the role of military professionals.

Recent studies of *Quirin* have been properly critical of the Court. According to Michal Belknap, Chief Justice Stone went to "such lengths to justify Roosevelt's proclamation" that he preserved the "form" of judicial review while "gutt[ing] it of substance."[2] So long as Justices marched to the beat of war drums, the Court "remained an unreliable guardian of the Bill of Rights."[3] In a separate article, Belknap describes Frankfurter in his "Soliloquy" essay as a "judge openly hostile to the accused and manifestly unwilling to afford them procedural safeguards."[4] David J. Danelski regarded the full opinion in *Quirin* as "a rush to judgment, an agonizing effort to justify a *fait accompli*."[5] The opinion signaled a victory for the executive branch but, for the Court, "an institutional defeat."[6] The lesson for the Court is to "be wary of departing from its established rules and practices, even in times of national crisis, for at such times the Court is especially susceptible to co-optation by the executive."[7]

Judicial rulings during World War II provided disturbing evidence of a Court in the midst of war forfeiting its role as the guardian of constitutional rights. Some of the district and appellate courts were more alert to governmental abuses and willing to confront military and executive authorities. With the war safely over, the Court began to reassert itself and place restrictions on military tribunals and courts-martial, gradually restoring the right of U.S. citizens to a jury trial in the civilian courts.

Matters changed abruptly with the 9/11 terrorist attacks on the World Trade Center and the Pentagon, followed by the Bush military order two

---

2. Michal R. Belknap, "The Supreme Court Goes to War: The Meaning and Implications of the Nazi Saboteur Case," 89 Mil. L. Rev. 59, 83 (1980).

3. Id. at 95.

4. Michal Belknap, "Frankfurter and the Nazi Saboteurs," Yearbook 1982: Supreme Court Historical Society, at 66.

5. David J. Danelski, "The Saboteurs' Case," 1 J. Sup. Ct. Hist. 61 (1996).

6. Id. at 80.

7. Id.

months later that authorized trials by military tribunal. Although the order applied only to noncitizens, within a short time the administration began to designate U.S. citizens as "enemy combatants" and hold them incommunicado, without access to an attorney or the opportunity for a trial. Issues seemingly long settled were once again actively debated. How many of the lessons learned over the past two centuries would guide the executive branch, Congress, the judiciary, and the general public to avoid repeating past mistakes or at least minimize them?

Military tribunals represent an unwise and ill-conceived concentration of power in the executive branch. In 1942, President Roosevelt issued a military order and proclamation to create the tribunal, appointed the generals to serve on the tribunal, and appointed the prosecutors and the defense counsel. When the military tribunal had finished its labors and produced a judgment, it was Roosevelt who served as final reviewing authority. Such a procedure in another country would be condemned by the United States as fundamentally flawed and at war with constitutional values.

Tribunals allow the President and his assistants to make law, handle prosecution, and then render final judgments. "Crimes" relating to the law of war come not from the legislative branch, enacted by statute, but from executive interpretations of international law. It was a mistake by the Roosevelt administration to have the Judge Advocate General share prosecutorial duties with the Attorney General in 1942. The Judge Advocate General adds integrity to the system of military justice by serving as a reviewing authority at the end of the process, not as a prosecutor at the start. Whatever the military tribunal decided should have been presented to the Judge Advocate General and his staff, acting in an independent capacity, and then to the President for possible clemency. That error was corrected in 1945.

It would be shallow and short-sighted to believe that whatever was tolerable in 1942, with the *Quirin* case, is acceptable today. It has always been the expectation and statutory policy that the rules and procedures for military tribunals conform, in general, with the rules and procedures for courts-martial. The procedures followed by courts-martial in contemporary times differ substantially from those in 1942. Courts-martial today "reflect evolving standards in both military and civilian criminal law."[8] It was therefore a miscalculation by the Bush administration in 2001 to accept the Roosevelt model of 1942 as an adequate model for tribunals. Whatever else

8. Kevin J. Barry, "Military Commissions: Trying American Justice," *Army Lawyer*, November 2003, at 2.

one might say of the post-9/11 military tribunal, it is at least to the credit of the Defense Department that it developed detailed rules on tribunal procedures and announced them in advance, rather than follow the 1942 experience of creating rules while the trial progressed. Still, a month after the Supreme Court national security decisions in 2004, defense lawyers objected that the military review panels established in Guantánamo were making up new rules "as they go along."[9]

Congress recognized the deficiencies of military law in 1950 when it enacted the Uniform Code of Military Justice. The statute represented an effort to unify, consolidate, and codify the Articles of War, the Articles for the Navy, and the Disciplinary Laws of the Coast Guard. A major purpose behind passage of the statute was the adoption of two levels of review. The Judge Advocate General of each of the armed forces would create one or more boards of review, "each composed of not less than three officers or civilians, each of whom shall be a member of the bar of a Federal court or of the highest court of a State of the United States."[10] Boards of review would receive cases in which the sentence of a court-martial "affects a general or flag officer or extends to death, dismissal of an officer, cadet, or midshipman, dishonorable or bad-conduct discharge, or confinement for one year or more."[11] The boards of review evolved into Courts of Criminal Appeals.

The second level of review provided by the 1950 statute is the Court of Military Appeals, now called the Court of Appeals for the Armed Forces. As an Article I court, it consisted originally of three judges (now five) appointed from civilian life by the President, with the advice and consent of the Senate. The term of office is 15 years. Judges on the court must be members of the bar of a federal court or of the highest court of a state. The statute empowers the court to prescribe its own rules of procedure.[12]

This civilian court originated out of complaints directed at the military system of justice. Too often it resulted in "unfair treatment accorded to civilian men," creating the need for a system of scrutiny by professional civilians who could assure that enlisted men "will get justice in the future which has been denied them in the past."[13] These remarks are similar to

---

9. Neil A Lewis, "U.S. Terrorism Tribunals Set to Begin Work," New York Times, August 22, 2004, at 17. See also Scott Higham, "Hearings Open with Challenge to Tribunals," Washington Post, August 29, 2004, at A12.

10. 64 Stat. 128, Art. 66(a) (1950).

11. Id., Art. 66(b).

12. Id. at 129, Art. 67(a).

13. 95 Cong. Rec. 5719 (1949) (remarks by Rep. Adolph Sabath).

concerns about the executive branch after 9/11 and its insistence on possessing exclusive and unreviewable authority over detainees and enemy combatants. Congressional debate on the Uniform Code of Military Justice reveals opposition to having appellate review conducted solely within the military departments: "This has resulted in widespread criticism by the general public, who, with or without cause, look with suspicion upon all things military and particularly matters involving military justice."[14] Consider these remarks offered during House debate in 1949, discussing the limitations and inadequacies of military justice found by both lawyers and laymen:

> It was disturbing to them to find that the same official was empowered to accuse, to draft and direct the charges, to select the prosecutor and defense counsel from the officers under his command, to choose the members of the court, to review and alter their decision, and to change any sentence imposed. . . . They were surprised to find that many of the judges, prosecutors, and defense counsel participating in courts martial were neither lawyers nor trained in the law, and that, in the naval services, there was not even the minimum requirement that a single law member be on a court.[15]

Identical words can be applied to the military order and proclamation issued by President Roosevelt in 1942, the tribunals used against Gen. Yamashita and other defendants during and immediately after World War II, martial law in Hawaii, and the military order issued by President Bush on November 13, 2001. Congress found it necessary in 1950 to pass legislation to regulate and check "arbitrary, capricious, and whimsical action of commanding officers at every level and every point."[16] Lawmakers wanted to do away with "autocratic, arrogant, pompous command-control brass in the Army and Navy."[17]

It was asked during House debate whether the Uniform Code of Military Justice would outlaw "the despotism that now exists in the occupied areas of foreign countries by which civilians are still being tried in military courts?" The floor manager answered that such individuals "are not tried under this code, they are tried under provost courts." The pending bill "has nothing to do with provost courts. Perhaps Congress should go ahead and

14. Id. at 5721 (remarks by Rep. Overton Brooks).
15. Id. at 5724 (remarks by Rep. Carl Durham).
16. Id. at 5726 (remarks by Rep. Philip Philbin).
17. Id. at 5727 (remarks by Rep. James Sutton).

legislate on that matter, but it is not sought to do so under this bill."[18] Congress is fully empowered by the Constitution to legislate on both provost courts and military tribunals.

The Uniform Code of Military Justice took other steps to add professionalism and expertise to military law. For the first time, Congress required that the Judge Advocate General of each service be a member of a federal or state bar, with at least eight years' experience of legal duties as commissioned officers.[19] In the past, those who served as Judge Advocate General usually had legal experience and training, but it was not required by statute.

In 1983, Congress passed legislation to authorize decisions by the Court of Appeals for the Armed Forces to be reviewed by the Supreme Court by writ of certiorari in a limited number of cases.[20] Part of the purpose of the statute was to grant the government an opportunity to appeal from adverse decisions issued by the Court of Appeals for the Armed Services.[21] The statute enabled either party to petition the Supreme Court for cert, with the granting of cert entirely discretionary on the part of the Court. Previously, the accused at times was able—through collateral proceedings (such as a petition for a writ of habeas corpus)—to initiate actions that might reach the Supreme Court. Such actions were denied to the government.[22]

Actions by the Bush administration after 9/11 have done much to impair the rights of defendants, going far beyond the boundaries mapped out by the Court in *Quirin*. Moving first against noncitizens with the military order of November 13, 2001, the administration next claimed the right to hold U.S. citizens as "enemy combatants" and detain them indefinitely without being charged, given counsel, or tried. Even those elementary rights and procedures were accorded the Nazi saboteurs in 1942. The framers rejected political models that concentrated power in a single branch, especially over matters of war. They relied on a system of checks and balances, separation of powers, judicial review, and republican principles. Those values have enriched the lives of Americans and attracted immigrants to our shores. To depart from those standards, under the pretext of emergency

18. Id. at 5728 (colloquy between Rep. Gross and Rep. Brooks).
19. 64 Stat. 147, Sec. 13 (1950). For further details on the legislative history of the Uniform Code of Military Justice and the provisions for review courts, see Jonathan Lurie, Military Justice in America: The U.S. Court of Appeals for the Armed Forces, 1775–1980, at 101–54 (2001 ed.).
20. 97 Stat. 1406 (1983).
21. S. Rept. No. 98-53, 98th Cong., 1st Sess. 8 (1983).
22. Id. at 9.

power and ever-present threats posed by terrorists, endangers fundamental constitutional rights and liberties of both citizens and noncitizens.

The Supreme Court has repeatedly expressed concern about the concentration of power that would result if the executive branch alone had the power to create military tribunals. In 1946, it emphasized the important constitutional principle that courts "and their procedural safeguards are indispensable to our system of government," and that the framers "were opposed to governments that placed in the hands of one man the power to make, interpret and enforce the laws."[23] In 1955, Justice Black wrote for the Court: "We find nothing in the history of constitutional treatment of military tribunals which entitles them to rank along with Article III courts as adjudicators of the guilt or innocence of people charged with offenses for which they can be deprived of their life, liberty or property."[24] Two years later, again writing for the majority, he warned that if the President "can provide rules of substantive law as well as procedure, then he and his military subordinates exercise legislative, executive and judicial powers with respect to those subject to military trials." Such a concentration of power, he said, ran counter to the core constitutional principle of separation of powers.[25]

Other federal judges have sounded the same alarm. U.S. District Judge Stern, in the 1979 Tiede case, rejected the government's position that the executive branch can determine by itself the availability of constitutional safeguards, such as the right to a jury trial. Such power, he said, would allow the government "to arrest any person without cause, to hold a person incommunicado, to deny an accused the benefit of counsel, to try a person summarily and to impose sentence—all as a part of the unreviewable exercise of foreign policy."[26] Those words fit perfectly with the Bush order of November 13, 2001, authorizing military tribunals. The Supreme Court's decisions on June 28, 2004, in the Hamdi, Padilla, and Guantánamo cases provided a welcome, needed, and long overdue check on this concentration of power in the presidency, but the rulings were in many respects vague and contradictory. Additional safeguards are needed, especially from the legislative branch and the public.

It is often argued that during war and emergencies, customary constitutional rights must be set aside or given secondary status. Thus the maxim:

23. Duncan v. Kahanamoku, 327 U.S. at 322.
24. Toth v. Quarles, 350 U.S. at 17.
25. Reid v. Covert, 354 U.S. at 38–39.
26. United States v. Tiede, 86 F.R.D. at 243.

inter armes silent leges. However much this aphorism describes the past, it does not deserve to be adopted as a principle of constitutional government. It is especially in time of war that the apparatus of the presidency poses the highest risk, executive errors inflict the greatest damage, and individual liberties are placed at maximum peril. Institutional checks are needed more, not less. Free speech, free press, public debate, and legislative deliberation are critically important in minimizing mistakes and miscalculations by executive officials. The Constitution was not written solely for tranquil intervals. The framers designed it for times of peace and war and expected republican government to meet the common danger.

BIBLIOGRAPHY

Abella, Alex, and Scott Gordon. Shadow Enemies: Hitler's Secret Terrorist Plot Against the United States (Guilford, Conn.: Lyons Press, 2002).

Aldrich, George H. "The Taliban, Al Qaeda, and the Determination of Illegal Combatants," 96 American Journal of International Law 891 (2002).

Anderson, Kenneth. "What to Do with Bin Laden and Al Qaeda Terrorists?: A Qualified Defense of Military Commissions and United States Policy on Detainees at Guantánamo Bay Naval Base," 25 Harvard Journal of Law and Public Policy 591 (2002).

Anthony, J. Garner. Hawaii Under Army Rule (Stanford: Stanford University Press, 1955).

———. "Martial Law in Hawaii," 30 California Law Review 371 (1942).

———. "Martial Law, Military Government and the Writ of Habeas Corpus in Hawaii," 31 California Law Review 477 (1943).

———. "Hawaiian Martial Law in the Supreme Court," 57 Yale Law Journal 27 (1947).

Appleman, John Alan. Military Tribunals and International Crimes (Indianapolis: Bobbs-Merrill, 1954).

Armstrong, Walter P. "Martial Law in Hawaii," 29 American Bar Association Journal 698 (1943).

Baldry, W. Y. "Early Articles of War," 4 Journal of the Society of Army Historical Research 166 (1926).

Ballantine, Henry Winthrop. "Martial Law," 12 Columbia Law Review 529 (1912).

Bantekas, Ilias. "The Contemporary Law of Superior Responsibility," 93 American Journal of International Law 573 (1999).

Barber, Charles F. "Trial of Unlawful Enemy Belligerents," 29 Cornell Law Quarterly 53 (1943).

Barry, Kevin J. "Military Commissions: Trying American Justice," The Army Lawyer (November 2003), pp. 1–9.

Bassett, John Spencer. The Life of Andrew Jackson (New York: Macmillan, 1931).

Battle, George Gordon. "Military Tribunals," 29 Virginia Law Review 255 (1942).

Baxter, R. R. "The First Modern Codification of the Law of War: Francis Lieber and General Orders No. 100 (Part I)," 25 International Review of the Red Cross 171 (1963).

———. "The First Modern Codification of the Law of War: Francis Lieber and General Orders No. 100 (Part II)," 26 International Review of the Red Cross 234 (1963).

Beale, Howard K., ed. The Diary of Edward Bates, 1859–1866 (Washington, D.C.: Government Printing Office, 1933).

Bederman, David J. "Article II Courts," 44 Mercer Law Review 825 (1993).

Belknap, Michal R., ed. American Political Trials (Westport, Conn.: Greenwood Press, 1981).

Belknap, Michal R. "A Putrid Pedigree: The Bush Administration's Military Tribunals in Historical Perspective," 38 California Western Law Review 433 (2002).

————. "Frankfurter and the Nazi Saboteurs," Yearbook 1982: Supreme Court Historical Society, pp. 66–71.

————. "The Supreme Court Goes to War: The Meaning and Implications of the Nazi Saboteur Case," 89 Military Law Review 59 (1980).

Bernstein, Cyrus. "The Saboteur Trial: A Case History," 11 George Washington Law Review 131 (1943).

Biddle, Francis. In Brief Authority (Garden City, N.Y.: Doubleday, 1962).

Birkhimer, William E. Military Government and Martial Law (Kansas City: Franklin Hudson, 1904).

Bittker, Boris I. "The World War II German Saboteur's Case and Writs of Certiorari Before Judgment by the Court of Appeals: A Tale of Nunc Pro Tunc Jurisdiction." 14 Constitutional Commentary 431 (1997).

Borch, Frederick L., III. "Why Military Commissions Are the Proper Forum and Why Terrorists Will Have 'Full and Fair' Trials," The Army Lawyer (November 2003), pp. 10–16.

Boskey, Bennett. "A Justice's Papers: Chief Justice Stone's Biographer and the Saboteur's Case," 14 Supreme Court Historical Society Quarterly 10 (1993).

Brackman, Arnold C. The Other Nuremberg: The Untold Story of the Tokyo War Crimes Trials (New York: William Morrow, 1987).

Bradley, Curtis A., and Jack L. Goldsmith. "The Constitutional Validity of Military Commissions," 5 Green Bag 2D 249 (2002).

Cain, Marvin R. Lincoln's Attorney General Edward Bates of Missouri (Columbia: University of Missouri Press, 1965).

Carley, Kenneth. The Sioux Uprising of 1862 (St. Paul: Minnesota Historical Society, 1976).

Carnahan, Burrus M. "Lincoln, Lieber and the Laws of War: The Origins and Limits of the Principle of Military Necessity," 92 American Journal of International Law 213 (1998).

Carr, Cecil T. "A Regulated Liberty," 42 Columbia Law Review 339 (1942).

Chamlee, Roy Z., Jr. Lincoln's Assassins: A Complete Account of Their Capture, Trial, and Punishment (Jefferson, N.C.: McFarland, 1990).

Childress, James F. "Francis Lieber's Interpretation of the Laws of War: General Orders No. 100 in the Context of His Life and Thought," 21 American Journal of Jurisprudence 34 (1976).

Chomsky, Carol. "The United States–Dakota War Trials: A Study in Military Injustice," 43 Stanford Law Review 13 (1990).

Clark, Gerald J. "Military Tribunals and the Separation of Powers," 63 University of Pittsburgh Law Review 837 (2002).

Cohen, Gary. "The Keystone Kommandos," Atlantic Monthly, February 2002, at 46–49.

Colby, Elbridge. "War Crimes," 23 Michigan Law Review 482 (1925).

————. "The Military Value of the Laws of War," 15 Georgetown Law Journal 24 (1926).

Cole, David. Enemy Aliens: Double Standards and Constitutional Freedoms in the War on Terrorism (New York: The New Press, 2003).

Cole, David, and James X. Dempsey. Terrorism and the Constitution (New York: The New Press, 2002).

Corwin, Edward S. Total War and the Constitution (New York: Knopf, 1947).

Cowles, William B. "Trials of War Criminals (Non-Nuremberg)," 42 American Journal of International Law 299 (1948).

———. "Trial of War Criminals by Military Tribunals," 30 American Bar Association Journal 330 (1944).

Cox, Albert L. "The Saboteur Story," Records of the Columbia History Society of Washington, D.C., 1957–1959, pp. 16–25.

Cramer, Myron C. "Military Commissions: Trial of the Eight Saboteurs," 17 Washington Law Review and State Bar Journal 247 (1942).

———. "The Lawyer in This War," 29 American Bar Association Journal 629 (1943).

———. "Military Justice and Trial Procedure," 29 American Bar Association Journal 368 (1943).

Crona, Spencer J., and Neal A. Richardson. "Justice for War Criminals of Invisible Armies: A New Legal and Military Approach to Terrorism," 21 Oklahoma City University Law Review 349 (1996).

Curran, John W. "Lincoln Conspiracy Trial and Military Jurisdiction over Civilians," 9 Notre Dame Lawyer 26 (1933).

Curtis, Michael Kent. "Lincoln, Vallandigham, and Anti-War Speech in the Civil War," 7 William and Mary Bill of Rights Journal 105 (1998).

Cushman, Robert E. "Ex parte Quirin et al.—The Nazi Saboteur Case," 28 Cornell Law Quarterly 54 (1942).

———. "The Case of the Nazi Saboteurs," 36 American Political Science Review 1082 (1942).

Danelski, David J. "The Saboteurs' Case," 1 Journal of Supreme Court History 61 (1996).

Dart, Henry P. "Andrew Jackson and Judge D. A. Hall," 5 Louisiana Historical Quarterly 509 (1922).

Dasch, George. Eight Spies Against America (New York: Robert M. McBride, 1959).

Davis, George B. "Doctor Francis Lieber's Instructions for the Government of Armies in the Field," 1 American Journal of International Law 13 (1907).

Decker, Malcolm. Ten Days of Infamy: An Illustrated Memoir of the Arnold-André Conspiracy (New York: Arno Press, 1969).

Detter, Delupis Ingrid. The Law of War (New York: Cambridge University Press, 2d ed. 2000).

Dickinson, Laura A. "Using Legal Process to Fight Terrorism: Detentions, Military Commissions, International Tribunals, and the Rule of Law," 75 Southern California Law Review 1407 (2002).

Dobbs, Michael. Saboteurs: The Nazi Raid in America (New York: Knopf, 2004).

Dowell, Cassius M. Military Aid to the Civil Power (Fort Leavenworth, Kans.: General Service Schools Press, 1925).

Dyer, Brainerd. "Francis Lieber and the American Civil War," 2 Huntington Library Quarterly 449 (1939).

Everett, Robinson O. "The Law of War: Military Tribunals and the War on Terrorism," The Federal Lawyer, November/December 2001, pp. 20–22.

———. "Possible Use of American Military Tribunals to Punish Offenses Against the Law of Nations," 34 Virginia Journal of International Law 289 (1994).

Everett, Robinson O., and Scott L. Silliman. "Forums for Punishing Offenses Against the Law of Nations," 29 Wake Forest Law Review 509 (1994).

Fairman, Charles. The Law of Martial Rule (Chicago: Callaghan, 1930).

———. "The Law of Martial Rule and the National Emergency," 55 Harvard Law Review 1253 (1942).

———. "The Supreme Court on Military Jurisdiction: Martial Rule in Hawaii and the Yamashita Case," 59 Harvard Law Review 833 (1946).

———. "Some New Problems of the Constitution Following the Flag," 1 Stanford Law Review 587 (1949).

———. Reconstruction and Reunion, 1964–88 (New York: Macmillan, 1971).

Farber, Daniel. Lincoln's Constitution (Chicago: University Press of Chicago, 2003).

Feldhaus, J. Gordon. "The Trial of Yamashita," 15 South Dakota Bar Journal 181 (1946).

Fidell, Eugene R. "The Culture of Change in Military Law," 126 Military Law Review 125 (1989).

———. "Military Commissions and Administrative Law," 6 Green Bag 2d 379 (2003).

Fidell, Eugene R., and Dwight H. Sullivan, eds. Evolving Military Justice (Annapolis: Naval Institute Press, 2002).

Filler, Daniel M. "Values We Can Afford—Protecting Constitutional Rights in an Age of Terrorism: A Response to Crona and Richardson," 21 Oklahoma City University Law Review 409 (1996).

Fisher, Louis. Presidential War Power (Lawrence: University Press of Kansas, 2d ed. 2004).

———. "Hijack in Berlin," Legal Times, July 12, 2004, at 50–51.

———. Nazi Saboteurs on Trial: A Military Tribunal and American Law (Lawrence: University Press of Kansas, 2003).

———. "Military Tribunals: A Sorry History," 33 Presidential Studies Quarterly 484 (2003).

Fisher, Sydney G. "The Suspension of Habeas Corpus During the War of the Rebellion," 3 Political Science Quarterly 454 (1888).

Fitzpatrick, Joan. "Jurisdiction of Military Commissions and the Ambiguous War on Terrorism," 96 American Journal of International Law 345 (2002).

Fletcher, George P. "On Justice and War: Contradictions in the Proposed Military Tribunals," 25 Harvard Journal of Law and Public Policy 635 (2002).

Fletcher, Henry J. "The Civilian and the War Power," 2 Minnesota Law Review 110 (1918).

Flexner, James Thomas. The Traitor and the Spy: Benedict Arnold and John André (Syracuse: Syracuse University Press, 1975).

Frank, John P. The Marble Palace: The Supreme Court in American Life (New York: Knopf, 1972).

———. "Ex parte Milligan v. The Five Companies: Martial Law in Hawaii," 44 Columbia Law Review 639 (1944).

Freidel, Frank. "General Orders 100 and Military Government," 32 Mississippi Valley Historical Review 541 (1946).

———. Francis Lieber: Nineteenth-Century Liberal (Baton Rouge: Louisiana State University Press, 1947).

Friedman, Leon, ed. The Law of War: A Documentary History (2 vols.; New York: Random House, 1972).

Gabriel, Ralph H. "American Experience with Military Government," 49 American Historical Review 630 (1944).

Gambone, Joseph G. "Ex parte Milligan: The Restoration of Judicial Prestige?," 16 Civil War History 246 (1970).

Garner, James G. "General Order 100 Revisited," 27 Military Law Review 1 (1965).

Garner, James W. "Treatment of Enemy Aliens," 12 American Journal of International Law 27 (1918).

———. "Treatment of Enemy Aliens," 13 American Journal of International Law 22 (1919).

Gimpel, Erich. Agent 146: The True Story of a Nazi Spy in America (New York: St. Martin's Press, 2003).

Glazier, David. "Kangaroo Court or Competent Tribunal? Judging the 21st Century Military Commission," 89 Virginia Law Review 2005 (2003).

Goldsmith, Jack, and Cass R. Sunstein. "Military Tribunals and Legal Culture: What a Difference Sixty Years Make," 19 Constitutional Commentary 261 (2002).

Golove, David. "Military Tribunals, International Law, and the Constitution: A Franckian-Madisonian Approach," 35 New York University Journal of International Law and Politics 363 (2003).

Green, A. Wigfall. "The Military Commission," 42 American Journal of International Law 832 (1948).

Guy, George F. "The Defense of Yamashita," 4 Wyoming Law Journal 153 (1950).

Halbert, Sherrill. "The Suspension of the Writ of Habeas Corpus by President Lincoln," 2 American Journal of Legal History 95 (1958).

Halleck, Henry Wager. International Law; or, Rules Regulating the Intercourse of States in Peace and War (San Francisco: H. H. Bancroft, 1861).

———. "Military Tribunals and Their Jurisdiction," 5 American Journal of International Law 958 (1911).

———. "Military Espionage," 5 American Journal of International Law 590 (1911).

Hanchett, William. The Lincoln Murder Conspiracies (Urbana: University of Illinois Press, 1983).

Hart, Franklin A. "Yamashita, Nuremberg and Vietnam: Command Responsibility Reappraised," 25 Naval War College Review 19 (1972).

Hartigan, Richard Shelly. Lieber's Code and the Law of War (Chicago: Precedent Publishing, 1983).

Henderson, Gordon D. "Courts-Martial and the Constitution: The Original Understanding," 71 Harvard Law Review 293 (1957).

Hentoff, Nat. The War on the Bill of Rights and the Gathering Resistance (New York: Seven Stories Press, 2003).

Hershey, Amos S. "Treatment of Enemy Aliens," 12 American Journal of International Law 156 (1918).

Holt, Joseph. Vindication of Hon. Joseph Holt (Washington: Chronicle, 1873).

Houston, Brahan. "Martial Law in Hawaii: A Defense of the War-Time Military Governor," 36 American Bar Association Journal 825 (1950).

Howard, J. Woodford, Jr. Mr. Justice Murphy: A Political Biography (Princeton: Princeton University Press, 1968).

Howard, Kenneth A. "Command Responsibility for War Crimes," 21 Journal of Public Law 7 (1972).

Howard, Michael, et al., eds. The Laws of War: Constraints on Warfare in the Western World (New Haven: Yale University Press, 1994).

Hughes, Charles E. "The Republic After the War," 53 American Law Review 661 (1919).

Hyde, Charles Cheney. "Aspects of the Saboteur Cases," 37 American Journal of International Law 88 (1943).

Irons, Peter. Justice at War (New York: Oxford University Press, 1983).

Israel, Fred L. "Military Justice in Hawaii, 1941–1944," 36 Pacific Historical Review 243 (1967).

Ives, Stephen B., Jr. "Vengeance Did Not Deliver Justice," Washington Post, December 30, 2001, at B2.

Jackson, Robert H. The Supreme Court in the American System of Government (Cambridge: Harvard University Press, 1955).

Johnson, Timothy D. Winfield Scott: The Quest for Military Glory (Lawrence: University Press of Kansas, 1998).

Jones, John Paul. Dr. Mudd and the Lincoln Assassination: The Case Reopened (Conshohocken, Pa.: Combined Books, 1995).

Kaplan, Harold L. "Constitutional Limitations on Trials by Military Commissions," 92 University of Pennsylvania Law Review 119, 272 (1943).

Katyal, Neal K., and Lawrence H. Tribe. "Waging War, Defending Guilt: Trying the Military Tribunals," 111 Yale Law Journal 1259 (2002).

King, Archibald. "The Legality of Martial Law in Hawaii," 30 California Law Review 599 (1942).

Klement, Frank L. "The Indianapolis Treason Trials and Ex Parte Milligan," in Michal R. Belknap, ed., American Political Trials (Westport, Conn.: Greenwood Press, 1981).

Koh, Harold Hongju. "The Case Against Military Commissions," 96 American Journal of International Law 337 (2002).

Kohn, Richard H. Eagle and Sword: The Federalists and the Creation of the Military Establishment in America, 1783–1802 (New York: The Free Press, 1975).

Kuhn, Arthur K. "International Law and National Legislation in the Trial of War Criminals—The Yamashita Case," 44 American Journal of International Law 559 (1950).

Kurland, Philip B., and Gerhard Casper, eds. Landmark Briefs and Arguments of the Supreme Court of the United States: Constitutional Law (Arlington, Va.: University Publications of America, 1975).

Lacey, Michael O. "Military Commissions: A Historical Survey," The Army Lawyer, March 2002, at 41.

Lael, Richard L. The Yamashita Precedent: War Crimes and Command Responsibility (Wilmington: Scholarly Resources, Inc., 1982).

Landau, Captain Henry. The Enemy Within: The Inside Story of German Sabotage in America (New York: G. P. Putnam's Sons, 1937).

Landrum, Bruce D. "The Yamashita War Crimes Trial: Command Responsibility Then and Now," 149 Military Law Review 293 (1995).

Lardner, George, Jr. "Nazi Saboteurs Captured!," Washington Post Magazine, January 13, 2002, at 12–16, 23–24.

Laska, Lewis L., and James M. Smith. "'Hell and the Devil': Andersonville and the Trial of Captain Henry Wirz, C.S.A., 1865," 68 Military Law Review 77 (1975).

Latimer, Hugh. "Tribunals and the Court: Misconstruing 'Quirin,'" National Law Journal, March 18, 2002, at A20.

Lawson, John D., ed. American State Trials (St. Louis: F. H. Thomas Law Book Co., 1917).

Lieber, G. Norman. The Justification of Martial Law (Washington, D.C.: Government Printing Office, 1898).

———. Use of the Army in Aid of the Civil Power (Washington, D.C.: Government Printing Office, 1898).

Lincoln, Abraham. The Collected Works of Abraham Lincoln (8 vols.; New Brunswick: Rutgers University Press, Roy P. Basler ed. 1953).

Linn, Brian McAllister. The U.S. Army and Counterinsurgency in the Philippine War, 1899–1902 (Chapel Hill: University of North Carolina Press, 1989).

Lurie, Jonathan. Arming Military Justice: The Origins of the United States Court of Military Appeals, 1775–1950 (Princeton: Princeton University Press, 1992).

———. Military Justice in America: The U.S. Court of Appeals for the Armed Forces, 1775–1980 (Lawrence: University Press of Kansas, 2001).

———. "Andrew Jackson, Martial Law, Civilian Control of the Military, and American Politics: An Intriguing Amalgam," 126 Military Law Review 133 (1989).

Macomb, Alexander. A Treatise on Martial Law and Courts-Martial (Charleston: J. Hoff, 1809).

———. The Practice of Courts Martial (New York: Harper and Bros., 1841).

Maddox, Heather Anne. "After the Dust Settles: Military Tribunal Justice for Terrorists After September 11, 2001," 28 North Carolina Journal of International Law and Commercial Regulation 421 (2002).

Maguire, Peter. Law and War: An American Story (New York: Columbia University Press, 2001).

Margulies, Herbert F. "The Articles of War, 1920: The History of a Forgotten Reform," 43 Military Affairs 85 (1979).

Mason, Alpheus Thomas. "Inter Arma Silent Leges: Chief Justice Stone's Views," 69 Harvard Law Review 806 (1956).

———. Harlan Fiske Stone: Pillar of the Law (New York: Viking Press, 1956).

Matheson, Michael J. "U.S. Military Commissions: One of Several Options," 96 American Journal of International Law 354 (2002).

McColloch, Claude. "Now It Can Be Told: Judge Metzger and the Military," 35 American Bar Association Journal 365 (1949).

Miller, Richard J., ed. The Law of War (Lexington, Mass.: Lexington Books, 1975).

Miller, Stuart Creighton. "Benevolent Assimilation": The American Conquest of the Philippines, 1899–1903 (New Haven: Yale University Press, 1982).

Miller, Theodore. "Relation of Military to Civil and Administrative Tribunals in Time of War," 7 Ohio State Law Journal 188, 400 (1941).

Morgan, Edmund M. "Court-Martial Jurisdiction Over Non-Military Persons Under the Articles of War," 4 Minnesota Law Review 79 (1920).

Mundis, Daryl A. "The Use of Military Commissions to Prosecute Individuals Accused of Terrorist Acts," 96 American Journal of International Law 320 (2002).

Munson, F. Granville. "The Arguments in the Saboteur Trial," 91 University of Pennsylvania Law Review 239 (1942).

Nardotti, Michael J., Jr. "Military Commissions," The Army Lawyer, March 2002, at 1.

National Institute of Military Justice. Military Commission Instructions: Sourcebook (Washington, D.C., 2003).

Neely, Mark E., Jr. The Fate of Liberty: Abraham Lincoln and Civil Liberties (New York: Oxford University Press, 1991).

Neier, Aryeh. "Military Tribunals on Trial," New York Review of Books, February 14, 2002, at 11–15.

Newton, Michael A. "Continuum Crimes: Military Jurisdiction Over Foreign Nationals Who Commit International Crimes," 153 Military Law Review 1 (1996).

Nichols, David A. Lincoln and the Indians: Civil War Policy and Politics (Urbana: University of Illinois Press, 2000 ed.).

"Note: Jurisdiction of Military Tribunals," 37 Illinois Law Review 265 (1942).

"Note: Federal Military Commissions: Procedure and 'Wartime Base' of Jurisdiction," 56 Harvard Law Review 631 (1943).

Nys, Ernest. "Francis Lieber—His Life and Work" (Part I), 5 American Journal of International Law 84, 355 (1911).

O'Brien, William V. "The Law of War, Command Responsibility and Vietnam," 60 Georgetown Law Journal 605 (1972).

Olshansky, Barbara. Secret Trials and Executions: Military Tribunals and the Threat to Democracy (New York: Seven Stories Press, 2002).

Orentlicher, Diane F., and Robert Kogod Goldman. "When Justice Goes to War: Prosecuting Terrorists Before Military Commissions," 25 Harvard Journal of Law and Public Policy 653 (2002).

Parks, William H. "Command Responsibility for War Crimes," 62 Military Law Review 1 (1973).

Paust, Jordan J. "Antiterrorism Military Commissions: Courting Illegality," 23 Michigan Journal of International Law 1 (2001).

Perlman, Philip B. "Habeas Corpus and Extraterritoriality: A Fundamental Question of Constitutional Law," 36 American Bar Association Journal 187 (1950).

Piccigallo, Philip R. The Japanese on Trial: Allied War Crimes Operations in the East, 1945–1951 (Austin: University of Texas Press, 1979).

Pittman, Benn. The Assassination of President Lincoln and the Trial of the Conspirators (New York: Moore, Wilstach and Baldwin, 1865).

Prior, Leon O. "Nazi Invasion of Florida," 49 Florida Historical Quarterly 129 (1970).

Rachlis, Eugene. They Came to Kill: The Story of Eight Saboteurs in America (New York: Random House, 1961).

Radin, Max. "Martial Law and the State of Siege," 30 California Law Review 634 (1942).

Randall, James G. Constitutional Problems Under Lincoln (Urbana: University of Illinois Press, 1964 ed.).

———. "The Indemnity Act of 1863: A Study in the Wartime Immunity of Governmental Officers," 20 Michigan Law Review 589 (1922).

Reel, A. Frank. The Case of General Yamashita (Chicago: University of Chicago Press, 1949).

Rehnquist, William H. All the Laws But One: Civil Liberties in Wartime (New York: Knopf, 1998).

Reid, John, and John Henry Eaton. The Life of Andrew Jackson (Philadelphia: M. Carey and Son, 1817).

Reisman, W. Michael, and Chris T. Antoniou, eds., The Laws of War (New York: Vintage Books, 1994).

Remini, Robert V. The Battle of New Orleans (New York: Penguin Books, 2001).

———. Andrew Jackson and the Course of American Empire, 1767–1821 (New York: Harper and Row, 1977).

Rice, Allen Thorndike. "New Facts About Mrs. Surratt," 147 North American Review 83 (1888).

Risvold, Floyd E., ed. A True History of the Assassination of Abraham Lincoln and of the Conspiracy of 1865 [by Louis J. Weichman] (New York: Knopf, 1975).

Roberts, Adam, and Richard Guelff, eds. Documents on the Laws of War (New York: Oxford University Press, 3d ed. 2000).

Root, Elihu. "Francis Lieber," 7 American Journal of International Law 453 (1913).

Rutherglen, George. "Structural Uncertainty Over Habeas Corpus and the Jurisdiction of Military Tribunals," 5 Green Bag 2D 397 (2002).

Rutman, Darrett B. "The War Crimes and Trial of Henry Wirz," 6 Civil War History 117 (1960).

Sabel, Stanley Law. "Court-Martial Decisions by Divided Courts," 28 Cornell Law Quarterly 165 (1943).

Sargent, Winthrop. The Life of Major John André (New York: D. Appleton, 1871).

Scheiber, Harry N., and Jane L. Scheiber. "The Roles of Lawyers in a Civil Liberties Crisis: Hawaii During World War II," in Sandra F. VanBurkleo et al., eds., Constitutionalism and American Culture: Writing the New Constitutional History (Lawrence: University Press of Kansas, 2002).

———. "Constitutional Liberty in World War II: Army Rule and Martial Law in Hawaii, 1941–1946," 3 Western Legal History 341 (1990).

Schilling, George T. "Saboteurs and the Jurisdiction of Military Commissions," 41 Michigan Law Review 481 (1942).

Schlueter, David A. Military Criminal Justice: Practice and Procedure (Charlottesville, Va.: Lexis Law Publishing, 5th ed. 1999).

Scott, Winfield. Memoirs of Lieut.-General Scott, LL.D. (Freeport, N.Y.: Books for Libraries Press, 1864).

Shepard, William S. "One Hundredth Anniversary of the Lieber Code," 21 Military Law Review 157 (1963).

Slattery, James J., Jr. "Federal Court Review of Decisions of Military Tribunals," 40 University of Cincinnati Law Review 569 (1971).

Smith, Joshua Hett. Narrative of the Death of Major André (1808; reprint, New York: Arno Press, 1969).

Smith, Justin H. The War with Mexico (2 vols.; New York: Macmillan, 1919).

Sofaer, Abraham D. "Emergency Power and the Hero of New Orleans," 2 Cardozo Law Review 233 (1981).

Solis, Gary D. "Military Commissions and Terrorists," in Eugene R. Fidell and Dwight H. Sullivan, eds., Evolving Military Justice (Annapolis: Naval Institute Press, 2002).

Speed, John. "The Assassins of Lincoln," 147 North American Review 314 (1888).

Sprague, Dean. Freedom Under Lincoln (Boston: Houghton Mifflin, 1965).

Spurlock, Paul E. "The Yokohama War Crimes Trials: The Truth About a Misunderstood Subject," 36 American Bar Association Journal 387 (1950).

Steers, Edward, Jr., ed. The Trial: The Assassination of President Lincoln and the Trial of the Conspirators (Lexington: University Press of Kentucky, 2003).

Stein, Kenneth E. "Judicial Review of Determinations of Federal Military Tribunals," 11 Brooklyn Law Review 30 (1941).

Sterck, Frank C., and Carl J. Schuck, "The Right of Resident Alien Enemies to Sue," 30 Georgetown Law Journal 421 (1942).

Stern, Herbert J. Judgment in Berlin (New York: Universe Books, 1984).

Stibbs, John Howard. "Andersonville and the Trial of Henry Wirz," 9 Iowa Journal of History and Politics 33 (1911).

Sutton, David Nelson. "The Trial of Tojo: The Most Important Trial in All History?," 36 American Bar Association Journal 93 (1950).

Swanberg, W. A. "The Spies Who Came in from the Sea," 21 American Heritage 66 (1970).

Taylor, Frank E. "Military Courts-Martial Procedure Under the Revised Articles of War," 12 Virginia Law Review 463 (1926).

Taylor, Lawrence. A Trial of Generals: Homma, Yamashita, MacArthur (South Bend: Icarus Press, 1981).

Trefousse, Hans L. Andrew Johnson: A Biography (New York: W.W. Norton, 1989).

Turley, Jonathan. "Tribunals and Tribulations: The Antithetical Elements of Military

Governance in a Madisonian Democracy," 70 George Washington Law Review 649 (2002).

Turner, Thomas R. "What Type of Trial? A Civil Versus a Military Trial for the Lincoln Assassination Conspirators," 4 Papers of the Abraham Lincoln Association 29 (1982).

Underhill, L. K. "Jurisdiction of Military Tribunals in the United States Over Civilians," 12 California Law Review 75, 159 (1924).

U.S. Congress. "Trial of Henry Wirz," House Executive Document No. 23, 40th Cong., 2d Sess. (1867).

U.S. War Department. A Source-Book on Military Law and War-Time Legislation (St. Paul: West Publishing, 1919).

Warren, Charles. "Spies, and the Power of Congress to Subject Certain Classes of Civilians to Trial by Military Tribunal," 53 American Law Review 195 (1919).

———. The Supreme Court in United States History (2 vols.; Boston: Little, Brown, 1937).

Warren, Earl. "The Bill of Rights and the Military," 37 New York University Law Review 181 (1962).

Watts, R. A. "The Trial and Execution of the Lincoln Conspirators," 6 Michigan History Magazine 81 (1922).

Wedgwood, Ruth. "Al Qaeda, Terrorism, and Military Commissions," 96 American Journal of International Law 328 (2002).

Welch, Richard E., Jr., "American Atrocities in the Philippines: The Indictment and the Response," 43 Pacific Historical Review 233 (1974).

Welles, Gideon. Diary of Gideon Welles (2 vols.; Boston: Houghton Mifflin, John T. Morse Jr. ed. 1911).

Wheless, Joseph. "Military Law and Courts in the United States," 15 Georgetown Law Journal 279 (1927).

White, G. Edward. "Felix Frankfurter's 'Soliloquy' in Ex parte Quirin," 5 Green Bag 2D 423 (2002).

Whiting, William. War Powers Under the Constitution (Boston: Little, Brown, 1864).

Wiener, Frederick Bernays, "American Military Law in the Light of the First Mutiny Act's Tricentennial," 126 Military Law Review 1 (1989).

———. "Courts-Martial and the Bill of Rights: The Original Practice," 72 Harvard Law Review 1, 266 (1958).

———. The New Articles of War (Washington, D.C.: Infantry Press Journal, 1948).

Winthrop, William. Military Law and Precedents (Washington, D.C.: Government Printing Office, 1920).

INDEX OF CASES

SUBJECT INDEX